Valparaiso Bound!

Valparaiso Bound!

European Pioneers on the Pacific Coast of South America

David J. Woods

ricaaventura
LIBRERIA Y EDITORIAL

Santiago, Chile

**"Valparaíso Bound! European Pioneers
on the Pacific Coast of South America"**

ISBN: 978-956-8449-20-9

First published (2016) by: Librería y Editorial Ricaaventura E.I.R.L.
editorial.ricaaventura@gmail.com
www.ricaaventura.cl

Derechos de autor N°: A-266339

Cover design:
Jenny Contente Guazzotti

For
Valentine, Sam and Scarlett
with the hope that they will grow up to understand
and enjoy their disparate roots

1795 map from the *"Nouvel Atlas Portatif"*, published in Paris by Didier Robert de Vaugondy and Charles-François Delamarche. The territories, then under Spanish rule, were quite different to those today. *Author's collection*

Contents

The three-masted steel barque "Garthsnaid" in rough seas off Cape Horn in 1920. The ship was en route from Iquique, Chile with a cargo of nitrate.

State Library of Queensland, Australia

Preface

European pioneers on the Pacific Coast of South America? Apart from a vague recollection from school of the Spanish colonial period – the conquistadors – few people in Europe know there were any such pioneers. It is a forgotten footnote in our collective history. And it is not well remembered in the region itself. Yet, for centuries the two continents were thoroughly entangled; their respective futures partially dictated by that entanglement. Gold, silver, copper and other mineral wealth had much to do with it. But so also did the strategic significance of that coast, the end of the Spanish monarchy's predominance in Europe, the impact of the Napoleonic Wars, the American Civil War, and the arms race that culminated in the First World War. Add to that elements of piracy, voyages of discovery, the rampant capitalism of the Industrial Revolution and the emigration of poverty-stricken farmers across the Atlantic, and you have a powerful melange. To do justice to such an epoch, in a non-academic, highly selective and readable manner, was a challenge. No less, to describe adequately the many colourful, larger-than-life personalities who permeate the story. To retell the voyages and new lives established in lands on the other side of the globe, and to see it all in human terms, required a personal journey by the author himself.

Yet it seemed a worthwhile journey to take on. Nearly a decade ago my wife and I started travelling regularly to the region, making close friends, exploring the coast, deserts, mountains and lakes, and eventually buying and restoring an old house in the historic centre of the Chilean port of Valparaíso. As in many such houses, constructed for Europeans in the nineteenth century, there was a tangible force circulating within its walls and its high-ceilinged rooms drawing us back to another era. In any event, I had caught the bug for writing history about the region from my earlier book on the bombardment of Valparaíso by the Spanish in 1866.

Somehow, the history of this region of the world – especially its impact on the Old Continent – is habitually neglected. Yet millions of European and North American tourists now travel to Chile and Peru and other states on the Pacific Coast. They stand fascinated in front of the remnants of what was part of their own history. They see names they recognize. They learn a little, but not much. This book is an attempt to help them understand more of the common heritage that binds these rapidly modernizing states to Europe.

Yes, the British presence was pervasive and influential. But the story is a truly European one. From Portugal and Ireland in the West to Croatia, Greece, Poland and Hungary in the East; from Scotland and Scandinavia to Italy and Greece, every part of today's Europe left a mark somewhere on these distant territories of South America.

It was not the kind of mass migrations that settled in Brazil, Argentina and Uruguay as well as much of the United States of America. True, many newcomers found themselves on the Pacific shores by accident or ill-luck. Many, however, were intrepid and enterprising individuals – sometimes with their families in tow – who pursued dreams and fulfilled their duty in some of the most challenging environments on earth. Most of all, the common element in each of their stories was the harsh voyage of three months or more from the great ports of Europe: from Liverpool, Hambourg, Copenhagen, Le Havre, Genoa and so on. Indeed, many never made it. The ships that still line the bottom of the sea around Cape Horn or the bed of the Strait of Magellan are testimony to the rigours and horrors of this unique journey.

Of course, much of the foundation of what the newcomers found and did in the nineteenth century was the Spanish colonial period lasting nearly 300 years until the 1820s. That at once glorious and shameful era needs an entire book to recount adequately. It will not be done here. Rather, the colonial influence on specific, mainly nineteenth and twentieth century, developments are treated in the relevant chapters. These include the great voyages of exploration and settlement; the military campaigns that pressed southwards but finally failed to tame the fierce and brave tribes of Araucania; the repressive measures that lead to the *encomienda* systems of near slavery in the fields and mines; the priests who strove to outlaw that system; the fight against piracy; the early traders and the corrupt administrators. These represent some, at least, of the most fascinating features of a dramatic epoch that ultimately imploded in the early nineteenth century with the independence movements and the painful expulsion of the Spaniards from the region.

What followed was a grand epoch, the early era of globalization. Yet it did not last long: natural disasters like earthquakes, fires and floods; wars and political crises; financial and commodities market bubbles; and the opening of the Panama Canal, all gradually helped eviscerate the foundations of affluent communities. Only in the past two decades has Chile, in particular, reasserted itself. But in their heydays these countries were hives of entrepreneurship, technological innovation and economic success. Poverty was rife alongside great fortunes. Yet the men and women who found or created wealth did so largely by their own efforts; they took risks and many paid a heavy personal price, even the ultimate price.

It was, and remains, a region of extremes, of passions, of adventure and of adversity. The emotions roused among the sailors, travellers and immigrants generated traditions of sea shanties, folksongs, music hall ditties, tango and the ballads of the *huasos*, or *gauchos*. The songs and poetry provide continuity for this extraordinary story.

Looking back, one cannot fail to be struck with parallels today. Globalization is the underlying dynamic of the past few decades, as it was in the nineteenth century. Great migratory movements are again underway, too often for the worst of reasons. The manner in which immigrants and refugees were treated – rejected or assimilated – is also a recurring theme in this book. But there is no denying the rich contributions that the European newcomers made to the emerging, independent nations of South America from 1810 onwards, and well into the twentieth century. It makes for colourful, adventurous but, above all, optimistic history.

I have had much help, advice and encouragement in researching and writing this book, notably from friends in Chile who know far more of the history than I will ever master. In particular I would like to thank Michelle Prain Brice, of the Universidad Adolfo Ibáñez and the Instituto Chileno Británico de Cultura in Vina del Mar; Fernando Vergara Benítez, director of the Budge Library at the Pontificia Universidad Católica de Valparaíso; Vice Admiral (ret) Kenneth Pugh of the Chilean Navy; John Marsh, Emeritus Professor of Geography at Trent University in Canada; Iain Hardy, the British Consul in Valparaíso, who shared his own family history; in California, my long-time friend and colleague Billie Blackhurst; and my enthusiastic publisher Guillermo Burgos Cuthbert of Ricaaventura in Santiago. Rhiannon Lewis was kind enough to share with me the story of her great-great-uncle, David Davies, who continued to serve on one of the Pacific coast mail steamers, commandeered by President Balmaceda, during the 1891 civil war in Chile. I owe a great debt to another old friend and colleague from the United Kingdom, Irene Lally, who yet again has subjected my text to the rigours of a real journalistic professional, asking all the right questions and insisting on some consistent style. But I should not forget Daniela Martinez, my dear friend and translator for the Spanish edition, who also pointed out discrepancies and errors during her work.

I also owe thanks to many librarians and archivists in, among others, the National Archive and the Guildhall Library in London, the Archivo Nacional de Chile in Santiago, the Universidad Católica del Norte in Antofagasta, and the Biblioteca Regional de Valparaíso "Santiago Severin." My friends at the Chateau de Lourmarin in France were good enough to let me use photographs of several engravings in the impressive Robert Laurent-Vibert Foundation collection.

1.

A Voyage

We did no more than linger at the mouth,
Imagining what drew Magellan in,
Then drove ahead a steady course still south
To where great seas like falling walls begin
With a Pacific din.

O, we were glad to see the outpost pass,
The wind less hard, the lookout less than blind.
To clean the Horn corrosion from the brass,
To shed the Horn corrosion from the mind,
With death outrun behind.

From *"Cape Horn"* by Ernest Kroll, 1952

It was a voyage like no other. For experienced sailors, the passage from the Atlantic Ocean to the Pacific, through the Magellan Strait or round Cape Horn, has always been regarded as probably the greatest nautical and physical challenge they were likely to face in their lives at sea. For the ordinary men, women and children who made the voyage from Europe to start new lives on the west coast of South America, the months of discomfort, privation, untreated disease or injury and, too often, tragedy, were a trial that few could possibly have accurately envisaged as they set out from Liverpool, Le Havre, Hamburg and other ports of the Old Continent. It was so for the Spanish conquistadores in the sixteenth century and not much less so for the miners, engineers, traders, farmers and their families embarking in relatively modern steamships in the 1920s and 1930s.

So great were the risks of this perilous passage that it is difficult to fathom quite why the adventurers and pioneers, let alone the ordinary folk, so easily accepted to put themselves and their kin so squarely in harm's way. That is the subject of other chapters. For the moment, the voyage itself is our focus. After all, it was not remotely the equivalent of an Atlantic crossing, from Le Havre to New York for instance, or even a passage from London to Rio or Buenos Aires. Such voyages were not without their dangers, especially in wartime or given the attention of pirates. Sometimes ships might be becalmed for days in

"The Doldrums", south of the equator. But these journeys were, nevertheless, relatively short. A sailing ship would reach land on the Atlantic coast of North America in a few weeks and, say, Buenos Aires in a week or so more. Steam propulsion pushed the times of passage down significantly, ultimately to a matter of days, not weeks. Tales of wrecks, disease and starvation are comparatively few – bar the horrors of the slave trade from the African coast.

The passage to Valparaíso by sail, on the other hand, was quite different. In the eighteenth century and most of the nineteenth the normal duration was three months at best. In earlier times it had been much more, often lasting a year or longer. Steam-assisted sailing ships began to reduce passage times even

Map engraved and printed by Tobius Lotter, in Augsburg, Germany, around 1770
Author's collection

before the Panama Canal opened in 1914, but the voyage remained lengthy and the chances of mishap to ships, crews and passengers alike stayed significant, and sometimes deadly.

What was it about the run between the Atlantic and the Pacific? The fears – or, at least, the sailor's profound respect – that attach to the passage round Cape Horn are amost as acute now as ever. Francis Chichester, the modern day, round-the-world, single-handed yachtsman, was as respectful as any. In a history of the old clipper ship routes he set out some of the physical attributes of the region which explain its vicious history of maritime harassment:

"The prevailing winds in the Forties and Fifties, between 40°South and 60° South, are westerly and pretty fresh on the average. For instance, off the Horn there are gales of Force 8 or more on one day in four in the spring and one day in eight in the summer. Winds have a lazy nature in that they refuse to climb over a mountain range if they can sweep past the end of it. South America has one of the greatest mountain ranges of the world, the Andes, which blocks the westerlies along a front of 1,200 miles from 35°South, right down to Cape Horn. All this powerful wind is crowding through Drake's Straight between Cape Horn and the South Shetland Islands, 500 miles to the south. The normal westerlies pouring through this gap are interfered with by the turbulent, vicious little cyclones rolling off the Andes."

Chichester went on to explain that the westerly winds generated sea currents flowing eastwards at average rates of ten to twenty miles a day. This is known as the Antarctic Circumpolar Current or the West Wind Drift. While the currents are complex in the area and sometimes the West Wind Drift is checked by easterly winds from the Atlantic, the prevailing stream can be as much as 50 miles a day eastwards.

"As with the winds, this great ocean river is forced to pass between South America and the South Shetland Islands. But there is another factor which greatly increases the turbulence. The bottom of the ocean shelves between the Horn and the Shetland Islands and this induces huge seas to break. [It get even worse] if there is an easterly gale blowing against the current flowing past the Horn."

As a result of all these mutually-reinforcing and contradictory forces, giant waves are produced, often over 20 metres in height and sometimes towering up to 40 metres. Chichester did battle with these elements in his historic single-handed circumnavigation in 1966-67 when he sailed the old clipper route from England to Australia and back, passing both the Cape of Good Hope and Cape Horn. He did it the 'easy' way, west to east, but the feat was extraordinary. His first-hand account added to the many harrowing tales, over five hundred years, of sailors and passengers who have made that journey and lived to describe it.

The Cape or the Strait?

The earliest European mariners to pass from the Atlantic into the Pacific were not even aware of the existence of Cape Horn. They made the tricky navigation through the Strait of Magellan, the first route to be discovered. When the Cape route was eventually found (see Chapter 3), the debate among sea captains on the best choice was a lively one and remained so. One French traveller in the mid-nineteenth century, Charles de Lambertie, reported that most sailors felt the option to pass by the Strait was under-used and not sufficiently appreciated. At the very least, the passage around Cape Horn added distance and time to the voyage. He quoted the Count de Bougainville, a French admiral and explorer, as an authority:

"'Despite the difficulties that we have undergone' says he, 'I always advise in favour of this [the Strait] route to that of Cape Horn, from the month of September to the end of March. In the other [winter] months of the year, when the nights are 16, 17, 18 hours in length, I would take the side of passing by the known sea route. The contrary wind and the high seas are not dangers, as an alternative to passing by groping between the lands.'"

De Lambertie noted that besides having the advantage of shortening the voyage considerably, the Strait offered the chance to procure supplies *en route* because of the proximity to land and fresh food like game, fish, shellfish and even plants which would act against scurvy and "repair the health of ailing sailors." Still, regardless of Bougainville's convictions, the Strait of Magellan was barely used by anything other than schooners and small brigs.

A supporter of the Cape Horn route was Captain James Cook who, in January 1769, had used it on his way to Tahiti. He had some poor weather on the way, but nothing too distressing. He passed the Cape smoothly and eventually entered the Pacific after taking a buffeting that drove the *Endeavour* far to the south. Making the comparison with a previous voyage – that of Samuel Wallis who had circumnavigated the globe in his ship *HMS Dolphin* for the second time during the years 1766-68 – Cook was clear about the advantages of a Cape Horn passage:

"The *Dolphin* in her last voyage, which she performed at the same season of the year with ours, was three months in getting through the Strait of Magellan, exclusive of the time she lay in Port Famine; and I am persuaded, from the winds we had, that if we had come by that passage, we should not at this time have been in these seas; that our people would have been fatigued, and our anchors, cables, sails and rigging much damaged."

Commodore (later Admiral of the Fleet) George Anson would have questioned Cook's confidence in Cape Horn. His 1741 voyage (see also Chapter 3), which ultimately turned into one of the most tragic of all circumnavigations, encountered not only the tempestuous sea and vicious weather conditions offered by the Cape but the hazards of poor diet and scurvy on such long voyages. His fleet suffered for a hundred days in passing Cape Horn and finally reaching the Pacific. The weather was bad, and the debilitation of the crew through illness drained the efficiency with which the ships were handled and navigated. The contemporary account states:

"Soon after our passing Streights Le Maire[1], the scurvy began to make its appearance amongst us, and our long continuance at sea, the fatigue we underwent, and the various disappointments we met with, had occasioned its spreading to such a degree that at the latter end of April there were but few on board who were not in some degree afflicted with it, and in that month no less than forty-three died of it on board the *Centurion*."

The same account described the nature of this seamen's malady which, then, was a common hazard on long voyages:

"These common appearances are large discoloured spots dispersed over the whole surface of the body, swelled legs, putrid gums and, above all, an extraordinary lassitude of the whole body, especially after any exercise, however inconsiderable; and this lassitude at last degenerates into a proneness to swoon, and even die, on the least exertion of strength, or even on the least motion. This disease is likewise usually attended with a strange dejection of the spirits, and with shivering, trembling, and a disposition to be seized with the most dreadful terrors on the slightest accident."

On the three of Anson's original eight ships that reached the Juan Fernandez Islands[2], the combined crews of 961 had been reduced by 626 to a total of 335 men, largely as a result of scurvy. It would take nearly another fifty years before the Admiralty required sailors to be provided with citrus fruit (vitamin C often in the form of lime juice) to fend off the killer disease.

Some mariners were later to scoff at the hardships the pioneers had experienced in passing Cape Horn. *HMS Conway*, under the command of Captain Basil Hall RN left port in England in August 1820. After calling at Rio de Janeiro and the River Plate, Hall received orders to sail to Valparaíso. He

---

1   The Le Maire Strait lies between the south-eastern tip of Tierra del Fuego and the more easterly Staten Island.

2   Around 670 km (362 nautical miles) west of Valparaiso, in the Pacific Ocean, they include the "Robinson Crusoe" island (Chapter 3)

noted how Anson's experience provoked nervousness among crews, but that improvements in navigation and seamanship had "stripped the Cape of most of its terrors." As they approached the Cape, the main point of interest for seamen on the *Conway* was a "brilliant light … at first of a bright red" which faded and re-ignited at intervals. The crew speculated that it was a lighthouse or a forest fire, but finally concluded, after taking bearings placing the light over 100 miles away, that it was a volcano. Perhaps it was this feature, or another like it, that spurred Magellan to name Tierra del Fuego. As for the passage itself, "little interest would be taken in the details of a voyage unaccompanied by hardship or dangers".

Hall recounts, nevertheless, that the ship struggled for a fortnight against the prevalent westerly winds, drifting to a latitude of 62 degrees south before finding the winds to turn north for the coast of Chile. A more representative and colourful first-hand account of the passage around Cape Horn would be written just twenty years later by an American, Henry Dana.

An extreme treatment for poor eyesight

Dana, born in Massachusetts in 1815, broke his studies at Harvard, in 1834, for a two-year voyage on the windjammer *Alert*. In part he was persuaded to sign up because a bout of measles had damaged his eyesight and he had been advised the sea could improve things. The modestly-crewed boat had left the port of San Diego to sail the West Coast southwards and round the Horn before returning via the East Coast. The timing was not propitious. Dana was well aware that their May departure meant an encounter with the Cape in July, the worst month of the year for weather and eighteen-hour nights.

He was not to be disappointed. Approaching from the west should normally have led to a rough but fast passage. Yet very soon the vessel showed that it could not deal easily with the huge swell that built up from the south.

"Being still so deep and heavy, she wanted the buoyancy which should have carried her over the seas, and she dropped heavily into them, the water rushing over the decks; and every now and then, when an unusually large sea met her fairly upon the bows, she struck it with a sound as dead and heavy as that which a sledge-hammer falls upon the pile, and took the whole of it in the forecastle, and, rising, carried it aft in the scuppers, washing the rigging off the pins, and carrying along with it everything which was loose on deck."

As one immense waves struck, the *Alert*'s deck was awash:

"The galley, the pigsty, the hencoop, and a large sheep-pen, which had been

Saturday 14th Mar. N.F.

Anna, (Ital. barq) from Genoa to Valparaiso
A telegram from Buenos Ayres
states this vessel has been totally
wrecked on Staten Island; crew saved. Agt. Genoa
bitel.

Western Bride from the Chinchas
Sinclair to England,
was lost in the Straits
of Magellan 8th March;
crew saved. Agt. M.te Vid

Panama, /s/ from Monte Video to
Valparaiso,
was lost in the straits
of Magellan 3rd May. Av. Do

Abbott's Reading, from Liverpool,
at anchor in
Valparaiso Bay,
was much damaged by
an explosion of gunpowder
12th Sept. & also the
undischarged portion
of her cargo; 2 men killed Af Valparai

Selected entries in the Lloyd's of London "Loss Book" for the year 1885
Guildhall Library, London

7

built upon the fore-hatch, were all gone in the twinkling of an eye – leaving the deck as clean as a chin new reaped – and not a stick left to show where anything had stood. In the scuppers lay the galley, bottom up, and a few boards floating about – the wreck of the sheep-pen – and half a dozen miserable sheep floating among them, wet through, and not a little frightened at the sudden change that had come upon them."

Much later, as they drifted south, came the snow and ice:

"Between daylight and dark … we saw thirty-four ice islands of various sizes … and at sundown of this day, a man at the mast-head saw large fields of floating ice, at the south-east. This kind of ice is much more dangerous than the large islands, for those can be seen at a distance, and kept away from; but the field-ice, floating in great quantities, and covering the ocean for miles and miles, in pieces of every size – large, flat and broken cakes, with here and there an island rising twenty or thirty feet, and as large as a ship's hull – this is very difficult to steer clear of. … To make our condition still worse, the wind came out due east, just after sundown, and it blew a gale dead ahead, with hail and sleet and thick fog, so that we could not see half of the length of the ship. … Here we were, nearly seven hundred miles to the westward of the Cape, with a gale dead from the eastward, and the weather so thick that we could not see the ice, with which we were surrounded, until it was directly under our bows."

Sent up the mast to bring in sail and slow the ship, Dana had the closest possible view of the appalling conditions:

"We had now got on our 'Cape Horn rig' – thick boots, southwesters coming down over our neck and ears, thick trousers and jackets, and some with oil-cloth suits over all. Mittens, too, we wore on deck, but it would not do to go aloft with them, as it was impossible to work with them. A man might fall; for all the hold he could get upon a rope; so we were obliged to work with bare hands, which, as well as our faces, were often cut with hailstones, which fell thick and large. Our ship was now all cased with ice – hull, spars, and standing rigging, and the running rigging so stiff that we could hardly bend it…"

The *Alert* had begun its run around the Horn on 19 June, 1834 and, finally, as the sky cleared for once, the crew spotted land just on the eastern side of the Cape on July 22. Whether or not Dana's eyesight improved as a result of this maritime experience, is not recounted.

Among the most celebrated voyages to the region in the nineteenth century was that of Charles Darwin in *H.M.S Beagle*. Not that it was as costly in terms of human misery as many others. Yet, while the great biologist had his mind mostly on higher things, Captain Robert FitzRoy, himself a serious scientist, needed to employ all his skills and experience. Initially, the ship approached Cape Horn with little trouble. In Darwin's own record:

"December 21st [1832]. The *Beagle* got under way: and on the succeeding day, favoured to an uncommon degree by a fine easterly breeze, we closed in with the Barnevelts, and running past Cape Deceit with its stony peaks, about three o'clock doubled the weather-beaten Cape Horn. The evening was calm and bright, and we enjoyed a fine view of the surrounding isles. Cape Horn, however, demanded his tribute, and before night sent us a gale of wind directly in our teeth. We stood out to sea, and on the second day again made the land, when we saw on our weather-bow this notorious promontory in its proper form - veiled in a mist, and its dim outline surrounded by a storm of wind and water. Great black clouds were rolling across the heavens, and squalls of rain, with hail, swept by us with such extreme violence, that the Captain determined to run into Wigwam Cove."

However, the "snug" little harbour could only be a refuge for a short while; the priority was to get on westwards into the Pacific.

"On the 13th [January 1833] the storm raged with its full fury: our horizon was narrowly limited by the sheets of spray borne by the wind. The sea looked ominous, like a dreary waving plain with patches of drifted snow: whilst the ship laboured heavily, the albatross glided with its expanded wings right up the wind. At noon a great sea broke over us, and filled one of the whale boats, which was obliged to be instantly cut away. The poor *Beagle* trembled at the shock, and for a few minutes would not obey her helm; but soon, like a good ship that she was, she righted and came up to the wind again. Had another sea followed the first, our fate would have been decided soon, and for ever. We had now been twenty-four days trying in vain to get westward; the men were worn out with fatigue, and they had not had for many nights or days a dry thing to put on. Captain FitzRoy gave up the attempt to get westward by the outside coast. In the evening we ran in behind False Cape Horn[3], and dropped our anchor in forty-seven fathoms, fire flashing from the windlass as the chain rushed round it. How delightful was that still night, after having been so long involved in the din of the warring elements!"

The voyage continued eventually into the Strait of Magellan with Darwin pursuing his researches on the climate, geology, flora and fauna as well as making contact with various Indian tribes. The *Beagle* zig-zagged between the

---

3   False Cape Horn lies about 56 kilometres north-west of the true Cape; it is the southern tip of the Tierra del Fuego archipelago.

Argentinian coast of Patagonia, the Falkland Islands and Tierra de Fuego for over a year before moving on up the west coast of Chile with Darwin observing and recording as they went. His observations are reported in his 1839 diary of the voyage and became part of the basis for his great works on evolution, notably *"On the Origin of Species"*. In July 1834, the ship finally weighed anchor in Valparaíso Bay. (See also Chapter 2)

A shocked young American sees Cape Horn for the first time

Charles Davis, born in New York in 1870, provided another graphic account

"Red Jacket", one of the fastest clipper ships ever built, in ice off Cape Horn on a passage from Australia to Liverpool.   *Library of Congress, Washington*

of a near-fatal encounter with Cape Horn. Davis became an accomplished yacht-design draftsman and artist. A the age of 22, he joined the 880-ton bark *James A. Wright* on a 10-month voyage, with a cargo of general merchandise, down the east coast of the United States, round the Horn to Chile and Peru, and back. Oddly, like Henry Dana, he went partly to improve failing eyesight. Unlike Dana, his vessel would take the feared east-to-west passage. Trouble arrived quickly when the ship entered the Le Maire Strait.

"It was an old whistler when it struck. For a few minutes I could hear no sound but the screeching wind and seething foam as it struck the weather side of the bark and hove her over until her rail was buried to leeward. The crew was making desperate efforts to reduce sail for there was weight enough in the wind to blow things away. Fred, one of the other watch, was up furling the main topgallant sail when it struck, and the whole topsails on that mast proved too great a strain for it. There was a report as if a gun had been fired on board, and a tremor ran through the bark. The old man [captain] ran forward and yelled to Fred at the top of his lungs to 'Lay down you fool! Lay down!'"

Fred and the rest of the crew survived that initial battering but the following day they were hit by another gale:

"When daylight showed us the height of the seas that were running, I was amazed. I thought I had seen some pretty big seas up north, but now with a Cape Horn sou'wester blowing I saw such seas as I hope never to see again. And every one seemed to get larger and larger for the gale had only just begun, and the wind blew with such force it seemed to slide the bark bodily to leeward. How she ever rose to some of those walls of solid green, or rather dirty-grey water that seems to prevail in those low latitudes where the sun never seems to shine, was a mystery to me."

What happened next is best told in Davis's own words:

"Once when we were 'sweating up' the lee fore braces, the whole crew came near to being washed overboard. We were bending our backs on the fore brace when the bark went over on her beam ends and a solid green sea broke over the lee rail. It took every one of us clean off our feet and those who were near the leading block on the rail were held down so the sea broke fully two feet over their heads and buried them completely. ... I was blinded and choked by the water that was washing me about, but when my knees hit something hard I caught it with my feet as well as I could, and hung on.

"... Every way we turned we were blinded by flying spray and, although our oilskins were lashed to our boots and tied about our waists, the water found its way inside and kept us chilled to the bone all the time. Dry feet were unknown. ... To make matters worse, the cook could not make a fire in his galley and our last comfort, the pot of hot tea or coffee, was cut off."

"Bill took the wheel to windward and I took hold to leeward. When the bark went over a sea and settled her stem, it was all the two of us could do to hold the wheel. We got along all right for about an hour and then I could tell by the way the bark lifted that an extra-heavy sea was coming, though we could not see five feet ahead of us. Bill let go of the wheel and hung on to the life-line, but what happened to me and the wheel I did not know for a minute. I thought

I had hold of a mule's leg instead of a ship's wheel. Then I felt a sharp pain in my left elbow and the next thing I knew, my head struck the deck behind Bill and my feet were up in the air on the wheel box. I was standing on my head but soon scrambled to my feet and saw the wheel going around like a buzz saw; over it went one way then back again the other so fast it looked like a pinwheel and I could not see the spokes. Then, just as it was about to spin back again, Bill grabbed it and I scrambled around to leeward and took hold again, but my left arm was powerless."

The gale went on for three days and three nights before one final "wild, furious outfly that tested things aboard to their utmost", and then came a lull. During the three days the ship had drifted one hundred miles sideways. Nor was the return voyage much easier. Davis was moved to observe in his diary:

"It would be impossible to convince a man, who thinks he has seen some high seas, of the enormous height a Cape Horn swell rises to. When I look at ships now, as they lie alongside the dock, and see the tons after tons that go into them, and run my eye along their mammoth hulls, and look aloft at the tremendous heights of their spars, it doesn't seem possible that such a large craft could be hurled about like a toy. What chance has such a mite of humanity, with his feeble strength, on the deck of such a vessel when the seas are smashing everything they hit into kindling wood?"

The days of commercial sailing ships lingered long after the advent of steam vessels, with many large, steel-built craft operating well into the early decades of the twentieth century. Running before the wind, these giant "tall ships", which had replaced the fine wooden clippers of an earlier epoch, could often outrun their motorized competitors. Yet the passage round Cape Horn and into the Pacific was no less challenging in these final days of sail. One of the most dramatic and tragic such voyages was that of the three-masted steel ship, *British Isles* between 1905 and 1909. Sailing for the first time as a 15-year-old apprentice was a boy called William Jones. Some fifty years later he was persuaded to recount the harrowing experience.

Jones's ship was one of the largest and fastest of its kind with a weight of 2,287 tons and capable of carrying 4,000 tons of cargo. Launched in 1884, it was admired in many ports around the globe as one of the finest ships ever built in the yards of Glasgow. The *British Isles* had broken speed records, once overhauling and passing the largest sailing ship afloat, the German five-master *Preussen* (5,081 tons), while crossing the Bay of Biscay.

But when Jones boarded for the very first time in the East India docks in London he found the glory days of the vessel were probably over. Freight rates were low so ship-owners insisted that their captains "keep the seas", avoiding the expense of any unnecessary port calls along the route. In the 'old days' commercial sailing ships regularly stopped for repairs and provisions at Rio de Janeiro or other ports on the Atlantic coast, before tackling Cape Horn. This was now forbidden by the owners. The manning of the ship was also cut to the bone. Just twenty seamen were taken on for this voyage against a more normal complement of twice that number. Among the crew were four boy apprentices, of whom Jones was the most junior, together with a carpenter, a sail maker, a steward, a cook, the first and second mates and the Master, the experienced Captain James Barker. And the voyage would be a long one, to the nitrate port of Pisagua in northern Chile (some 10,000 miles, or over 16,000 kilometres, via Cape Horn) to deliver 4,200 tons of coal from Port Talbot in Wales. It was a common run in that era.

Tragedy, misery and a fire in the coal cargo

Every minute of the voyage engraved itself on Jones's memory. That he lived to tell the tale, given the number of ships lost that same year, was remarkable enough. But there is no denying the share of misery and physical hardship that he and his crew-mates would be required to bear as they set sail from Port Talbot docks on 11 June 1905. And not merely the crew; Captain Barker had brought along his wife and child for the voyage.

From the start, conditions on board – meeting the owners' specifications – were desolate. Jones describes the diet – if that is an appropriate term:

"At 7 a.m., one boy of the watch below, and one man, would each take a 'bread barge' – an oblong box – to the cabin door, where the steward would dole out the day's allowance of 'Liverpool pantiles' [more often known as 'dog biscuits' or 'hardtack'], a hard baked biscuit which was the substitute for bread throughout the whole voyage, and the sailor's Staff of Life. At seven bells [later, depending on the sailor's watch] the same two would go to the galley to receive a billy [a seven-pound jam tin] of tea."

The midday dinner would include a small piece of salt-beef with pantiles. And that was about it, at least as far as routine sustenance was concerned. Twice a week, there was a small ration of sugar, tinned milk and tinned butter, just enough to last a day. On Sundays and Thursdays there was salt pork for dinner. The one boiled potato dished out, also on Sundays and Thursdays, was the only vegetable available, but only for as long as there was stock that had not rotted – perhaps for three weeks at the start of a three-month passage. There was still no refrigeration on such vessels, so fresh food was almost never served. The classic mariner's disease of scurvy – itself a result of the absence of fresh fruit – was still countered by stores of lime-juice.

Essentially, this was the diet that ship-owners considered the bare minimum to sustain their sailors – and the minimum was sufficient. Anything more – in the case of the *British Isles*, jam was available – and the seamen had to pay for it themselves, out of pay that was yet to be received. Naturally, the captain, his family and senior members of the crew ate from a much more appetizing table. The refusal of owners to feed their crews adequately was potentially self-defeating. After all, ships were valuable assets and many, including the *British Isles* on this voyage, were not insured. The owners relied wholly on their under-manned crews to ensure delivery of cargoes in the face of every hazard.

Among such hazards, was the risk of fire on board vessels carrying coal as a cargo. As Jones's ship moved southwards into the tropics the coal in the hold naturally warmed. Thermometer readings soon suggested temperatures well above normal in the centre of the vast heaps of fuel, meaning spontaneous com-bustion was a real possibility. It had happened before; ships and crews had been lost to uncontrollable fires of this kind. Yet, the Captain, doggedly kept the interests of the ship-owners as his priority, refusing advice from the first mate that the ship put in to Rio. It was a gamble that very nearly ended in disaster.

On July 24, the cry of "Fire! Fire! All hands on deck" reverberated. The coal was indeed smoking, somewhere down in the bowels of the hold. The Captain made his decision almost instantly: members of the crew would have to get down into the hold and dig out the smouldering coal, wherever it could be found. "Stripped to the waist, they set to with a will, and were soon in a lather of sweat, half suffocated by the smoke and fumes, and blackened by dust." The ordeal lasted four days, getting steadily worse as the source of the combustion got closer. The thermometer read up to 200 degrees F (over 90 degrees C). Jones commented: "The fire-walking fakirs of India might have felt at home in that hold, but to us it was hell." Still, for a tot of rum, the crew did their work and saved the owner's cargo; finally, the smouldering and flaming coal was reached, dug out and thrown overboard.

Yet, this might be considered only a mildly dramatic start to a devastat-ing voyage. Some 46 days and 6000 miles out from England, the ship entered the 'Roaring Forties'[4], some 350 miles south of Buenos Aires. The initial gale lasted just four days and nights and brought the first serious casualty: a badly broken leg for a seaman who would be strapped to his bunk for the rest of the

---

4   Latitudes between 40 and 50 degrees in the Atlantic Ocean

voyage. It was also Jones's first experience of some of the worst that a passage to the west coast of South America could bring. Far, far worse was to come.

On 7 August, 1905, the vessel passed St John's Point on Staten Island. The order was given to steer south-west. To start with, all was fine, weather included. The Captain's pale-looking wife and children came out on to the deck for the first time in many days. The crew relaxed a little. Cape Horn came and went. Yet the respite was over almost before it had begun. The barometer was falling, and with it the temperature plummeted and the first snow started to collect on the spars. A "dense mass of cloud" could be seen on the approaching horizon.

William Jones's ship "British Isles", built in 1884 in Glasgow
Collection Guillermo Burgos

"The long oily-looking swell from the west took on a sinister look and feel as we breasted it. Suddenly, in the wall of darkness to the westward, a line of vivid white is glimpsed advancing relentlessly towards us. It is the surface of the water churned up by the violence of the approaching storm, about a mile from us, so that it seethes as though boiling in a gigantic cauldron".

When the storm hit the *British Isles* it did so with sustained virulence.

"Squall follows squall in unremitting succession. The drumming of the wind, the wild plunging and rolling of the ship in the cross sea, the masses of cloud hurtling past near the mastheads, the heavens opening to let loose on us a deluge of snow, hail and sleet, would provide an awe-inspiring, perhaps terrifying, spectacle – if we had time to pause and ponder and observe them at

15

leisure."

The crew and the ship prevailed against all the odds, for a time. Yet, they were being driven backwards. Cape Horn, which had been behind them a day earlier, was now ahead of them again. An albatross hovered above, observing the plight of *British Isles*, a plight that would not last just a few hours or even just a few days, but weeks. Seeking to tack west and south, the ship was, in practice, driven relentlessly south and east towards the ice-packs of the Antarctic. Colder and colder, with snow and hail ceaselessly bombarding the distressed vessel, and with visibility virtually nil for much of the time, the tiny crew was perpetually exhausted, avoiding only a total capitulation to the weather. Such a capitulation – turning and running before the unforgiving winds – would have meant absolute retreat eastwards, probably to shelter around the Falkland Islands. This, the "Old Man", as the Captain was known, sometimes fondly, would not countenance.

Almost inevitably, tragedy struck. High above the deck balanced on a spar, a seaman was struggling with a damaged and frozen sail. When a squall hit the ship he was catapulted forward before plunging into the sea. There was no possibility of launching a lifeboat for a rescue attempt in which other mariners would probably have been doomed also. The desperate mariner fought briefly to stay afloat, before being lost forever. During the three following weeks, nine of the remaining seventeen seamen were put out of action by frost-bite to their fingers or toes. There was no effective treatment on board; intensely painful at best, limbs and lives could eventually be lost if gangrene set in.

As days went by, the *British Isles* continued to drift southwards, arriving well over 500 miles south east of Cape Horn and within 105 miles of the Antarctic Circle. Even with his wife and children strapped to their bunks for days on end, Captain Barker refused to concede and turn eastwards to shelter. There were mutinous mutterings among a dwindling crew, many of whom failed to appreciate the over-riding interests of the ship-owner in the face of conditions almost beyond endurance. The Old Man prevailed, as always.

In a short period of relative calm, the ship was turned on a north-westward tack, at least moving away from the ice packs. But when the squalls restarted, disaster struck once more. As the crew fought to clear the wreckage of a fallen mast and its yards, a Greek seaman's leg was crushed and then a Danish mariner was lost overboard. At that point the Captain had no other course open than to run for shelter, the crew had been reduced to "six worn-out seamen and four equally worn out boys." After four days with the vast waves now heaving the ship up from behind, they reached the shelter of Staten Island and found other distressed vessels whose passages had been blocked by the appalling weather. It was 17 September, 1905.

For two days all the available hands were set to work on basic repairs. On the third day, the wind changed to the East. The Captain did not hesitate. Some 45 days after it had left Staten Island, for the first time, westwards, *British Isles* set course for the Pacific from exactly the same place once more. It took just one day for the wind to change again, for the barometer to start falling, signalling gales, rough seas and freezing temperatures. This time, with a drastically depleted crew, coping with such stormy weather was an extreme challenge, if not impossible. There was no longer room for mistakes or further losses. With "a full gale shrieking through the rigging", the men were at the limits of weariness and disheartenment. Sails had to be stowed, while the wind raged about them. In one such effort, as the mainsail was being brought down, yet another seaman had his frozen fingers crushed, lost his grip and fell over 60 feet (20 meters), to be lost among the towering waves.

Only after "that last blast of hate" did the weather relent. Some 52 days after passing it for the first time, Cape Horn was left behind. Of the ship's initial compliment of twenty seamen, three had been lost overboard, three more were seriously injured, six were out of action because of severe frostbite and another two were partly incapacitated by frost bite. Gangrene was spreading, and with it the smell. The leg of the Greek seaman reached the point where the only means of saving his life was a makeshift amputation performed by the Captain who had no training in such an operation. But he did the job without blinking, his patient deeply unconscious, and a life was duly saved. But another was lost within a few days, as a seaman who had sustained serious head injuries gave up his personal fight for survival. Two other injured men would die later after hospital treatment ashore.

The ship had taken 71 days to complete the passage around Cape Horn. On 20 October 1905, it passed Valparaíso, but did not stop. On the 28th, *British Isles* finally lay a few miles off its destination, Pisagua, some 139 days out from Port Talbot on a voyage scheduled to last just eighty. Of the handful of seamen left standing after the voyage, several deserted as soon as they set foot on dry land. It was common among mariners landing for the first time on the Pacific Coast, even after relatively uneventful voyages. Those left, as well as the boy apprentices, received little comfort for their troubles and efforts over so many months. They were expected to unload the coal themselves – once more to avoid the expense to the owners of hiring additional local labour.

The *British Isles* was refitted and a new crew enlisted. It sailed on to

Australia where it collected coal for delivery in Valparaiso. William Jones's first voyage had lasted two-and-a-half years when he arrived home at the end of January 1908. And, despite what many men would regard as an experience not to be repeated, he would return within a year to once more brave the waters around Cape Horn.

The horrors experienced by the crew and passengers of the *British Isles* were perhaps the worst of many dreadful stories of Cape Horn which belong to the twentieth century. Yet, the losses continued without end. The Australian newspaper reporter, A J Villiers, wrote one classic modern account of a voyage via the Cape, filming and photographing as he went. His ship was the 1,750-ton three-masted, full-rigged, steel ship, *Grace Harwar*. She sailed east from Australia in 1929, and this large, strong vessel survived a passage as tough as any. One man was lost overboard between New Zealand and the Cape and another was almost lost during the passage. Rounding the Horn took the ship and crew fifty-seven days. When they finally found themselves next to Staten Island, feelings among the crew were mixed:

"The discovery that the position was four degrees out – over one hundred and fifty miles – brought home to us to what extent we had been sailing in the lap of the gods, down there, running blindly on through fog and storm and gale, rain and sleet and snow, lightless, alone, not even knowing where we were. We were glad we were round Cape Horn at last. ... A good many lovely ships, members of that grand old sisterhood to which *Grace Harwar* belonged, have gone to their doom there; a good many wraiths of sailors rise nightly from the sea just hereabouts, and spring into the rigging of their ghost ships and cry airily in the clammy air. We were permitted to slip slowly by, now that we have come around the Horn, and we allowed ourselves to hope that our share of tragedy was done for the voyage.

Especially in the summer months, many thousands of ships, sailors and passengers passed Cape Horn or groped their way through the Strait of Magellan to the Pacific without accident or even excessive discomfort. Yet there was no guarantee of survival; the risks were always clear, the tragedies of previous passages well known. Nonetheless, few were deterred. It is perhaps one of the forgotten realities of Chile's story that, over centuries, has helped forge such a proud, determined and rugged nation.

2

First impressions: Paradise or purgatory?

But when we got to bully ol' Valaparaiser,
In the Bay we dropped our mud hook far from shore;
The ol' Man he refused ter let us raise 'er,
An' he stopped the boardin'-masters comin' aboard.

I quickly made me mind up that I'd jump 'er,
I'd leave the beggar an' git a job ashore;
I swum across the Bay an' went an' left 'er,
An' in the English Bar I found a whore.

Paddy, lay back!
Take in yer slack !
Take a turn around the capstan, heave a pawl!
'Bout ship, stations, boys, be handy!
For we're bound for Valaparaiser 'round the Horn!

Traditional sea shanty

It is reasonable to imagine that after two or three months at sea, in either normally uncomfortable or wholly desperate conditions, crews and passengers would be unanimous in their delight at finally glimpsing land as their ships entered the shelter of Valparaíso Bay. Certainly, many were relieved. Others were largely oblivious as they were helped ashore, ill or injured. Others still were simply grumpy that paradise was not all it had been made out to be. Old maps showed the place as "Val Paraíso" (Valley of Paradise), a title perhaps bestowed by the first Spanish arrivals or the indigenous local "Chango" tribes or one of several other early visitors. Nevertheless, whether or not it was a heaven on earth, the first impressions of what in many cases was to be the site of a new life were important, and often recorded.

Charles Davis had arrived from New York aboard the sailing bark *James A Wright* in 1892, after an eventful 115-day passage around Cape Horn:

"Then, as the view of the bay opened up, we saw a large fleet of steamers and sailing vessels at anchor. Built up on the side of a mountain that ran up from the shores of the bay, lay the city of Valparaíso, basking in the sun.

"As we sailed in, a ridge of land, which came out from the mountain to the point we had rounded, shut off the view to the south'ard. To the north'ard the mountains gradually sloped down to a level plain backed in the distance by mountain ranges.

"Land was such a welcome sight that I hung a long time over the rail, just gazing at the city and the other ships. The city seemed stuck up the side of the mountain's base and was composed almost entirely of square, flat-topped houses either a grey or brownish colour. Down in the heart of the city, though, there were many white marble buildings; grand old affairs with all the finery of Spanish carving under the eaves and on the columns. What few trees there were looked dried up and stunted on the bare, brown hills."

In 1889, William Howard Russell, once a star reporter and war correspondent of The Times of London, accompanied John Thomas North, the "Nitrate King," to Chile[1]:

"Next morning the *Chiloé* came to her moorings in the roadstead of Valparaíso. I was surprised and pleased at the appearance of the city. At the foot of a deeply-indented and rugged-looking bright-red mountain range, some 1,200 feet to 1,600 feet high, which comes quite close to the shore as if threatening to squeeze it into the sea, there is a long semi-circular curve of white buildings, church spires, warehouses, and public edifices bordering the bay behind a forest of masts. The mountain range, over which peers the frosted head of the giant Aconcagua, 23,000 feet high, is furrowed by deep cuts, which were doubtless the beds of torrents when the drainage of the upland continent was in progress; between the ravines, and on the shoulders of their moraine-like banks, houses are built, tier above tier, thrown up, as it were, in clusters, from the long main street, which extends for miles along the shore, which is bordered by quays and factories. The roadstead is open to the north, and as the water is very deep the anchorage is insecure in winter when the north winds prevail, but it is well sheltered on the south, west and east."

In 1861, Annie Williamson, the new wife of the well-known partner in the trading house Balfour, Williamson, (see chapter 10) arrived for the first time with her husband. She was deeply impressed:

"At last we saw the flagstaff and signal post above Valparaíso; then the lighthouse and powder magazine, and at last we rounded a certain point at which we had been gazing for hours – and the beautiful bay of Valparaíso was before us. It really was an extraordinary sight. The hills on which the town is built are

---

1   See chapters 11 and 12.

so unlike the hills at home, and at once strike you with the idea of the dreadful earthquakes when the earth has opened. Each hill is divided from its neighbour by a deep ravine, and all round the bay there are the same narrow brown hills rising from the port and stretching far back – some almost covered with villas, others with huts.

"The mole was black with people. Doctor Trumbull has kindly sent his carriage for us, for our house is very high up on Cerro Alegre (the Happy Hill)

Arrival in Valparaiso Bay, around 1840.
From "Voyages pittoresque dans les deux Ameriques", Alcides d'Orbigny, Paris 1841

which is entirely monopolised by the English. ... Our garden would charm you exceedingly, but of all things the view is the best. From the veranda we have the bay stretched out before us.

"But the moonlight here! – it is beyond all things beautiful and brilliant. It throws a silver mantle over Aconcagua, and you wonder that you could ever admire the gaudy light of the sun again, but would wish ever to live in the moonlight."

Darwin takes a first look

Charles Darwin had also observed the sunnier side of the town in July 1834, arriving nearly three years after his departure from England in *HMS Beagle*:

"July 23rd. — The *Beagle* anchored late at night in the bay of Valparaíso, the chief seaport of Chile. When morning came, everything appeared delightful. After Tierra del Fuego, the climate felt quite delicious - the atmosphere so dry, and the heavens so clear and blue with the sun shining brightly, that all nature seemed sparkling with life. The view from the anchorage is very pretty. The town is built at the very foot of a range of hills, about 1600 feet high, and rather steep. From its position, it consists of one long, straggling street, which runs parallel to the beach, and wherever a ravine comes down, the houses are piled up on each side of it. The rounded hills, being only partially protected by a very scanty vegetation, are worn into numberless little gullies, which expose a singularly bright red soil. From this cause, and from the low whitewashed houses with tile roofs, the view reminded me of St Cruz in Tenerife."

Disappointments, there were many. Captain Basil Hall, commanding the English naval vessel *Conway*, arrived in the Bay of Valparaíso, after a voyage of three and a half months, on 19 December 1820.

"After a perilous and protracted voyage, seamen are ready to consider any coast delightful; and it was probably from such a cause that the early Spanish adventurers named this place the Vale of Paradise, a designation which its present appearance by no means justifies."

However, Hall later relents when a picnic party takes him into the hills above the city:

"Here we found ourselves seated in the cool veranda of a neatly built cottage; and the sea breeze settling in was delightfully refreshing after our dusty drive in the *caretta*[2]. Our situation on the side of the mountain commanded a full view of the bay and shipping, as well as the long line of houses skirting the shore; and the cottage being surrounded by fruit trees such as figs, apples, peaches and oranges, and shaded by lofty tamarinds, [the name] "The Vale of Paradise" appeared no longer inappropriate."

Robert O Cunningham (1841-1918), a Scottish scientist, was appointed official naturalist on *HMS Nassau* for its 1866-9 voyage to South America to survey the Straits of Magellan and the islands and coastline to the west of the continent. He did not suffer too much discomfort in the south but clearly failed to find the sight of Valparaíso Bay the relief that many travellers found:

"I must confess that my first impressions of the city and surrounding country were those of great disappointment. I suppose I had formed extravagant ideas of the attractions of Valparaíso, from the various accounts of it which I had heard, and was surprised to behold a shabby-looking large town, the

---

2   Simple horse-drawn carriage

main streets of which straggled along a narrow strip of ground at the foot of bare, rugged, steep, saddle-backed, reddish-coloured range of hills upwards of 1400 feet in height, furrowed with numerous narrow ravines or *quebradas*, with their sides piled up with dwellings of a very mean description of architecture, tenanted chiefly by the poorer part of the population. ... Wherever we directed our gaze around the sides of the bay, we beheld an entire destitution of vegetation higher than low shrubs, with the exception of a very few trees in the gardens of some houses near the top of one of the hills, the Cerro Alegre, and which we afterwards learned were chiefly tenanted by English merchants. But if there is little that is interesting or attractive in the immediate vicinity of the city, there is amply sufficient in the distant prospect to satisfy the observer's sense of wonder and beauty; for on casting the eye eastward on a clear day, he will see the horizon bounded by the snow-clad range of the Andes, including the magnificent precipitous mass of Aconcagua, upwards of 23,000 feet in height, and generally regarded as the highest mountain of the New World."

One American lady, Mrs George Merwin, who was to set up house and live three years in Valparaíso in the early 1850s, had her mildly sarcastic expectations dashed immediately:

"We rose early, packed our trunks and went on deck, eager for the first glimpse of that terrestrial paradise, in whose delicious climate of perpetual sunshine, amid orange groves filled with birds of gorgeous plumage, we were to live without care and without effort. We had such fond dreams of Chilean existence as nearly everyone has of southern lands, but it was soon dispelled. The morn was cool and dark, and we shivered under out heavy shawls, while the Promised Land remained invisible until we entered the port, and then only showed itself vaguely."

The land route to Valparaíso from Santiago offered many early travellers a more impressive initial glimpse of the town than that from the sea. One British diplomat and traveller, Alexander Caldcleugh, having slept the night in the town of Casablanca, describes the scene thus:

"... on gaining the summit of another chain, the deep blue waters of the Pacific at once burst on my sight. The sun, which had broken through a thick fog, gave me all the advantages I could wish, and the Bay of Valparaíso, with the ships at anchor, immediately under my feet, presented a most beautiful and interesting scene, and one that remains deeply impressed on my memory."

But even this perspective failed to impress everyone. In 1818, John Miers, a mining engineer, who became more famous as a botanist, received a commission to construct copper refining plants in Chile. He left England in January

1819 and crossed the Atlantic to Buenos Aires. From there, he travelled cross-country, over the Andes to Santiago and, ultimately, to Valparaíso.

"Everybody who arrives here is disappointed, having been misled by exaggerated accounts given of this place, which has been absurdly named Val Paraíso, the Vale of Paradise, with its Almendral, or almond grove, although no almonds ever grew here. A stranger finds none of the beautiful trees, rich foliage, superb edifices, delightful walks and rides, which have been painted to his fancy, he finds it to consist of a few miserable houses, built irregularly on the margin of a steep hollow basin, formed by a semi-circular ridge of hills which rises 1200 feet above its level. ... the aspect, therefore, of the town and bay to a new comer is the most dreary that can be conceived."

The port of Valparaiso in the 1860s.   *A Handbook to Valparaiso, 1862*

A port bustling with the ships of all nations

Still, in those days, and for many decades after, Valparaíso was first and foremost a port, Santiago's link to the ocean and the world. And it was the vivacity of the port that struck the mariners arriving there for the first time. Charles Davis, from the United States, for instance:

"The harbour was full of vessels of all nationalities; from a little full-rigged Chilean bark of about one hundred tons ... to a monster of a four-masted German ship with ... more apprentices than there were men in our whole crew, and whose tonnage was close to two thousand.

"All the ships lay anchored stern to stern in rows across the harbour. From the mud batteries there was a stone seawall built around the shore of the bay, with a mole or landing stage projecting out from the main street, where all the rowboats landed. Along the wall at intervals were placed iron cranes to hoist the cargoes out of the lighters that ferried the cargoes to and from the anchored ships.

"The lighters were large, clumsy open boats built from lumber hewn out of native wood and with adz marks visible on every part. ... They carried from eight to ten tons each and were rowed by two *'launcheros'* using immense oars fully twenty feet long."

The Frenchman, Count Eugène de Robiano, who travelled to Chile around 1880 and explored the country for nearly eighteen months was also struck by the intense activity in the port of Valparaíso:

"And see the movement, the animation of the port! Apart from the fortifications and the steamers offering services along the coast, there are more than 3000 merchant ships that make their arrivals and departures every year. Many of them are engaged in a perpetual trade with Peru: gold, silver, platinum, wool, tallow and skins. The sums involved in the business [of Valparaíso] are enormous; and if Santiago, as capital and the seat of government, has the monopoly of diplomacy, it is here that reside the great majority of foreign consulates."

One travel-writer was moved to compare resistance to the weather-blown orientation of Valparaíso towards the north to the nation's virile fighting spirit. The celebrated travelogues of the American Burton Holmes, at the beginning of the twentieth century, were rife with over-coloured, over-opinionated description:

"The harbour is enormous in extent but not protected as it should be from the fury of the winter storms, which have wrought fearful havoc here from time to time, demolishing the quays and wrecking buildings near the water front. But Valparaíso, being a Chilean city, takes her annual punishment with the courage of a fighting cock. Chile fears neither Nature's furies nor the forces of her foes. Chile is today the dominating power of the western coast – and if a natty little navy and a well-drilled German-looking army, animated by a fighting spirit and backed by a nation of born belligerents count for anything, Chile will for a long time maintain her present prominence; naval, military and political."

Holmes called Valparaíso "the San Francisco of South America". And he was not alone. Frank Wiborg, a commercial traveller assessing investment prospects in the region in 1905, declared: "Valparaíso is the finest harbour next to 'Frisco on the western coast of America." They were probably right since vast land reclamation and port development had taken place in the city in the closing years of the nineteenth century. The English journalist William Howard Russell had noted those efforts in 1890.

Valparaiso Bound!

"Valparaíso is ceasing to be like a mathematical line – length without breadth; the city authorities have already retrieved many hundreds of acres from the sea and are busily engaged in acquiring more. Workmen are engaged in bedding out the earth into the ocean and casting stones of which the mountains furnish near and inexhaustible supplies, and thus establishing foundations for houses already rising or built on quays similarly constructed, so that there are now short cross streets from the main thoroughfare, which has also small offshoots nearly parallel to its course at the Plaza and the Railway Station."

Finding a good bed after months at sea

Yet, if the bay and its port were impressive and the setting quite striking to most new arrivals, the first thought as they stepped on dry land for the first time in months was the hope of finding a comfortable bed and a decent meal. From the early part of the nineteenth century, Valparaíso had catered for European visitors of every kind. By the middle of the century, hotels, taverns, seamen's hostels, boarding houses and spare bedrooms in private dwellings abounded. Mostly they were owned and run by Europeans, but not necessarily run to the best European standards to which visitors had previously been accustomed. William Howard Russell was especially unimpressed by a French establishment:

"Our hostelry, the *Hotel de France*, is half way up the main street. It is kept by a Frenchman, a great deal of a *petit maître*, and, except in the matter of the bill, very little of a landlord; his wife who was good enough to take her meals in the *salle-à-manger*, where she could criticize, if she could not attend to, her guests, was a suitable helpmate. The internal arrangements were discreditable and abominable in every way, and a fair table and the merits of a good chef did not reconcile us to the want of decency, not to speak of comfort, in the domestic economy of the hotel."

A few weeks later, Russell's group led by John Thomas North, chose the *Hotel Colon* instead:

"The landlord, Karl Bernhardt, very indignant when I asked naturally enough, if he was a German. The possibilities, judging from his name, were that he was a Jew of Alsace. 'Allemand! Comment donc? Non, monsieur! Je suis Breton! Je suis le Bre-r-r-eton des Bretons!' Anyway, an excellent host. He told me he was the great Sarah's uncle: 'une gloire pour la France! une honte pour sa famille!'[3] After the experience of the *Hotel de France* it was quite a surprise to the Paymaster-General to have a moderate bill to discharge when

---

3   Sarah Bernhardt, the famous French actress.

we were leaving."

With or without a comfortable first night ashore in good, hospitable company, the first serious observations of the town itself would be made the following day. Here again, initial impressions varied widely. Few were greatly impressed by the local architecture, but it was the life in the streets that caught the attention of those who later bothered to record their early thoughts. Some were delighted by the gaiety and enterprise. Others saw just crime, poverty and misery. Their comments were often coloured by a level of European class snobbism that would be considered unacceptable, if not outrageous, today.

Hotel Colon, Valparaiso, 1867
Photo: William Letts Oliver

Captain Basil Hall and his crew, arriving in time for Christmas 1820, warmed to the town:

"We were fortunate in having reached Valparaíso at a moment when the Christmas festivities were at their height; and multitudes of people had been attracted from the country to witness bull-fights and other shows. On the evening of Christmas, which corresponds with our Midsummer, everybody had strolled abroad to enjoy cool air in the moonlight. Groups of merry dancers were seen at every turn, and crowds of people listening to singers bawling out their old romances to the sound of a guitar; gay parties sauntering along laughing and talking at the full stretch of their voices; wild-looking horsemen pranced about in all quarters, mixing amongst the people on foot, drinking and talking with them, but never dismounting. From one extremity of the town to the other, in short, along the base of the cliffs, and all around the beach of the Almendral, there was an uninterrupted scene of noise and revelry."

John Miers, arriving at much the same period, was his dismissive, easily-irritated and superior self:

"The population of Valparaíso has been greatly exaggerated: when I arrived here it was said to contain 10,000 souls, and is now reported to contain 15,000 of whom at least 3000 are Englishmen; but this, like all reports of Spanish origin, is an exaggeration[4]. Valparaíso cannot contain above 5000, or at most 6000 persons, and certainly not more than four hundred Englishmen, and this number includes the masters and supercargoes of vessels, and naval officers who are continually coming and going. But by far the greater portion of this number consists of sailors, or persons of the lowest sphere of life, thus reducing the actual respectable residents to a very small number. ... The few English families residing here associate wholly among themselves. Like all sea-port towns there exists much low life and debauchery; and the place, from one end to the other, even into the recesses of the ravines and concealed hollows, is filled with *pulperias*, or grog shops, where ardent spirits are copiously consumed and much depravity results therefrom."

The intricate written observations of Maria Graham in the 1820s would become the supreme marker for future historians of Chile[5]. Her descriptions of people, their traditions and their habits were, and probably remain, unrivalled.

"The dress of the Chilian men resembles that of the peasants of the south of Europe; linen shirts and drawers, cloth waistcoats, jackets, and breeches with a coloured listing at the seams; left unbuttoned at the knee, and displaying the drawers. In the neighbourhood of Valparaíso trowsers are fast superseding the short breeches, however. White woollen or cotton stockings, and black leather shoes, are worn by the decent class of men: the very lowest seldom wear stockings; and in lieu of shoes they have either wooden clogs or *oxotas*, made of a square piece of hide bent to the foot, and tied in shape while green... the hair is usually braided in one large braid hanging down behind, and a coloured handkerchief is tied over the head, above which a straw hat is fastened with black cord."

Yet Graham too had a merciless eye for behaviour unbecoming of her ideas of proper Englishness:

"It is not unpleasant to have one's solitude now and then broken in upon by persons who...have characters of their own; but there is a sad proportion in the English society here of trash. However, as vulgarity, ignorance, and coarseness, often disguise kindness of heart, and as I have experienced the latter from

---

4   In this, at least, Miers was certainly correct; even by the time of the 1865 census, only around one thousand English citizens were recorded for the entire province of Valparaiso.

5   Maria Graham's personal history is covered in Chapter 7.

all, it scarcely becomes me to complain of the roughness of the coat of the pine-apple while enjoying the flavour of the fruit"

William Howard Russell, many years later, at least found reason to praise the city's institutions, but little else:

"Many things might be said to the disparagement of Valparaíso – the atrocious pavement of the streets and *trottoirs*, the exorbitant prices in the shops, the foul purlieus and the drinking dens on the quays; but there is much to admire in the well-conducted hospitals, the charitable and educational institutions, the libraries, schools, and public buildings; the facilities for locomotion, the lighting and police of the streets, the extension of electric lighting and acoustics, the telephone, the tram-car, and the railway."

Much to test British nerves and humour

Russell ventured heroically into the surrounding hills (the *"cerros"*) to visit English entrepreneurs and families, but spared no adjectives in describing the abject conditions through which it was necessary to pass:

"Before a visitor can reach one of those pleasant retreats he must pass through several ordeals. I am aware that there are to be found nearer home scenes of misery, squalor, vice and drunkenness, but the purlieus of this city offend every sense at least as much as those of any I have ever seen. They are peopled by a heterogeneous mass, indigenous and foreign. They seem to have come in swarms like insects, carrying with them the debris of rotten tenements, of dust heaps, deserted slums, rag shops, marine dealers' stores – all kinds of odds and ends of planks, doors window-frames, pieces of zinc, and corrugated iron, sacking, tiles, iron piping, &c. – and to have established their suburbs as they listed, each swarm in its own nook. The inhabitants are various: there are industrious men for several days till they have earned a few dollars – then laborious drunkards till the money is gone; artificers, muleteers, sailors, boatmen, carmen, loafers – no doubt honest but poor people – swelter in and about these shanties like bees around a hive; flies innumerable, children almost emulating the flies; dust ever rising, ever falling; drinking-shops hemmed in by mules and horses awaiting their riders; men speechless on the roadside or reeling in the street.

"That and the like was what I saw when I went to visit friends whose charming villas, luxuriously furnished, the centres of pleasant gardens fenced in by belts of natural forest, offered a contrast to the suburbs through which I clombe to reach them – clombe is the word – and visitors of the horses must "climb" to reach the recesses of *The Foxes* or of the *Beautiful Retreat*, and must, if they

29

be nervous, prepare for disagreeable experiences as they descend to the level of the city on which they look down."

One rather grand American lady traveller, May Crommelin, found herself in Valparaíso, in the mid-1890s, after crossing the Andes from Argentina. In 1894, Mrs. Crommelin naturally stayed in a villa on Cerro Alegre. One day she ventured down to the commercial streets below:

"Prancing down these steps we entered a wicked street, that of the brokers. This is the Stock Exchange, and from nine till dusk the pavements are crowded with groups of eager men, for stockbroking is at present laughingly described as 'about the only paying profession in Chili'. No lady alone, or even two ladies, would be bold enough to risk the passage of the Calle Prat, 'for those men do nothing but gossip and make remarks'. Collectively they form a street club, and

Turn-of-the-century elegance. Valparaiso before the 1906 earthquake.
From "Chile" by G.F. Scott Elliot

everyone knows what horrid places clubs are for gossip."

To say the lady had a blinkered view of the city is to understate:

"There are few poor in Valparaíso, either foreign or Chilian, so sewing and some visits to the hospital are the only outlets for the indwelling charity of most British bosoms. But during the late war[6] the English ladies nursed the wounded with praiseworthy devotion. Of other amusements there are football, cricket

6   Probably a reference to the civil war of 1891.

and polo at Viña del Mar, with occasional balls and acting, much music, reading and debating clubs."

Indeed, by the end of the nineteenth century, many diversions were available to foreign residents and visitors of Valparaíso (see Chapter 7). It had not always been so, as John Miers had protested during his stay:

"...in a short time the place becomes nearly intolerable, since, independent of the want of society, there exists to public amusement, no theatre, commercial reading, or news room; no parade, not even a single spot to walk on, except up the fatiguing steep hills, or in the narrow dirty streets, where, in consequence of the continually violent south winds the dust and sand are raised in clouds, to the great annoyance of passengers. In short, in spite of its matchless and beautiful climate, its most agreeable temperature throughout the year, I do not know a more uncomfortable and cheerless place of residence for a being of sense and feeling than Valparaíso."

By the turn of the century – but before the 1906 earthquake struck – the city had a more attractive face for the visiting American businessman, Frank Wiborg, who noted that "... the public buildings and business blocks are handsome, imposing edifices, and there are stores and shops filled with all the beautiful things that money and taste can demand, and everywhere the bustle of much business is going on and a great deal of shipping." The same commercial traveller was struck by the eccentricities of the city, not least, finding that the double-deck buses had women as conductors. "I would suggest to American women seeking new fields of industry to consider the street cars," he proposed with the macho impertinence that was common at the time.

Less than ten years later, with Valparaíso still a mess of earthquake rubble, another American visitor, Robert Mansfield, was understandably less than enthusiastic on his first glimpse of the town:

"Valparaíso is as cosmopolitan in architecture as it is in population. It possesses no architectural features that can be considered national in character; it has few public buildings worthy of the name, no system of parks or boulevards - nothing to distinguish it except a consistent mismanagement of municipal affairs."

Yet, perhaps one of the most colourful descriptions of the joys and irritations of a first encounter with Valparaíso came from a Chilean. Josè Joaquín Vallejo wrote some hilarious but penetrating social commentaries during the 1840s. He lived and worked, for the most part, in the mining town of Copiapó in the Atacama region. His limited travels further south, especially in Santiago and Valparaíso, were cautious, critical and full of suspicions of the city-dwellers. Writing in *El Mercurio* in August 1843, under his pen-name "Jotabeche" he displayed the same mixed feelings as the European arrivals. His first glimpse was euphoric:

"At dawn, the hills of Valparaíso directly ahead. The chill on deck was unbearable, but who could tear their eyes away from the beautiful view about to unfold before our eyes in scene after glorious scene. The telegraph office, the cliffs above the port and their windmills, the winding roads that go to Santiago and Quillota: a forest of masts and, amid all this confusion, all the bright, proud flags of the earth; ships spreading their sails to head out to sea like birds taking flight; the barrios of [Cerro] Arrayán with their houses as close together as the numbers on a logarithm table; all those ravines and canyons where man has stuck his dwellings the way shellfish planted their conches in past millennia when those heights were covered by the sea; the elegant little towers that crown the Planchada and the Almendral or some other section, huge new objects gradually coming into view as we approach by sea this dazzling city that time must mean to symbolize the white star on our flag. Our entrance into Valparaíso was like a festival to me."

But once he set foot in the town, the enthusiasm quickly receded:

"Let's move ahead. But who the devil can move ahead in this Valparaíso? Where can you go without running into obstacles? Where does a poor provincial go who's used to walking down the streets of his own town without the risk of being crushed under a load of freight, without having to stand aside for some cart, without some gringo giving him a shove this way, a second gringo pushing him that way, and a third elbowing him, a fourth knocking him down, and a fifth and sixth trampling him underfoot – a 'Careful, sir!' here, a 'Careful, sir!' there, another 'Careful, sir!' in front of him, a 'Step aside!' in back of him, and they assist you with a shove; 'Get out of the way!' and before long they've knocked off your hat, which rolls down another street where the hooves of a horse or the wheels of a public carriage happen to run over it?

And it only got worse:

"There's nothing to do here if you aren't buying or selling; in order to have dealings with human beings you have to sign a contract. ... Amid this babel, an elegant dresser is an exotic plant, the absent-minded professor a suicide, the provincial a ball rolling every which way, and the poet just another wanderer through the crowded desert, a desert without illusions or mirages to nourish him, beauties to inspire him, or (and this is the worst lack of all) any other cross to make him melancholy but the Cross of Kings on coins he'll never own.

32

... I, who never saw the people of my town run about in such a tremendous tumult and hubbub over any business of this world, was nearly suffocating in this plaza; perturbed, maimed and oppressed by its bustling, rude multitude, it seemed to me that the prophecy of Judgment Day in the Valley of Jehoshaphat must be coming to pass, a gathering in which, more likely than not, we'll be similarly piled on top of each other, three to a shoe."

First impressions are one thing, but what of parting? One French traveller in 1850 had hardly been short of critical comments throughout his stay. But as his ship drew further out into the Bay, on its way back to San Francisco, Charles de Lambertie reflected sadly:

"Sitting on the poop-deck while the boat, pushed by a good breeze, gained the open sea speedily, I could see disappearing little by little this likeable city which had offered, after a long voyage on troubled seas, such agreeable hospitality. I thought of its lively, playful people, so loving of pleasures, of their games, of their traditions so full of charm for a foreigner. I seemed to see again the handkerchief waved so gracefully as the queca was danced, the harp and *vihuela* singing in my ears as delightful concerts. The more the land receded from my eyes the more I reflected deeply on this society that I believed to have bid farewell for the last time. That is the incessant sadness of the traveller."

Valparaiso Bound!

3.

Explorers, pirates, admirals and deserters

Then came the cry of "Call all hands on deck!"
The Dauber knew its meaning; it was come:
Cape Horn, that tramples beauty into wreck,
And crumples steel and smites the strong man dumb.
Down clattered flying kites and staysails; some
Sang out in quick, high calls: the fair-leads skirled,
And from the south-west came the end of the world...

Rounding the Horn from *"Dauber"* by John Masefield

For two hundred years after the arrival of the Spaniards in the early six-teenth century, the coasts of Chile and Peru remained largely uncharted. For the European pioneers it was necessarily a time of exploration and discovery. Trade was retained as a monopoly by the Spanish, and managed from Lima. All commerce had to pass through Peru, whether between the colonial territories or back and forth to the mother country. So piracy thrived. And, later, as the independence movements began their hesitant course, so the sailors of other countries – especially the British – engaged themselves with a force and enthusiasm that would one day provide a foundation for the continuing European role in free nations on the west coast of South America.

Not that there was a clear demarcation between these various maritime endeavours. Pirates became explorers and map-makers. Otherwise respectable traders engaged in illegal as well as legitimate commerce. Naval commanders were often as gifted in looting and taking the treasure of 'enemy' vessels as they were in defending national interests. To the monarchs of Europe, a sea captain returning with a hold full of gold, silver and other valuables, was more welcome than one entering port with no more than a batch of weakened prisoners and tales of valiant patriotic action to take distant territory of little obvious value.

Mastery of the interior by Spain, achieved initially by conquests fanning out southwards and westwards from the coasts of the Spanish Main[1], ultimately required dominance on the Pacific coast. That could only come with a direct

---

1   Essentially, what are now the northern coasts of Panama, Colombia and Venezuela

passage from the Atlantic to the Pacific. Initially, the search was for an east-west route to the Spice Islands – now part of Indonesia. By the fifteenth century, access to spices made fortunes, so control of the trade became a strategic priority for European nations.

A route south and westwards?

The routes to the Orient were well-known, commonly passing by the Cape of Good Hope and on across the Indian Ocean. But was there a shorter or easier way? Could trading ships sail south and westwards instead? To find out, the accomplished Portuguese sea captain Fernão de Magalhães (Ferdinand Magellan), financed by the Spanish crown, left Seville on 10 August 1519 commanding five small ships, none larger than 130 tons or with more than a 60-man crew. Conditions were sufficiently tough and discipline cruel for mutiny to break out in three of the vessels while the fleet was wintering at Port St Julian in southern Argentina. Some accounts suggest that at least two of the Spanish captains were implicated. Magellan quickly restored his own authority by trying and executing one of the commanders along with a number of accomplices. Another of the captains was left ashore. Up to forty other death sentences were handed out although the mutineers were later reprieved.

On 21 October 1520, well over a year after leaving Spain, the four remaining ships sighted Cape Virgins[2] at the eastern (Atlantic) end of what would become known as the Strait of Magellan. Observing a wide opening to the south, Magellan sent two vessels ahead to explore while he waited. Only when news was received that there was indeed a passage did Magellan proceed. By 27 November the group emerged from the western limit and entered the Pacific. On the way, not only did they become the European discoverers of Chile but they noted the large land mass to the south of the Strait and named it Tierra del Fuego. This 'Land of Fire', was presumed to be a reference to the fires of Indian settlements though some accounts speak of an active volcano.

The voyage continued to be beset by accidents, illness and mutiny. Having passed into the Pacific, Magellan made not for the Spice Islands but towards China. When he arrived in the Philippines he rashly, and unnecessarily, got himself involved in the bloody feuds rumbling incessantly among the native tribes. On 8 September 1522 Magellan was duly murdered on the island of Zebu. The very next day thirty of his mariners were massacred having, even more rashly, accepted an invitation to a native feast on shore.

Only two ships of the original fleet remained and just enough crew to man

---

2   Initially named "Cape of 11,000 Virgins" by Magellan after the legend of Saint Ursula

them both. They finally navigated back to the Spice Islands. One of them, Magellan's original vessel, the *Trinidad*, was leaking badly and, after some repairs, it was decided it should turn east and sail to Mexico. The *Victoria*, now under the command of Juan Sebastián Elcano sailed on. He became the first man to circumnavigate the globe when he arrived back in Spain, on 8

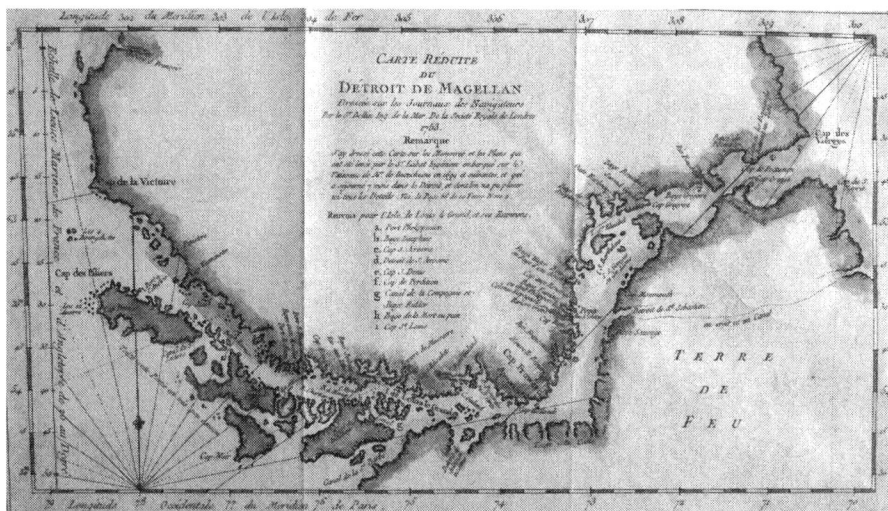

Navigators' map of the Strait of Magellan, 1753. From seven months of observations made during a 1699 voyage. *Author's collection*

September 1522 after a voyage of over three years. Elcano was accompanied by just 35 survivors from the original combined 230-strong crew.

Elcano was received as a hero and was eventually properly rewarded. Very soon he was given a new command as part of a second expedition of seven ships under Commander Garcia Jofre de Loaisa, to reassert Spanish preeminence over the Spice Islands and to improve navigation charts of the Magellan Strait. The fleet departed from the Spanish port of Coruna on 24 July 1524. Though several ships were lost early in the voyage, they passed through the Strait successfully. However de Loaisa died suddenly, leaving command of the fleet to Elcano who himself expired from illness just six days later. The expedition held out for several years against Portuguese attacks and in the absence of reinforcement and supplies from Madrid. Ultimately, the king of Spain, Charles V, gave up, sold the islands to King John III of Portugal and the few Spanish survivors of the original de Loaisa fleet were given passage back to Lisbon.

Two expeditions had been initiated in Spain to relieve the de Loaisa fleet. Both failed. That of Sebastian Cabot got no further than the River Plate. The second, to be commanded by a Portuguese, Simon de Alcazaba, was abandoned when the Spanish king sold the Spice Islands. Nevertheless, Alcazaba had powerful friends in the Spanish court and, in 1534, was granted a large slice of Patagonia – the territory immediately to the south of the Chilean concession granted to the conquistador Diego de Almagro (see Chapter 4). It was 300 leagues in length (approximately 1250 kilometers) and was named Nueva León. The concession included the Strait of Magellan. Two ships set off that year with Alcazaba and 250 crew and passengers to take possession.

It was to be another voyage marked by poor leadership, starvation, treachery and death. Vital supplies were inadequate from the start – so rations were short and a continual source of discontent and dissent. The ships entered the Magellan Strait briefly in 1535 but poor weather drove them back into the Atlantic. Giving up on any further attempts, they anchored finally on the Patagonian coast of Argentina in a natural harbor which the commander named Puerto de los Leones. Alcazaba had himself sworn in as governor and then set off inland with a large party. The conditions were appalling. Soon there was a mutiny, resulting finally in the murder of Alcazaba. With the deaths by illness and starvation of most of the rest of the crew only a handful of survivors eventually made it back to San Domingo (Dominican Republic). The settlement and the dead governor's realm were never revived.

Indeed, the successful passage through the Strait of Magellan by de Loaisa's ships was an exception in that epoch. That of Alcazaba was nearer the rule. Most expeditions were lost and many never even reached Cape Virgins. The Spaniards practically abandoned the route, preferring to reach the Pacific coast of South America via an overland crossing of the Panama peninsula and then sailing southwards to Peru. Much later, they would establish routes from Buenos Aires and Mendoza, across the Andes. From the 1550s, further attempts were made to explore the lower coastline of Chile but were not often productive. Juan Ladrilleros was among the most admired scientific explorers of his time, but even he lost seventy men from his original crew during his 1557 voyage from which only he and two others survived to return northwards.

The detail of the mainland coast, and the thousands of islands and fjords that make up the south-western edge of Chile were mapped over hundreds of years by explorers of many nations. The church also played a role. The Jesuits settled on the large, fertile island of Chiloé[3] in 1609 and subsequent missionary

3 Some 1000 km south of Santiago, Chiloé is Chile's largest island – discounting Tierra

journeys led to the complex geography of the region becoming better under-stood. Father José Garcia explored a long length of coastline, which he mapped roughly. But only in 1787 and 1796 was a detailed topographical survey under-taken, between 41 and 46 degrees south, this time by a lieutenant in the Spanish Navy, Don José de Moraleda y Montero. Much of his work was carried out in specially-fitted Indian canoes. Thereafter, it was mainly British and American expeditions that carried out the detailed mapping and survey of the coastline in the nineteenth century. Such was British involvement in the charting of this part of the world that King Edward VII was named arbitrator in deciding the trace of the Argentine-Chilean border from north to south, along the Andes. His award, at the end of 1902, settled matters once and for all, including the sensitive division of Tierra del Fuego.

Call it trade promotion ... or piracy

What then of the pirates and privateers who sometimes doubled as explor-ers and map-makers? And what is the difference between the two vocations? Daniel Defoe wrote:

"I shall not repeat what I have said in the History concerning the Privateers of the West-Indies, where I have taken Notice they live upon Spoil; and as Custom is second Nature, it is no Wonder that, when an honest Livlyhood is not easily had, they run into one so like their own; so that it may be said, that Privateers in Time of War are a Nursery for Pyrates against a Peace."

It was common practice for European monarchs and governments to issue *Letters of Marque* to *privateers* – sometimes known as *corsairs* – to take and loot the ships of enemies in wartime. These were private individuals sailing privately-owned, but armed, sailing vessels, profiting from the treasure taken from their victims. The demarcation with the role of *pirates* in peacetime, as suggested by Defoe, may be vaguer and more illusory than he believed, with outright pirates (or *buccaneers* operating against the Spanish in the West Indies) taking frequent advantage of the known existence of letters of marque.

Whatever they were called – and we will often term them *pirates* regardless of their 'legality' – for at least two-hundred years from the late 16th century onwards, there were many to be found generating fear and outrage not only on the Spanish Main but up and down the length of the Pacific Coast of South America. Their role may have been provoked in part by the continual states of war existing among European nations of the period and in part by the attempts of Spain to monopolize trade between the mother country and its colonies

---

del Fuego, which is divided between Chile and Argentina.

and among the colonies themselves. If other Europeans expected a slice of the action – and especially that yielding gold – then there were not many options available other than taking it by force.

The favourite pirate of Queen Elizabeth I of England was Francis Drake. Born in the town of Tavistock in 1540, Drake spent several years of his youth living with cousins in the seafaring Hawkins family a few miles away. One cousin, John Hawkins – later Sir John – seems to have given him his first chances to undertake significant sea voyages and, under his command, the young Drake learned the skills and art of piracy. With John Hawkins he sailed the west coast of Africa collecting and stealing slaves and crossed the Atlantic to sell them. Then, in 1567, Hawkins assembled a fleet of six ships, including two contributed by Queen Elizabeth, and gave Drake his first command, that

Sir Francis Drake by Jodocus Hondius
Library of Congress, Washington

of the tiny 50-ton *Judith*.

Having collected slaves with difficulty, the ships eventually headed off towards the Caribbean where Hawkins attempted to sell his captives. It was to be a troubled expedition, John Hawkins eventually finding himself trapped by bad weather and a Spanish fleet in the port of San Juan de Ulúa, off Veracruz, Mexico. By Hawkins' account, Drake and the *Judith* sailed away just when instructed to go to the aid of another captain under a surprise attack by the Spanish. The consequent rift between the two men festered. While Drake had learned a lot from his cousin – including a taste for good living at the Captain's table and a tendency towards harsh and rapid punishment to maintain discipline – the pair had very different characters. In 1577, he was commissioned by the Queen and a group of investors to undertake a trading and exploration voyage around the tip of South America. Quite what was to be traded was never clear. But the investors would certainly have had reason to believe that piracy, not trade, was the true objective. Drake constructed his own ship – the 150-ton, heavily-armed *Pelican* – financed by wealth acquired from earlier voyages of piracy and plunder. The armada had four principal vessels and a total complement of around 170 crewmen.

It was an extraordinary voyage, and the subject of often differing accounts. After a false start which was abruptly ended by a squall, the fleet made sail from Plymouth on 13 December 1577. Drake's touchy and difficult temperament was soon apparent. Trouble struck just a month out, in the Cape Verde Islands. A

HMS Meander in a squall in the Strait of Magellan, 1851.

The Illustrated London News

large Portuguese merchant ship, *Santa Maria*, was captured with a valuable cargo. Adding the vessel to his fleet, Drake named Thomas Doughty (one of his "equal" partners) as captain. Shortly afterwards, Doughty discovered Drake's brother, Thomas, stealing from the Portuguese cargo. He should probably have said nothing; instead, rashly, he reported the matter to the commander.

A heated quarrel ensued between Francis Drake and Doughty. Drake, taking the accusation as a personal attack, could not be pacified. Eventually, Drake changed ships to the *Mary,* as the *Santa Maria* had been re-named, now under the command of Thomas Drake. The *Pelican* would be captained by Thomas Doughty. Nevertheless, a fundamental problem of authority remained. Drake was constantly obsessed with what he regarded as a betrayal and sought out the smallest items of gossip that might confirm Doughty's insolence and disobedience. By the time the ships had crossed the Atlantic and reached the estuary of the River Plate, the persecution of Thomas Doughty, and his brother John, had attained extreme proportions.

Drake eventually considered he had sufficient reason to strip Thomas Doughty of his command. A furious row ensued with Drake, attacked verbally, striking out with his fists and then having Doughty bound to the mast. The two brothers were later isolated with Drake contending they were magicians or conjurors and therefore a danger to the fleet. Seamen who sided with the Doughtys were themselves condemned. Displaying all the signs of paranoia, Drake forced a trial of Thomas Doughty for mutiny and by manipulating the jury secured a guilty verdict. Despite general distaste among officers and men alike, Doughty's head was chopped off and displayed as a 'traitor'. Drake could offer no documentary proof that he had the Queen's authority for such an execution and his obsession with Doughty has never been satisfactorily explained, though there was gossip that Doughty had seduced Drake's wife. Whatever the case, the treatment and demise of Doughty would stain the entire voyage.

By the end of October 1578 – more than ten and a half months after leaving Plymouth – the small fleet emerged from the Strait of Magellan and began sailing north. With heavy losses sustained in the passage through the Strait, partly from hunger and disease and partly because several ships were wrecked or separated, the total crew was now around 80 men. Violent encounters with indigenous Indian tribes in the south led Drake and his expedition to push on towards Valparaíso and Quintero expecting to find valuable cargoes to plunder.

They finally arrived in what was then the small port and village of Valparaíso on 5 December 1578. Drake immediately took an old Spanish ship, *La Capitana,* which reaped him as much as 200,000 pesos of gold as well as stores of wine and lumber. Some of the crew landed in the speedily-evacuated town and took wine, food and a number of religious ornaments from a church. Most valuable of all, however, seems to have been a set of charts detailing the ports on the coast. The ships moved progressively northwards, from harbour to harbour, plundering as they went. They seized much treasure, especially silver, but also wine, food and clothing. The fleet arrived in Guatulco – a port just south of Acapulco – around 13 April 1579. From there, unexpectedly, Drake set off west to circumnavigate the globe.

Drake arrived back in Plymouth late in September 1580, not far short of three years after his departure. Drake returned with his ships' holds bulging with treasure, including several tons of gold. But he arrived to multiple legal claims against him by the Spanish government which wanted restitution of lost treasure. Queen Elizabeth seems to have given authority for Drake to take a good share of the gold for himself, with the crews sharing another portion and the expedition's investors receiving double their original outlay. The balance of treasure was moved from place to place, including the Tower of London to avoid the legal clutches of the Spanish. Sir Francis Drake thus became one of the richest men in the country.

Another notorious English pirate of the time was Thomas Cavendish (often referred to as Thomas Candish). Cavendish was born in Suffolk in England, of a wealthy family with a large estate and interests in foreign trade. The young man had an enthusiasm for the sea and did not hesitate to sell and mortgage his estate to finance a series of adventures, the most celebrated of which was a voyage around the world, from 1586 to 1588. With a commission from the Queen, he built two ships and set out with a crew of 123, including men who had sailed with Drake. After looting along the West African coast he crossed the Atlantic and made a relatively easy passage through the Magellan Strait, even if the crews nearly starved for want of provisions on the barren and dangerous coast.

The little fleet then made its way northwards calling at the ports of Concepción, Quintero and Arica, raiding as it went. They had bloody encounters with Araucanian Indians and later with Spanish soldiers. Reaching Mexico, and then setting sail westwards, Cavendish circumnavigated the globe in two years and two months and returned with much treasure. A few years later he tried again. This time, he planned badly, met extreme weather in the Magellan Strait and eventually turned back into the Atlantic. The expedition was ruined, there was dissention among the captains and Cavendish finally died of illness on his own ship without seeing England again.

Sir Richard Hawkins, the son of Sir John, seems to have had some difficulty in deciding whether he was an explorer or pirate. Certainly, his voyage to the Pacific from 1594, was marked by the taking of abundant treasure from Spanish and other interests along the way. But it would end disastrously, with Hawkins imprisoned first in Lima and then Spain.

His first major plundering raid was to be Valparaíso itself where he arrived in late April 1594. In his personal account, Hawkins took delight in the ease with which he excised the contents of the ships in the bay and that of the town's merchants and residents. Spotting four anchored ships in the harbour, Hawkins immediately lowered armed row-boats the sight of which quickly persuaded the crews of the vessels to get ashore. The following morning as the holds were ransacked, the disappointment was intense: rather than the copious quantities of gold expected, there were just normal ships' stores including three thousand chickens, bread, dried beef, bacon and merchandise of no use to Hawkins. So he sold three of the vessels back to their captains: "... for a small price, rather than to burne them." The fourth he hung on to since his crew was convinced there was much gold stashed away on her somewhere, and would not be per-

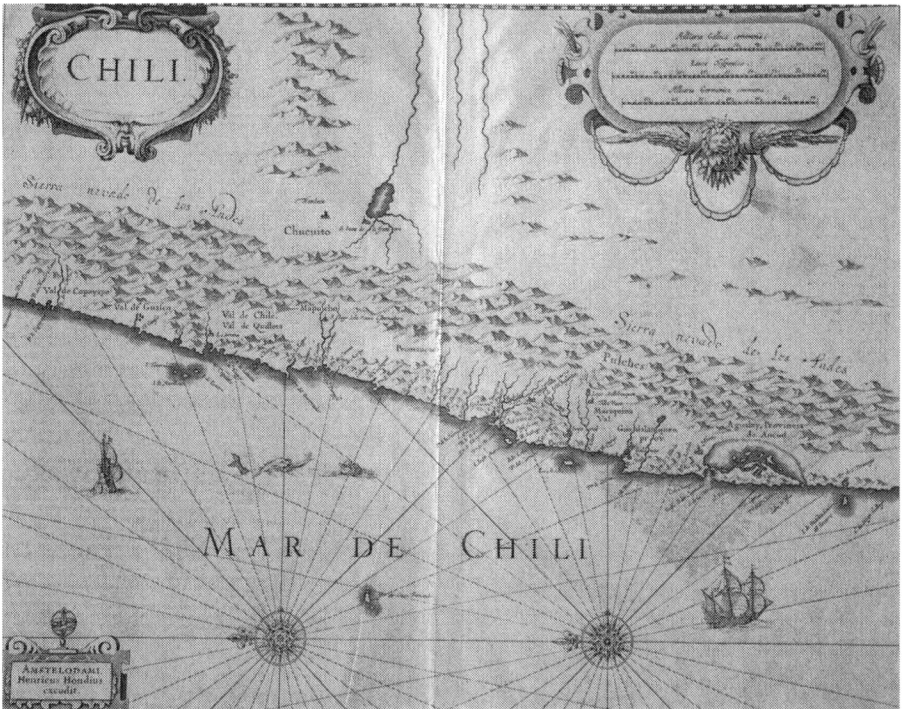

Part of the coast of Chile by the Dutch master engraver and cartographer Hendrik Hondius, 1638. "Val Parayso" is marked near the centre, with "S. Iago" inland.

Author's collection

suaded otherwise.

Happily for Hawkins, another ship entered the Bay soon after and was instantly captured. This time gold was found in large quantities. The ship and pilot, who knew the coast well, were taken along as the little fleet later moved northwards. However, the pilot, was put ashore in Peru: Hawkins being "moved by compassion (for that he was a man charged with wife and children)". The owner, who accompanied Hawkins up to Lima, had his ship returned there.

Hawkins marvelled that his 75 men and boys had been able to maintain control of five captured ships during their stay in Valparaíso, especially when he learned later that there had been military units onshore waiting their chance if the crews showed any lack of attention in watching over the vessels. Yet he claimed to have had more fear of the taverns of the town: "But the enemy I feared not so much as the wine; which, notwithstanding all the diligence and prevention I could use day and night, overthrew many of my people."

Finally, however, the enemy would prevail. Having taken many ships and much treasure on the coasts of Chile and Peru, the fleet was finally run down by a powerful Spanish naval force. After a three-day battle in which Hawkins was severely wounded the English ships surrendered. The commander was jailed in Lima before being transferred to various prisons in Spain and finally released to return to his Devon home some ten years after he had first set sail.

The Dutch take their turn

The British were notorious pirates and privateers. But the Dutch were not far behind, even if they called it commerce. In 1595, having finally rid itself of Spanish rule, the United Provinces of the Netherlands saw its future in global trade and especially in controlling the European market for spices from Asia. For that, there was no alternative but to build the best and the most ships available to any naval power of the time. It was also necessary to encourage the most capable navigators, chart-makers and sea captains to challenge the Spanish and Portuguese. After all, Madrid retained the naval strength to undermine Dutch trading ambitions and the will to do so.

In 1602 the Dutch East India Company was established as probably the world's first stock company and multinational corporation. It had a charter to engage in whatever activity was necessary to promote a monopoly in trade with Asian suppliers. That included waging war, establishing colonies, minting coinage and negotiating treaties. Access to the Pacific was a priority.

Already, in 1598, a group of rich and ambitious Dutch merchants had fixed on Oliver van Noort to command an expedition through the Strait of Magellan, employing Sir Thomas Cavendish's pilot to help navigate the difficult waters. He did so with the greatest difficulty, gales constantly driving the Dutch vessels back from the entrance. The fleet reached the Pacific nearly eighteen months after departing from its home port, the island of Goeree, in Holland. Van

Noort, who had lost several of his ships along the way, took a Spanish vessel off the island of Mocha, between Valdivia and Concepción, and others in Valparaíso before moving north to Arica and Callao – without discovering the gold they were told was being carried by Spanish vessels in those seas. He went on to cross the Pacific to Guam, the Philippines and on round the world. Van Noort turned out to be the pioneer who would be followed by many more Dutch

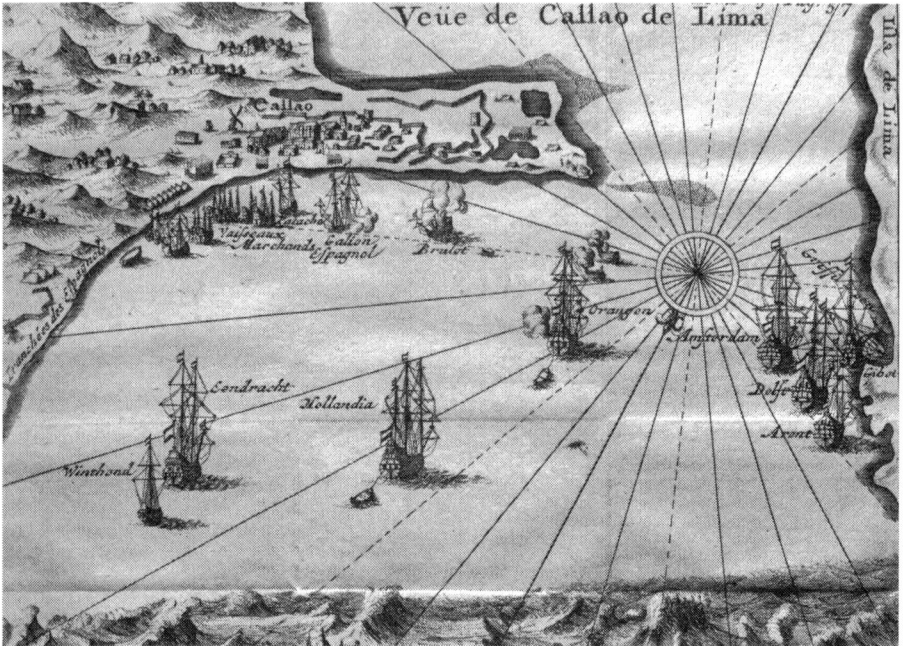

Blockade of Lima's port, Callao, in May 1624 by the Dutch fleet.

Author's collection

sailors, pirates and explorers.

Still, the Dutch East India Company's ambition to secure maritime dominance was far from achieved. It would await the success of another circumnavigation, taking nearly three years, this time by Admiral George Spilbergen whose fleet of six vessels set out in 1614. They passed through the Strait with little problem apart from skirmishes with indigenous tribes and the terrified sighting – replicating reports from many expeditions of the time, including those of Magellan and Schouten – of "a man of gigantic stature climbing a high hill on the southern shore of the straits, called Tierra del Fuego.'[4]

The route up the coast of Chile and Peru – including calls at Mocha Island, Valparaíso and Quintero – was well chosen to avoid strong Spanish naval and coastal defences but yielded little treasure. Off Callao, Spilbergen was forced into a heavy naval engagement with a powerful, eight-vessel Spanish fleet commanded by Admiral Don Rodrigo de Mendoza, a kinsman to the viceroy. Accounts of what ensued are confused, as was the engagement, with ships being sunk by their own side and a general lack of experienced and decisive command. In the event, however, the Dutch were judged to have had the better of the Spanish whose own admiral went down with his ship during an attempted escape. The reputation of the Dutch as a naval power in the Pacific was thus secured and Spilbergen was welcomed home as a national hero and a champion of the Dutch East India Company.

One discovery changes everything

Yet the monopolistic advantages enjoyed, courtesy of the state, by the East India Company, rankled with other Dutch merchants. Unexpectedly, an effort by two of them to circumvent the monopoly led to one of the greatest discoveries of all, that of Cape Horn. Isaac Le Maire, a rich merchant in Amsterdam, and Wilhelm Cornelisz Schouten of Hoorn, argued that while the Company's monopoly applied to commercial activity west of the Strait of Magellan, there would be nothing to stop them exploiting opportunities to the south. It was a specious claim since there was absolutely no evidence of anything like the Spice Islands to the south of Tierra del Fuego and only the vague and little known report from the voyage of Francis Drake suggesting that there was even open sea to that region. But the argument was sufficiently sound legally for an expedition to be mounted.

Le Maire agreed to provide half of the necessary funds to equip two ships while Schouten and other wealthy figures from Hoorn found the rest. Schouten was appointed commander of the two vessels and Isaac's eldest son, Jacob was to be president of the expedition and supercargo[5]. They set out in June 1615

---

4   These sightings were probably of Indians of the Onas (Selk'nam) tribe of Tierra del Fuego who stood well above average European heights of the time. Some fanciful reports assessed them at as much as eleven-foot high (3.4 metres). When he explored the island in the 1830s, Charles Darwin was less impressed: "The tallest amongst the Fuegians was evidently much pleased at his height being noticed. When placed back to back with the tallest of the boat's crew, he tried his best to edge on higher ground, and to stand on tiptoe." (Darwin, *Journal of Researches into the Geology and Natural History of the Various Countries Visited by the H.M.S. Beagle, Under the Command of Captain Fitzroy from 1832 to 1836. 1839*)

5   The officer having responsibility for the cargo and commercial activity on the voyage.

from the island of Texel but it was only in October, after they had left the African coast for Brazil, that the two crews were told the objective of the voyage: to discover a new route into the South Sea. As they journeyed south along the coast of Patagonia, one of the two ships – ironically, perhaps, the one called the *Horne* – was lost in a fire and the remaining vessel *Eendracht* (Concord) had to sail on alone with both crews aboard.

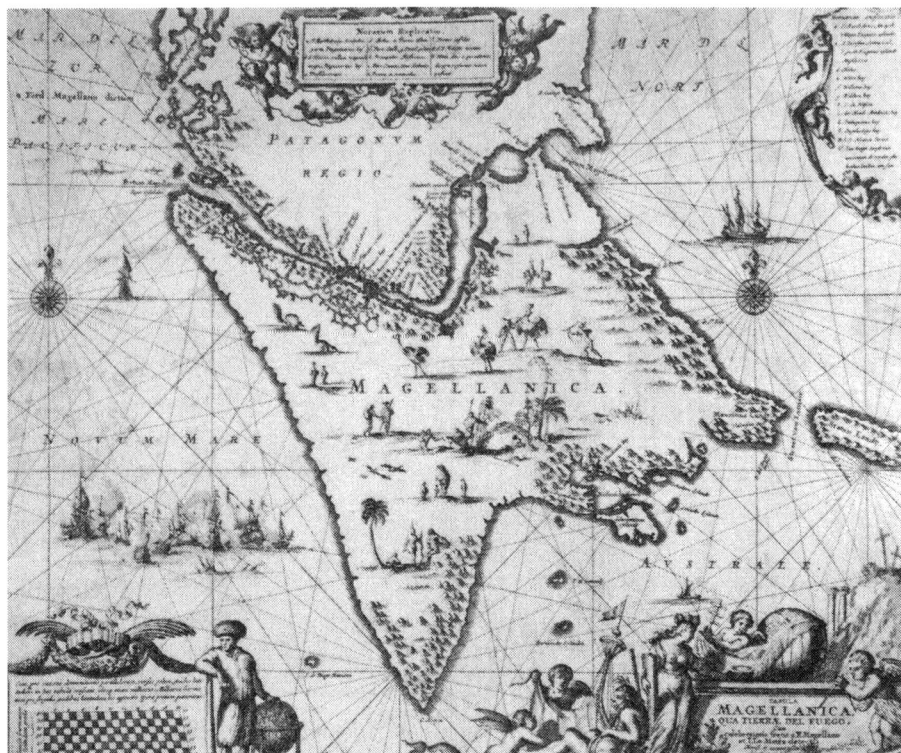

A 1671 map by Arnold Montanus of Amsterdam showing early notions of the Strait of Magellan and with Cape Horn incorrectly placed at the southern tip of Tierra del Fuego.   *Fondation Laurent-Vibert, Lourmarin, France*

By the following January they had sailed well to the south, passing the Falkland Islands, which are almost due east of the entrance to the Magellan Strait, before heading west and finding the coast of Tierra del Fuego. By 25 January the vessel had reached the passage which would be named the Le Maire Strait, with the coast of Tierra del Fuego to the north-west and Isla de los Estados (or, originally, Staten Land in honour of the States of Holland) to the south-east. A few days later, after heavy buffeting by an angry sea and freezing temperatures a look-out perched high on the main mast spotted a point of land which was soon named Cape Hoorn.

They headed on westwards but contrary winds seem to have blown the ship back south and probably east of the Cape at least once. Nevertheless, they were eventually able to turn northwards and, after fighting violent storms, found the western entrance of the Magellan Strait on 12 February. There the crew was treated to a celebration with plenty of wine. Another month on and they were at anchor off Juan Fernandez Island. They took on stores before heading north-westwards across the Pacific to Java and eventually Jakarta (then known as Batavia), discovering various islands in the Dutch East Indies (now Indonesia) along the way. There, after what had otherwise been a successful voyage, the entire expedition was ended prematurely when the local head of the Dutch East India Company seized the ship, its crew and cargo, claiming the *Eendracht* had been sailing illegally in waters protected by the company's charter. The shocked officers and crews were provided berths on other ships for their return to Holland, but Jacob Le Maire died at sea, aged 31, without seeing his home country again.

It was a tragic end to a remarkable voyage of discovery, the greatest since that of Magellan. Even if Le Maire did not live to see it, the lives of sailors and travellers to the Pacific coast of South America would never be the same. The passage round Cape Horn, however difficult, transformed the voyage from Europe.

The Dutch Admiral, Hendrik Brouwer, was another example of a mixture of explorer, mercenary and pirate on Company business. In 1644, Brouwer was commissioned by the Dutch West India Company to establish a national presence in southern Chile that would provide the company with a maritime springboard for its commercial links across the Pacific. On his way towards Cape Horn – and perhaps accidentally – he navigated in a southerly direction across the Le Maire Strait and down the coast of Staten Land. He soon discovered that far from being the edge of the great land mass that had previously been imagined (effectively one extremity of Antarctica) Staten Land was, in reality, an island that could be rounded, opening up another approach to the Cape.

The Dutch commander landed on Chiloé Island in 1644, destroying the Spanish settlements there. His men crossed to the mainland and captured Valdivia, establishing their own fortress there. The Araucanian tribes at first formed what amounted to a military alliance with the Dutch, helping to supply the town. Indeed, for a while it looked like southern Chile might become a Dutch territory. But when Brouwer died suddenly, the Indians became suspicious of the real intentions of the expedition's leaders and promptly disappeared. The Dutch garrison's provisions ran short and the remnants of Brouwer's expedition preferred to abandon both Valdivia and Chiloé.

The British reassert themselves

Through the later part of the seventeenth century and well into the eighteenth, British pirates and privateers again dominated the waters off Peru and Chile. For much of that time there was a succession of wars – declared or assumed - between Spain and England so piracy became intricately linked with strategic interests especially as it required the commitment of warships half the world away from where the real battles were taking place. The French usually sided with the Spanish, and thus could be expected to help obstruct British commerce off the South American coast. But pirates went about their business largely unperturbed.

Indeed, trade with Spain and among her colonies was upset to such an extent that the authorities could eventually no longer stand meekly by. In 1682, Chile's new governor, Don José de Garro, decided that some minimal riposte and basic defences were necessary. He fortified Valparaíso, Coquimbo and other ports and ordered that their inhabitants be trained to handle arms. Coastguard sentinels were also established. Shortly after these measures were put in place, the English pirate, Charles Swan, was driven out of Valdivia, and Edward Davis's ships fared little better. Davis went first to Juan Fernandez Island, for provisions. He then went on to plunder ports on the Peruvian coast, even taking Guayaquil. However, in 1686, he and his crew hit trouble when they moved south again, landing near Coquimbo to get stores and cattle. They were taken on by a detachment of cavalry and driven back to the shore, leaving three men dead. Later the same year, two of Davis's ships anchored in Coquimbo Bay, landing before dawn in an effort to take La Serena. Reaching the city, they quickly found themselves surrounded by soldiers. For thirty hours they were besieged inside St Domingo's church before making a run back to their ships, this time carrying eight or nine dead and with no stores. The Spanish took further action against the pirates: for instance depopulating some small islands, including Mocha, north of Valdivia, which was a popular port of call after the passage round Cape Horn and where provisions were often secured. Another initiative was an attempt to destroy all the goats on Juan Fernandez Island, a move that did not improve relations between the resident Spanish and Indian communities.

50

The English Captain William Dampier made several voyages to the South Sea and two circumnavigations. In 1683, he made an easy passage through the Magellan Strait and on to Juan Fernandez Island where he made copious observations of the flora and fauna. After taking several Spanish vessels as prizes off the Chilean mainland, he sailed on to the Galapagos Islands where he again recorded detailed hydrographic data and descriptions of the natural features. Sailing much of the time with the ships of Swan, Davis and John Eaton, the combined pirate force created havoc up and down the coasts of Peru, Chile, and Ecuador despite the Spanish effort to improve defences. In all, Dampier's second circumnavigation lasted eight years, a constantly varying mixture of piracy and discovery and observation.

The man who became Robinson Crusoe

Yet, Dampier's most celebrated historical footnote is his association with the castaway who became the model for the story of Robinson Crusoe by Daniel Defoe. Alexander Selkirk was a troublesome Scottish crew member of the *Cinque Ports* which set sail from Kinsale in Ireland in September 1703. The vessel was part of the expedition commanded by Dampier who sailed in the *St George* with letters of marque from Prince George, Britain's Lord High Admiral and husband of Queen Anne. A stormy passage around Cape Horn and a botched attempt to capture a large, well-armed French merchant ship was followed by mostly ineffectual operations up the Pacific Coast to Mexico. Eventually, two of the captains fell out and their ships parted company. *Cinque Ports* found its way to the Juan Fernandez Islands where, after some especially ill-tempered clashes with the captain over the sea-worthiness of the *Cinque Ports* (on which he was later proved right as the ship sank off the coast of what is now Colombia), Selkirk was abandoned ashore.

The castaway seemed not to have envisaged a long period alone, no doubt expecting one or other merchant or pirate ships to come quickly to his aid. While awaiting deliverance, he survived by adapting to his wild surroundings and being highly resourceful – helped by a pleasant climate and plenty of wild goats. In the event, only a couple of Spanish naval ships were ever spotted by Selkirk and he knew better than to seek help from them. Finally, in February 1709, a friendly vessel, the privateer *Duke* under the command of Captain Woodes Rogers, came to his aid. Ironically, the *Duke's* sailing master was William Dampier who had been dismissed from the Royal Navy in 1702 by a court martial which found him guilty of cruelty to a crew-member during an expedition to Australia. Selkirk had lived alone on the island for four years and four months. He did not, however, retire gracefully to a quiet life in Scotland. Rather, given officer responsibilities in several vessels, he carried on eagerly and successfully plundering in the Pacific for another two years before completing a circumnavigation via the Cape of Good Hope.

One of the most colourful tales of pirates and privateers operating off the Pacific coast of South America in the eighteenth century is that of William

Juan Fernandez Island in 1890   *Library of Congress, Washington*

Betagh. Having set sail a year earlier, in 1720 Betagh took part in raids in the region perpetrated by an expedition lead by John Clipperton and George Shelvocke commanding the ships *Success* and *Speedwell* respectively. This was during another period when England was at war with Spain. So, as privateers carrying King George's commission, the expedition was almost immune from prosecution. Initially, Betagh was Shelvocke's captain of marines, thus commanding the small contingent of soldiers often carried by such privateering expeditions.

Speedwell arrived in the region after a desperate passage around Cape Horn during which many men were lost and the rest reduced to a diet of mussels and wild celery. The captain had been prepared to resort to anything to get a respite from the cruel storms. According to Shelvocke himself, the situation was so dire that he allowed one of his officers to shoot an albatross which he believed was bringing bad luck to the ship. This incident later inspired a theme in *The*

Rime of the Ancient Mariner, the narrative poem by Samuel Taylor Coleridge.

Once in the Pacific the two small ships with skilled, experienced commanders and able crews made life miserable for the Spanish. In the case of Shelvocke, however, the success was interrupted when *Speedwell* was wrecked off Juan Fernandez Island. Having been marooned there for five months, the crew managed to build a boat from the wreckage and local trees to escape. The rest of the expedition was carried out in ships taken as prizes. Betagh found himself commanding a tiny vessel called *Mercury,* a fruit bark he had seized. He took two further prizes, taking command of one of them, but was captured by a Spanish warship under the command of Admiral Don Pedro Miranda. Happily for Betagh, the Admiral had once been a prisoner of Sir Charles Wager. This British naval officer had treated the Spaniard so generously that Betagh, in his turn, was received in captivity with the same lavish treatment. He dined and toasted good wine routinely at the captain's table.

Eventually Betagh was taken to Lima where the Viceroy also refused to take harsh measures against the English buccaneer. At much the same time, a group of Captain Clipperton's men were brought to Lima as prisoners. According to Betagh, as a means of avoiding the worst punishment for piracy these men agreed to be converted to Catholicism. Celebrating their baptisms, with a bowl of punch in a local public house, they became so drunk that a saintly image was knocked over and smashed. Even the Inquisition was remarkably easy-going with the rowdy British contingent, simply locking them up for five days to cool off. Unbowed, the same group then hatched a plot to take a ship in Callao port for their escape. To raise money for firearms, they had the nerve to beg for it in the streets of Lima, labelling themselves: 'poor English, newly baptized'. It might have been seen as one provocation too many, yet, even then, they were jailed only briefly.

It has to be noted that lenient treatment of pirates by the church was not the rule. The Inquisition did not often take piracy lightly. In 1592, for instance, four English sailors were captured after their ship was wrecked off Guayaquil. They were paraded at an *auto-da-fé*. One was burnt alive after four years of imprisonment, two were executed otherwise and the fourth was saved only by his youth and willingness to be converted. John Oxenham, a friend of Drake, was hanged in Lima with several of his sailors, all regarded by the authorities as heretics as well as pirates. Four Dutch corsairs, from the fleet of Admiral Spilbergen, were dragged before the Inquisition in 1615.

Anson's losses and Byron's near-death experience

With the onset of the War of Austrian Succession[6], one of the largest naval fleets ever to be sent by Britain to harass the Spanish in the Pacific was despatched, in 1740, under Commodore George Anson. He sailed with his flagship *Centurian*, four other men-of-war, an armed sloop and two store ships. The crews numbered over 1500 in total and the fleet collectively brandished 235 guns. Thus, in principle, it was a heavy and impressive squadron for any belligerent – or innocent – crossing its course. Unfortunately for Anson, that was without reckoning on the dangers inherent in the voyage to the other side of the world. As we have seen in Chapter 1, by the time the flagship had rounded the Horn and reached a point of rendezvous at the Juan Fernandez Islands, in June 1741, only three vessels remained. The total complement of men had been reduced to around 335.

Nevertheless, with what was left and new vessels taken as prizes, Anson caused mayhem for the Spanish during nearly four years. Having taken a Spanish treasure ship – one of the Manila Galleons, *Nuestra Señora de Covadonga*, on its way from Mexico with some one and a half million dollars of valuables on board – he set sail for home via the Cape of Good Hope with a fortune. It is estimated that he returned with more than a million pounds worth of gold alone and one account suggests he entered the Solent (Portsmouth) with large golden Spanish candlesticks hanging from the yard arms of his ship, *Centurion*. True or not, his ultimate arrival in the capital was triumphant. As the *General Advertiser* of London reported on 5 July, 1743:

"Yesterday the money taken by Admiral Anson was carried through the City in thirty-two wagons, preceded by a kettle-drum, trumpets and French horns, guarded by the seamen, commanded by Officers richly dressed, and was lodged in the Tower... Their Royal Highnesses, the Prince and Princess of Wales, and Admiral Anson were at the house in Pall Mall to see the procession."

Anson was promoted to Rear-Admiral on his return to England and eventually became a much-appreciated First Lord of the Admiralty. His voyage around the world and his deadly harassment of the Spanish became a celebrated feat of navigation and maritime warfare. Yet perhaps the more remarkable story was that of the crew of one of the ships that had been lost in the fight to pass Cape Horn, *HMS Wager*. On board that unlucky vessel was one John Byron, the grand-father of the famous English poet.

When he eventually got round to telling his story of near death and unlikely survival, nearly twenty years later, the emotionally bruised Byron had not

---

6   From 1740 to 1748 much of Europe was at war, initially over the succession of Maria Theresa, daughter of Charles VI, as head of the royal House of Habsburg.

mellowed in his dislike of Chile, however ill-observed:

"...a country scarce to be paralleled in any part of the globe, in that it affords neither fruit, grain nor even roots proper for the sustenance of man, and what is still more rare, the very sea, which yields a plentiful support to many a barren coast, on this tempestuous and inhospitable shore is found to be almost as barren as the land ..."

Certainly, the *Wager* was another ship fated with ill-fortune from the start. Exploring the Western approaches to the Strait of Magellan, HMS Nassau at anchor near Mount Burney in 1869.   *Robert O. Cunningham*

An old store-ship made up to be a man-of-war, weighed down with materials for use by other ships in Anson's squadron, *Wager* was manned by an ill-kempt, inadequate crew. Many of these men had been pressed into service with barely time to rest after previous voyages. Further, the ship carried a contingent of marines "no more than a poor detachment of infirm and decrepit invalids from Chelsea hospital..." according to John Byron.

The *Wager* was struggling to keep up by the time it arrived at the eastern end of the Le Maire Strait and came close to being wrecked off Staten Island. The weather was at its unforgiving worst and barely calmed for an hour during the entire passage. Damaged, the ship soon lost contact with the rest of the squadron. *Wager's* commander, Captain David Cheap, headed for the island of Socorro (Isla Guamblin) off the Chilean coast northwest of Aisen. The crew, with "the greater part of the men being disabled through fatigue and sickness," were unable to cope with a series of accidents that brought down the fore-yard among other essential parts of the sailing rig.

"[It was] blowing now a perfect hurricane, and right in upon the shore,

[and] rendered our endeavours (for we were now only twelve hands fit for duty) entirely fruitless. The night came on, dreadful beyond description, in which, attempting to throw out our topsails to claw off the shore, they were immediately blown from the yards. In the morning, about four o'clock, the ship struck … we were soon undeceived [in believing the first shock was just the impact of a heavy sea] by her striking again more violently than before, which laid her upon her beam ends, the sea making a fair breach over her.

"In this dreadful situation she lay for some little time, every soul on board looking upon the present minute as his last. However, a mountainous sea hove her off from thence; but she presently struck again, and broke the tiller."

The men were becoming deranged in the vicious, unrelenting and untameable sea:

"… one, in the raving despair brought upon him, was seen stalking about the deck, flourishing a cutlass over his head, and calling himself king of the country, and striking everybody he came near, till his companion, seeing no other security against the tyranny, knocked him down. Some, reduced before by long sickness and scurvy, became… as it were petrified and bereaved of all sense, like inanimate logs, and were bandied to and fro by the jerks and rolls of the ship, without exerting and efforts to help themselves. … Yet there was valour too. A few brave men ensured that the crippled ship ran in towards the shore and at a reasonable distance the boats were lowered and they escaped to the barren coast that would ensnare them for months to come."

Ashore in the Golfo de Penas, between 47 and 48 degrees south (probably on what is now Isla Wager), the survivors – about half the initial complement of 160 men - were lost and starving. Some were contemplating cannibalism, there being no shortage of corpses after the wreck. Contact was eventually made with groups of Indians, but the basic food they offered brought little relief. In desperation, there was a revolt against and among the officers and what was left of the crew divided. The larger group, led by the ship's gunner, went south in several boats, hoping to get back home to England by way of the Strait of Magellan – which a handful did about five years later. The rest, including Byron and Captain Cheap, went north, hoping to reach the island of Chiloé, by rowing the longboat.

Their first attempt was defeated very quickly by mountainous seas. Cheap and his companions resigned themselves to staying in place for a while, feeding on seal meat, some berries (like gooseberries), and when possible shellfish. The conditions were Spartan. There was great hardship and a prevailing sense of hopelessness. Eventually six of the crew, too frustrated to stay put, rowed away

56

with the boat, leaving six others stranded, including the captain, Byron and the ship's surgeon. This remaining group, with no means of moving on, eventually made a deal with some Indians which allowed them to set out northwards in canoes, with guides. At one point they rowed for three days, eating nothing but roots. To make a bad situation worse the surgeon became ill and died.

When they finally made it to the Spanish garrison in the south of Chiloé there were just three left, including Byron and Captain Cheap. Emaciated from starvation and effort, they were mere skeletons, with sores over their bodies and barely any clothes left to hang from their bones. They were received kindly by the Spanish governor in Chacao, on the north coast of the island, and stayed with him in relative comfort until the annual ship that would take them north-wards arrived on 2 January 1742. Seventeen months after leaving England, they embarked for Valparaíso.

On arrival, the Spanish governor initially locked them up in the fort above the port. After a few days, Captain Cheap and Lieutenant Hamilton (who had been left behind during the journey because of exhaustion but found his way to Chiloé independently), were sent to Santiago – while the other two remained imprisoned, suffering rough treatment on top of all their previous trials. It was several weeks before the four were reunited in Santiago where they were received by the president and stayed, living well, for another two years.

On 20 December 1744 the group was finally embarked on the frigate *Lys* in Valparaíso, bound for St Malo. Yet, even the return voyage was dogged by persistent bad luck. It was not until January 1746 that the group landed in Dover. Even then there were problems for Cheap, Hamilton and Byron who found they did not have the money to get them home. Byron eventually rode to Marlborough to a friend's house only to find it shut up. Although he was later reunited with his sister who had married Lord Carlisle and lived in Soho Square, London, he came to the uncomfortable conclusion that after five years he no longer knew who was alive and who dead among his family and friends. It was an experience common to many sailors and travellers of the time.

What of the men who had decided to go south rather than north from Wager Island after the wreck? The 80 men set out in a longboat, a cutter and a barge. Within a few days the barge returned north, and the cutter was destroyed on rocks. The longboat continued with 72 men. Some were put ashore, others died of exhaustion or illness before they made it to Rio Grande do Sul in Brazil on 28 January the following year. The few dozen who finally made it back home in two parties, were welcomed by difficult questions about mutiny and desertion, despite their having survived an heroic escape in an open boat in some of the world's most savage seas.

Deserters' misery

Looking back on these many tales of heroism, accident and ill-treatment, it is hardly surprising that many sailors jumped ship in the Pacific ports. Even at the end of the nineteenth century it was common to see European mariners drifting between ship-berths, taverns, prison, odd jobs and the gutter. One American sailor heard a first-hand account in 1892:

"He was a typical old salt and a thorough seaman. In the course of his conversation he told us there were between two and three hundred 'beachcombers' ashore in Valparaíso. Sailors who had run away from ships and were now begging a miserable living around the streets and docks rather than undergoing the hardship of rounding the "Corner" as they called the "Horn". He also said that all these beachcombers had been gathered by the police and locked up. Several American men-of-war were expected any day and the authorities feared another outbreak such as had occurred a few months ago and resulted in the death of a sailor named Riggin from one of the American war vessels[7].

"The beachcombers, he said, slept in caves in the mountains or about the streets, and early in the morning they went from house to house offering to empty the slops for the price of a drink. There were no sewers and everyone had to dump their slops off the seawall. As soon as a beachcomber had earned a few centavos he went and got drunk and so lived from day to day.

"But there was one thing the beachcombers feared, and that was the mounted police. Nor do I blame them, for I saw a man arrested and it was a wonder he ever lived to reach the station house. It was a policeman or *'gendarme'* as they are called, in hot pursuit of a ragged, tattered tramp whose bare feet went pat, pat, pat as fast as he could go, the very picture of desperation. ... Just as I got there, I saw the gendarme swing a lasso around his head and then let it fly, catching the tramp just below the shoulders, pinning his arms to his side. I expected to see the gendarme dismount and arrest his man, but no, on went the horse with the poor tramp, already exhausted from his flight, endeavouring to keep pace with it. Just before they reached the corner, the tramp fell, but without a halt the gendarme galloped on dragging his victim along the stones."

By night, the streets of the port of Valparaíso were a rough and dangerous

---

7   Certainly a reference to the deaths, in 1891, of two sailors from the *USS Baltimore* in the aftermath of a bar-room brawl between American and Chilean mariners. Some reports insisted that one of the deaths was due to a shot fired by a Chilean policeman. Washington treated the incident as a full-scale diplomatic affront and sent warships to demonstrate its anger.

place to be. Men carried knives almost without exception. The mariners stayed put while they had money to spend in the taverns, brothels, cock-fight arenas and hostels. Then they begged, stole or took on minor jobs to sustain themselves. Inevitably, the day came when they had no other option than to sign up for a voyage home to Europe – or they were taken by the *enganchedores* (press gangs). A small number, mainly those with shore-bound skills, headed out of Valparaíso to take their chances further north in the mines or south to become farmers or fishermen.

Valparaiso Bound!

4.

The Spanish and a defiant outpost of empire

While beating off Magellan Strait it blew exceeding hard;
Whilst shortening sail two gallant tars fell from the topsail yard.
By angry seas the ropes we threw from their poor hands were torn
And we were forced to leave them to the sharks that prowl around
Cape Horn.

"Rounding the Horn", traditional sea song

The origins of Spanish rule, as well as the failure to cement that rule in Chile's Araucanían forests and the territories to the south, are found in the lives of two soldiers, two *conquistadores*: Francisco Pizarro González and Diego de Almagro. In the beginning, they were joined by a priest, Hernando de Luque, the spiritual leader of the first Spanish settlement in Panama. After a tentative voyage south by Pizarro, during the 1520s, to view the fabled Incan civilization around the then unexplored Pacific coast, a well-armed expedition, largely financed by Luque, was launched in 1532 to conquer that civilization and seize access to the gold that went with it. A year later Pizarro and Almagro took the capital of the Incas, Cuzco. The spoils were divided between the two soldiers, since Luque was already dead. The influx into Peru of Spanish adventurers could begin. The only question was how far and how easily they could progress – east, into the highlands, and south to what would become Chile.

Pizarro founded Lima as the capital of Peru, in 1534, but was soon quarrelling with Almagro, notably over who would control the riches of Cuzco. With that decision in abeyance, the King of Spain offered Almagro the royal licence to explore and annex for the crown the vast territories to the south of Cuzco, a region to be called "New Toledo". Pizarro had domination of a large swathe of territory to the north, now known as "New Castile".

In 1536 Almagro set off, for the first time, to take possession of the King's new realm. The expeditionary force of around five hundred Spaniards and many thousands of captive Indians struggled across the desert and up the Andean passes: an estimated 10,000 natives were reported to have died along the way, unprotected victims of the bitterly cold nights and intolerably rugged conditions. Many of the horses also perished. The Spanish survived by virtue

61

of the warm clothing and other supplies with which they had been equipped through Almagro's lavish preparations.

The expedition eventually descended from the mountains to Copiapó where it rested for some weeks. Almagro then moved on southwards, sending out advance parties to garner as broad an assessment of Chile's potential as possible. He was disappointed with the reports that came back. The priority had been gold, and there was none; at least, there was not the proliferation of the precious metal that the adventurers had seen, and spent, in Peru. The people were poor and often fierce, the climate stark. The basis for establishing secure new Spanish settlements was far from apparent. There were violent encounters

Cuzco. The ruins of the old Inca capital, overlaid with Spanish architecture. A representation by John Ogilby, dated 1671. *Fondation Laurent-Vibert, Lourmarin, France*

with local tribes before Almagro, running short of supplies, was persuaded to turn back to Cuzco, this time crossing the Atacama Desert. On the way, his men compensated for their disappointments through their vicious treatment of the Indians; but they themselves ended up weakened and exhausted by the conditions.

Arriving back in early 1537, Almagro found Cuzco under siege by Inca rebels with two of Francisco Pizarro's brothers and the garrison trapped inside. He raised the siege but was forced to go to war with the brothers for ultimate control of the city. By 1538, his supporters were defeated and Almagro summarily executed by Pizarro, his corpse displayed in the central square of Cuzco. Pizzaro lived on until 1541 when followers of Almagro's son, looking for revenge, cut him down in his palace in Lima. Ultimately, it would be another *conquistador*, Pedro de Valdivia, who would establish Spanish domination of the north and centre of what is now Chile.

Valdivia was a seasoned soldier under Pizarro, and of high rank, . But he was much more, possessing rare judgment, wide learning and a probably-exaggerated view of his own abilities. He was also pious while not being burdened by too many scruples. Valdivia had arrived in Peru just as the confrontation between Almagro and Pizarro was turning bloody and in time to make his name in overcoming the subsequent Indian uprising. He was given a large estate as a prize and Pizarro named him Lieutenant-Governor of Chile with the right – at his own expense – to conquer the country over which Spain had so far failed to establish even the slightest authority. He put together a small army with the financial backing of a Spanish merchant called Francisco Martínez and some of the assets of his own mistress, Inés Suárez, to whose fortitude he would eventually be deeply indebted.

A third powerful partner was Pedro Sancho de la Hoz, a conquistador who had played a role in the submission of Peru and who had returned from a visit to Spain in 1539 with the King's mandate to explore and take control of whatever territories he could discover south of the Strait of Magellan. Since Sancho de la Hoz was also the secretary of Francisco Pizarro, Valdivia had little choice but to work with him. Their agreement, signed in Pizarro's dining room in Cuzco in December 1539, required Sancho de la Hoz to seek ships and supplies to support Valdivia who would move southwards by land.

In January 1540, Valdivia set off with a force of 150 Spaniards and some one thousand Indians. This time the trek was without serious loss, across the desert and as far as Copiapó. Yet it was hardly without incident. Sancho de la Hoz, far from meeting his part of the contract, became over-indebted and found himself in a prison cell in Lima. His creditors, with little hope of being repaid, decided to let him pursue Valdivia into the Atacama and recoup their money by whatever means. De la Hoz chose assassination. However, arriving at Valdivia's camp in the desert, a handful of his murderous followers – mostly from La Rioja in Spain like their leader – made an elementary mistake. Instead of falling on Valdivia himself they stumbled into the presence of the fiery Inés Suárez who promptly detained them. Sancho lost face, was forced to sign away all his rights in the Chilean enterprise in favour of Valdivia and deported back to Peru.

Evidently a persistent man, Sancho de la Hoz tried a second time, returning to Chile with a troop of soldiers, intent on provoking dissent in the ranks of Valdivia's army and ultimately a mutiny. Again the commander was elsewhere but his warrior-like mistress, Inés, soon picked up signals of unrest and had the troop's unfortunate captain swiftly executed. Once again, though, Sancho escaped with his life, Valdivia knowing too well the influence of his treacherous would-be partner in the royal court. The expedition forged on south, eventually settling in the verdant valley of the Mapocho where Valdivia fixed on the site of his future capital, Santiago (or St Jago as it was then titled). The city, described as "a miserable little hamlet of straw-roofed huts," was founded formally on 12 February 1541.

A Chilean Boadicea defends Santiago

This is not to say the country, or even the region around Santiago, was pacified. On the first occasion when Valdivia ventured out, some eight to ten thousand Indians attacked the town and set it alight. By most accounts, the defence of the capital was led by the remarkable and beautiful Inés Suárez. She was said to have personally beheaded six Indian chiefs, taken from the prison, and then led a last-ditch charge from the besieged and over-run city to bloodily push the Indians out. Nevertheless, the occupants of Santiago were effectively sealed off from supplies of any sort and starvation set in, despite valiant attempts quickly to develop local farming. The town was only saved when one of Valdivia's friends provisioned a ship that arrived in Valparaíso in September 1543.

Moreover, Valdivia and Inés had not seen the last of Sancho de la Hoz. In 1542, he tried again to sow the seeds of discord, this time exploiting bickering over the division of land in the central region between colonists and conquistadores. Yet again it was Inés who spotted the danger and put Sancho back in a prison cell before having him exiled to the countryside. Yet rancour can die hard: Pedro Sancho would try one last time, in 1547, during a period when there was outrage among conquistadores in Santiago against Valdivia who they believed (rightly it seems) had cheated them of their treasure. On this occasion Sancho was not the principal ring-leader. But that did not prevent his execution and the display of his head in Santiago's main square.

Meanwhile, Valdivia had sought to battle his way south to take control of a much larger swathe of the country; the land thus far secured was limited and Valdivia had many friends to satisfy. He spent from 1544 to 1546 taking possession of some of Chile's most fertile land down to the Rio Maule. Huge estates, or *hacien-das*, were established with Indians attached to the land, under a system of forced-labour called *encomienda* (see Chapters 8 and 9). At much the same time, Valdivia's own author-ity in Santiago was under threat, with plots in Peru to depose him by rebellion. He prevailed, although only after standing trial in Lima – capital of the Viceroyalty to whose courts Chile was still subject – on largely fabricated charges of dis-loyalty to the crown.

When he returned to Chile in 1549 he found Indian uprisings in several cities including Santiago. Nevertheless, he was determined,

Pedro de Valdivia

once again, to push south to conquer new territory. After a succession of skir-mishes that generated huge casualties on both sides, Valdivia eventually reached what was to become the city of Concepción. But however many men he had to defend the small tracts of land gained, they were never enough to withstand storming, almost suicidal, assaults by tens of thousands of brave, ferocious Araucanían warriors. South of Concepción he founded the city of Valdivia but his limited, though well-equipped forces were always fighting against the odds – in numbers and audacity. Finally, Valdivia found himself isolated at Tucapel, heavily outnumbered by several thousand warriors commanded by the famous chief Lautaro. Not a single Spaniard escaped alive. Pedro de Valdivia himself met his death in a ghastly manner.

A succession of governors of Chile failed to tame the indomitable Araucaníans, and several died in their attempts. Battles were often won, but it made no difference to the determination of the native Indians to fight to the last for their freedom. They employed guerrilla tactics: avoiding confrontation, but striking when least expected and when the enemy was most vulnerable. Towns and cities were secured by the Spanish at great cost, only to be over-run and torched when the indigenous tribes had regrouped. Chillan, Valdivia, Concepción, Imperial, Villarrica and Osorno were all lost, retaken and lost again over many years.

Alonso Garcia Ramón became governor in March 1605. He too lost many men in futile attempts to push south from the Biobío River[1] frontier. In 1607, he reported to King Philip III, in Madrid, as follows:

"Since my childhood I have served your Highness, being present in the war before Granada, in the naval battle of Navarino, and in the garrison at Espoleto. I have soldiered in Sicily, in Naples, in Lombardy and latterly in Flanders, where I enjoyed the greatest honours, but I certify to your Majesty that there is not in the whole world so laborious a war as this. It is such that there are many soldiers who have not for six years either tasted bread, heard a Church bell or seen a Spanish woman. ... After having marched 6 or 7 leagues, and sitting up the whole night afterward, they cannot so much as eat a tortilla without grinding the corn to make it."

The policy towards taming Araucanía lurched periodically between quiet, persuasive pacification, normally led by priests, and military campaigns of extreme cruelty. Neither approach worked. Finally, in 1639, the Marquis de Baydes signed the Treaty of Quillan, on behalf of the King of Spain, together with the Indian *caciques* (tribal chiefs). In effect, the treaty ended Spanish attempts to conquer Araucanía, establishing a *de facto* frontier at the Biobío River, while allowing Catholic missionaries to enter the territories southwards. It was the only such treaty that the Spanish colonial authorities ever signed with indigenous Indian peoples anywhere in the empire. It recognized the power of the Mapuches of Araucanía and gave them a form of sovereignty which would only end when the country of Chile itself won its independence nearly two centuries later.

Sarmiento's tragedy

A solution to the Araucanían problem might have been simply to ignore those territories that remained unconquerable but to settle the lands much further south, around the Strait of Magellan and Tierra del Fuego. One of the most tragic attempts to do so was that led by Pedro Sarmiento de Gamboa.

---

1   Chile's second largest river which flows from the Andes, north-west to the city of Concepcion.

In 1579, the viceroy of Peru decided that the fear among Spanish sailors of the direct sea passage to Spain had to be broken. His objective was the precise identification and charting of the elusive western opening of the Magellan Strait, which was difficult to distinguish among the dozens of inlets and blind passages at the southern tip of mainland Chile. His motivation was to secure the capacity to block the Strait to non-Spanish shipping, so outraged was he by the rampages of Francis Drake and his like. An expedition was fitted out under the command of Captain Pedro Sarmiento. It consisted of two ships and a largely reluctant crew of 112. The initial voyage was comparatively successful: Sarmiento found the western entrance of the Strait on 2 February 1580 and, with some difficulty, the eastern opening three weeks later. On his way, he took formal possession of important locations on behalf of the King, before sailing on to Spain.

Thus, equipped with improved charts, the government in Madrid decided to settle strategic sites in the Magellan Strait. Two forts with two hundred soldiers and one hundred settlers and their families would make up the basis of the new settlements. Under the command of Admiral Diego de la Ribera, some twenty-three ships carrying 3000 people (including 600 settlers and families accompanying the new Governor of Chile, Alonso de Sotomayor) sailed from Sanlúcar de Barrameda on September 15, 1581. Pedro Sarmiento went along as the newly-designated Governor and Captain-General of the Strait.

The entire enterprise was ill-fated from the start. In a storm outside the port of departure, five ships went down and 800 men were lost. Not far to the south, another ship was lost leaving Cadiz and there followed some 150 deaths on the Atlantic crossing to Rio de Janeiro. The expedition wintered in Rio in 1582, but suffered another one hundred deaths from illness during the stay. A few days out from Rio, in especially rough weather, a large ship went down with 350 people and many stores. Shortly after, yet another vessel was lost. At that point dissent began to emerge among the disparate leaders of the expedition as to whether the enterprise was still viable, some arguing that their losses were already such that they should turn back for home. Alonso de Sotomayor, with his soldiers and settlers, left the fleet at the River Plate having decided to try his luck taking three ships up river and then journeying over the Andes to Chile.

When the Magellan Strait was finally sighted there were just five of 23 ships remaining. Since the tiny fleet was no longer viable for the settlement operation, the fleet commander forced Sarmiento to return to Rio. There the would-be governor of the Strait found four new vessels with fresh supplies from Spain and set out again, once more reaching the eastern end of the Strait on 1 February, 1584.

While initially driven eastwards by fierce winds the five ships finally reached the site of the first settlement at Cape Virgins. Some 300 civilians, as well as soldiers and stores named their new township 'La Ciudad de Nombre de Jesus' (City of the Name of Jesus). A plan of the future town was marked out on the ground by Sarmiento. As homes were being constructed, the weather worsened out at sea where the small fleet lay. One of the five ships was beached. So alarmed was Admiral de la Ribera that he decided to flee north with three of the four remaining vessels. Left to his own devices, Sarmiento sent the final ship westwards along the Strait towards Cape Santa Ana, designated as the site of the second settlement. The governor himself headed inland with 100 soldiers, tracing an overland route to the same location. It was a debilitating struggle but the party finally arrived

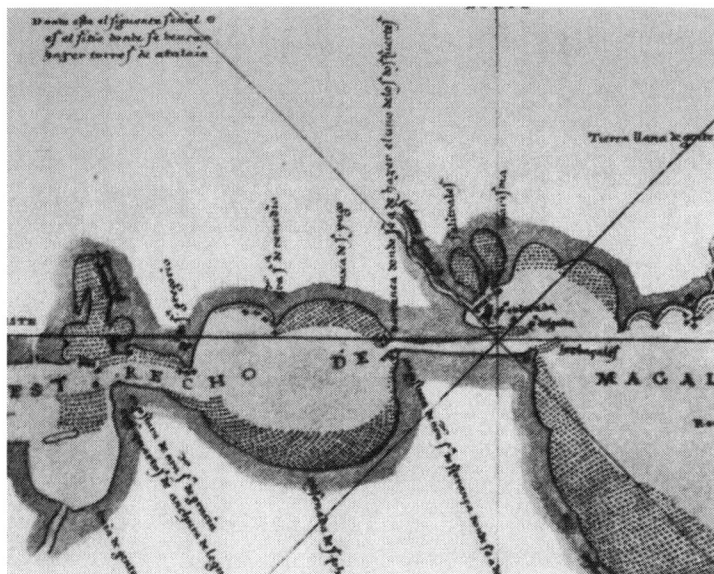

Strait of Magellan as drawn by Pedro de Sarmiento in 1580.
"Monumenta Chartografica Indiana" 1942

at Cape Santa Ana, exhausted and near starvation. They identified a site for a fort, tussled with Indian tribes and eventually reunited with the ship and crew sent along the Strait.

The new settlement was traced out and named "La Ciudad del Rey Don Felipe" (The City of the King Don Felipe). A church was built and accommodation erected for 500 people and what was left of their provisions. The town was fortified – but was hardly impregnable. Nevertheless, by the end of May 1584, Sarmiento had left the fledgling community to fend for itself and sailed back to Cape Virgins. There the saga of misfortune worsened. Gales prevented any landing. Sarmiento was forced to flee north up the Patagonian coast and seek provisions. Then, on his return voyage he was hit by a storm so severe he was left with no alternative but to throw much of these precious new supplies overboard.

At this point Sarmiento had neither adequate provisions for the settlements nor the resources to purchase them. With few options open, he decided to return to Spain to seek additional support from the King. Again fate was against him. Initially, he was captured by the fleet of Sir Richard Granville and taken to England. There he was treated kindly by the Queen and her nobles, including Sir Walter Raleigh. Then, on being sent back to Spain, in December 1586, he was captured by the French. Only after a ransom of gold and fine horses was paid was he released. Crippled, exhausted and ill, he reached home to finally seek out the relief needed for his settlements.

It was too late. After over three years, almost no one was left alive in The City of the King Don Felipe. The place had been observed by the English commander, explorer and privateer Thomas Cavendish, who subsequently promised then refused to rescue the few souls left from both settlements. With Sarmiento long gone, the people of The City of the Name of Jesus had eventually joined the second group. They had lived on berries and what seafood they could find. Believing Sarmiento had himself been lost, the survivors built two small boats and tried to reach the eastern end of the strait. They were not sailors; one boat was run ashore and the other sunk. By the summer of 1586, there were 15 men and 3 women left. The remainder had died of hunger and illness. Witnesses spoke of corpses strewn around the settlement. What became of the few left alive is not known. Cavendish took just one man with him and some looted armaments. Before sailing away, he renamed The City of the King Don Felipe as Port Famine (Puerto Hambre), as it is still known. The place was seen by the Dutch mariner Oliver Noort in 1600. What he described as 'just a pile of stones' was a few kilometers south of modern-day Punta Arenas, which demonstrates only that Sarmiento was not wrong in his conviction that the region could successfully be settled.

Three centuries and a mixed legacy

These few episodes serve to show that even if Spanish rule was lengthy, it was very far from trouble-free. The relatively small numbers of conquistadores and those that followed them to Peru, Chile and southern Patagonia always struggled to dominate the region, to do justice to the ambitions and expectations of the King and court back in Madrid. This is not the place for a detailed description of three centuries of rule. Some specific aspects of the colonial period – farming and mining, as well as trade, among them – will be taken up in the appropriate chapters. Nevertheless, if we are to understand the nineteenth century, during and after independence, a judgment is necessary on the tally of Spanish supremacy. Was colonial domination all bad? The conquistadores certainly get a bad press now, but more-careful observers have long considered the record a mixed one.

How did the Spanish rule their dominions in South and Central America? First, the 'colonies' were considered an integral part of the Kingdom of Spain – less like India to Great Britain, under what was the British Empire, than Martinique and Guadeloupe to modern-day France. The territories were fiefdoms held by the Spanish crown by virtue of a grant from the Pope. And, while they were in principle regulated directly by the monarch, assisted by his "Council of the Indies", in practice they were run, day-to-day, by ministers of the crown.

The territories were divided among viceroys, captains-general, governors and other administrative sub-divisions. Chile – or, at least, those parts finally subdued – was ruled by the Viceroy of Peru in Lima. In all, it was a huge and heavy bureaucracy with every administrative position overseen and disciplined by several others. The Viceroy was, in theory, controlled by the Real Audiencia, whose members were European Spaniards who could not hold land, or marry into the country. In practice, when it counted, the viceroys had unlimited powers and, while they operated within a legal code known as the Laws of the Indies, they were easily able to overrule the administrative, and ecclesiastical powers. Of 170 viceroys appointed during nearly 300 years, only four were of South American birth; of 610 captains-general and governors, only fourteen were other than Spanish. Sharing no common interest with, or feeling for, the local inhabitants – largely because these senior appointments were normally purchased in Madrid – dreadful abuses of the native populations were routine. For gifted locally-born citizens, there was "the utter hopelessness that any merit could lead to useful distinction". The expression of public opinion was repressed totally.

This stifling of native talent applied not only to administration; locals were prohibited from engaging in commercial agriculture, manufacturing, trade and even the arts: literature was forbidden. Indeed, trade, outside the narrow confines of the colonial framework, was forbidden on pain of death. Furthermore, foreigners were not permitted to set foot in these Spanish territories without special permission or a license, and that for a short period. Plenty of unauthorized visitors, especially mariners, ended up in hideous prisons, shackled in irons, some finally dying from the cruelty and harsh conditions. Even contact between the provinces was suppressed outside the administrative and military structures.

The justice system was largely either inoperative or dysfunctional. As Captain Basil Hall was told by a resident with personal experience: "Sir, they

1671 map of Peru by Arnold Montanus of Amsterdam

Fondation Laurent-Vibert Lourmarin, France

put you in prison, whatever the case be; they turn the key, and never think more of you". After the capture of Lima from the Spanish by General José Francisco de San Martín, in 1821, the dungeons were found to be filled with prisoners, long forgotten by the courts, and against whom no charge was on record. Having visited one Lima prison San Martín himself immediately ordered many prisoners to be released. An extract from *Biblioteca Americana No. 3*, a contemporary periodical published in London, stated:

"It is impossible to paint in colours sufficiently vivid the miseries to which all prisoners were subjected, or the inhumanity with which they were treated by their keepers. They were stripped of everything, deprived of all motive to exertion – occasionally put to torture to confess imaginary crimes, and in all prisons corporal punishment was allowed. Such was the state of the prisons all over South America during the dominion of the Spaniards."

Taxes, tithes and duties were heavily and severely applied throughout the dominions. High duties on precious metals deterred industrial development, while tobacco, gunpowder and mercury were closed royal monopolies. Yet, contraband and piracy conducted by other European nations gradually wore down the system, As Captain Hall noted:

"Along with the goods which the contraband trade forced into the colonies, no small portion of knowledge found entrance, in spite of the increased exertions of the Inquisition, and church influence, aided by the redoubled vigilance of government, who enforced every penalty with the utmost rigour. Many foreigners too, by means of bribes and other arts, succeeded in getting into the country, so that the progress of intelligence was gradually encouraged, to the utter despair of the Spaniards, who knew no other method of governing the colonies but that of mere brute force, unsupported by the least shadow of opinion, or of good-will."

Ultimately, however, the same observer and author, as many others, after searing criticism of their behaviour, gives the Spanish the benefit of much doubt. He praises the large and beautiful cities, the new sea ports with their fortifications, the roads and communications, the development of mining. He admires the progress made in agriculture and the introduction of horses, cattle, mules, sheep and pigs, all of which abounded by the early nineteenth century. Further, and with the self-righteous paternalism that was a mark of the time in Europe, he concludes:

"The civil institutions of the country too, with all their defects, are infinitely superior to the rude establishments of the aboriginal inhabitant. And it may therefore be said, with strict historical truth, that for all those advantages by which civilization is distinguished from barbarism – Christianity from Paganism – knowledge, in short, from ignorance – this vast portion of the globe must forever stand indebted to the Spaniards."

5.

Independence, with help
from European friends

Lord of the sea come to us
We are as water and sand oppressed,
We are a people mute and beseiged
Lord of the sea, we call you, singing, to battle
Spanish chains deny us the seas.
Our hopes wither in the Spanish night.
Lord of the sea, grief and rage await you in the harbour.
Southern seas are calling you, Lord of the sea...

From *"Cochrane de Chile"* (1970) by Pablo Neruda

It is not the intent of this chapter to follow all the twists and turns of the long trek towards independence in Chile, Peru and Bolivia; rather, it is to give an impression of the sometimes splendid, sometimes dubious roles taken by European officers and soldiers in that struggle. It is a heritage that remains vivid and mostly glorious in national perceptions of the period, even if sometimes controversial also.

By the end of the 18th century, the collapse of the Spanish colonial system was looking inevitable. In Chile, National Day *('Las Fiestas Patrias')* is celebrated on 18 September and is the anniversary of events that took place on that day in 1810. That it is not to say it was the day on which Spanish rule ended. The end of Spain in Chile – as in the rest of South America – followed progressively.

In large part, the pursuit of freedom from colonial domination shadowed violent confrontation in Europe. Napoleon's Peninsular War (1807-1814) in Europe, triggered change around the world. The Emperor of France effectively deposed the Bourbon monarchy of Fernando VII and installed his own brother on the Spanish throne. The popular response in provincial Spain was the establishment of local "juntas" to govern outside the new, central, French-run bureaucracy. In the colonies the old monarchy's demise initially drew outrage; but several countries of South America followed the example of the homeland by establishing their own juntas.

Among the first to do so was Chile. This act of "independence" and the oaths sworn in its name said nothing specifically of independence. Rather, it installed a junta in Santiago committed to: "public security and the conservation of this integral part of the Monarchy for our much missed Monarch don Fernando VII." Thus, in principle at least, the Chilean junta was established – as were those in other parts of the disintegrating Empire – to rule and defend the country on behalf of the deposed Bourbon King. Nevertheless, rule from Lima was clearly over: the new government in Santiago set about various liberal reforms, including the opening of the ports to the world and freedom of trade. By the middle of 1811 the first National Congress was in place, although its members were still required to swear allegiance to Fernando VII.

Very soon, however, separatist sentiment developed together with a growing sense of solidarity with anti-royalist movements across the continent. For a while, reformers sparred politically with royalists and a clear declaration of Chilean independence seemed out of reach. In December 1811, a military revolt led by José Miguel Carrera and his two brothers – enthusiastic supporters of absolute independence – secured the dissolution of Congress and of the ruling junta. Carrera assumed command of the country as a military dictator, though pursuing significant reforms, including a primary-school building programme and new institutions for secondary and higher education.

Chile began to look lost to Spain, a situation that the hard-line defender of Spanish supremacy, José Fernando Abascal, Viceroy of Peru, found intolerable. To the viceroy, it amounted to insurrection. So, early in 1813, he sent one force to Buenos Aires to counter the separatist movement in Argentina and another, under Brigadier Antonio Pareja to the island of Chiloé and the mainland town of Valdivia to raise a royalist army in Chile and fight back. Pareja quickly gathered a force of 2000 but, wintering in Chillán, that same year, he fell seriously ill and died of pneumonia. Despite the loss of Pareja, the royalist army grew and began moving north, quickly taking Talca. In Santiago, sprits dropped, and there was some public and political pressure for a settlement with the royalists. A new separatist leadership was needed. The Carrera brothers were relieved of their army commands with José Miguel being replaced as commander-in-chief by Bernardo O'Higgins. At the same time, Colonel Francisco de la Lastra, the governor of Valparaíso, was installed as the nation's first all-powerful Supreme Director, heading a new junta.

The passage north of the royalists was halted only temporarily by the heroic stands of the 'Patriot army', largely under the command of Bernardo O'Higgins, notably at Rancagua in October 1814. O'Higgins, the defining figure of Chile's independence, was the son of Ambrosio Bernardo O'Higgins, born Ambrose Bernard O'Higgins in Ballinary, County Sligo, Ireland. After the family fortunes ebbed away, O'Higgins senior first established himself as a trader in Cadiz, Spain, before emigrating to South America where he was appointed by the Spanish to a succession of official posts, culminating in that of Governor of Chile. His son was born illegitimately, in 1778, during a period when Ambrosio

Ambrose O'Higgins, a reforming Governor of Chile under Spanish rule

Son, Bernardo O'Higgins, led the country to independence as Supreme Director

held the office of Governor of Concepción. Bernardo was raised by his mother with the financial support of his father, but little else; the two barely knew each other. Ambrosio O'Higgins was responsible for important reforms in Chile during the colonial period, as well as a succession of major public works like the construction of a respectable and much needed road between the capital and Valparaíso. Yet, his son would take a dramatically more radical path to secure the final break with the "mother" country.

However, in 1814, defeated and without hope of reinforcement, O'Higgins and some two thousand supporters were forced to flee across the Andes to Argentina and into exile. By that time, with Napoleon's increasing military reverses, Fernando VII had been restored to the Spanish throne and was keen to take a hard line with his recalcitrant colonies. The Chilean Junta's modest patriot reforms were dismantled and the old forms of rule reinstated. Repression of the patriots themselves followed; some were banished to misery on the Juan Fernandez Islands, lost in the Pacific some 700 kilometres west of

The Battle of Maipú, 1818. *From an oil painting by Juan Mauricio Rugendas*

Valparaíso. Others were murdered by Spanish soldiers. Indeed, the repression was so severe that even those who had supported the separatist cause began to doubt whether an independence movement could ever succeed.

In fact, real freedom was neither far away nor a long time coming. Across the Andes, O'Higgins had made a powerful ally in General José de San Martín, Governor of Cuyo Province and a visceral enemy of Spain. The Argentine general yearned to attack the Viceroy of Peru through Chile. In early 1817, the two leaders took an army of more than four thousand men over the Andean passes to engage unprepared royalist troops at Chacabuco, north of Santiago. The patriot victory, on 12 February, is still regarded as a remarkable military feat, accomplished under the most extreme conditions. A cavalry charge by O'Higgins' division was decisive. Within nine days of the triumph, O'Higgins was in Santiago, appointed the second Supreme Director of the State of Chile.

He formed a national army and began prosecuting a vigorous and definitive war of independence.

A year later, in February 1818, O'Higgins declared Chile an independent republic. That still did not mean peace; the national army continued to sustain losses from royalist assaults – O'Higgins himself being wounded at Talca on 19 March. Finally, however, San Martín, still unable to pursue his ambitions in Peru, again brought salvation to Chile. His battered Army of the Andes took on the royalists at Maipú, close to Santiago, on 5 April, 1818, inflicting a stinging defeat which rumbled through the old Spanish empire. Some two thousand royalist soldiers are believed to have died in the action and around three thousand more were captured; the national army lost some one thousand dead.

The "sea wolf" takes control of the seas

For practical and legal purposes, Chile was a free country; but the job was not finished for O'Higgins. For a start, he needed control of the seas. Strongly pro-British throughout his life, he engineered the installation of Admiral Lord Thomas Cochrane[1] as commander of Chile's small navy. Famously audacious, the Scottish-born Admiral was, at the time, in national disgrace because of scandal at home. Yet, he was to become a legend in South America and, in particular, in Chile.

Cochrane had inspired terror in the French and Spanish fleets alike in the first decade or so of the nineteenth century. In just one year, commanding a 14-gun sloop and a 92-strong crew, he was given credit for capturing fifty ships, with a total of 122 guns, and taking 534 prisoners. One of his triumphs was to outfox the large Spanish 32-gun frigate *El Gamo*, finally storming the vessel with his entire crew bar the ship's surgeon. Napoleon referred to Cochrane as the 'Sea Wolf'.

However, Cochrane was unpopular with the Admiralty establishment and in political circles. He should have stayed at sea. Misfortune – accidental or contrived – struck in February 1814 when Cochrane was accused of a fraud on the London stock exchange. Large amounts of money had been made in government bonds on the basis of a hoax rumour about the death of Napoleon. In a probably politically-inspired trial, Cochrane was found guilty by association with the Prussian aristocrat who had fomented the rumour. He was sentenced to 12 months imprisonment, a £1000 fine, and required to stand in the "pillory"

---

1   Cochrane was the main inspiration for Captain Jack Aubrey, the principle character in the seafaring novels written by Patrick O'Brian, as well as for Captain Horatio Hornblower, created by C.S.Forester, and the novels of Captain Frederick Marryat who served under Cochrane.

in the City of London for one hour. He was dismissed from the Royal Navy, expelled from his seat in Parliament and deprived of his knighthood in a ceremony at Westminster Abbey in which his banner was taken down from its place in Henry VII's Chapel and kicked down the steps outside. Disgrace was total though Cochrane never stopped insisting on his innocence.

In any event, his popular support was such that within a month, he was re-elected to his House of Commons seat and the sentence of pillory was rescinded for fear of creating a riot. In the meantime, national disgrace or not, his swashbuckling skills and tactical brilliance were needed in the Pacific. With the land war against Spain under control, O'Higgins wanted maritime dominance and was convinced that Chile's security depended also on securing Peru's independence. Cochrane took command of the frigate *O'Higgins* on his arrival with his wife in Valparaíso, in November 1818. Initially, he had very few vessels under his command but the fleet slowly expanded as Spanish ships fell to the same intrepid operations that had decimated the navy of the Spanish monarchy in Europe. The British admiral also set about re-organizing the navy.

In 1820, Cochrane's squadron captured the fortress city of Valdivia. Cochrane had won Chile command of its own seas. Only the island of Chiloé and its archipelago would remain in Spanish hands for some years. Soon after the crucial success in Valdivia, the fleet of seven warships and 4,500 soldiers was sent north by O'Higgins to engage in the struggle for Peru's independence. At the same time, General San Martín moved by land with an army of liberation. Having blockaded the port of Callao, the English admiral famously took Spain's most powerful vessel in the region, *Esmeralda*, on 5 November, 1820. She not only added firepower to the Chilean fleet of the time, but her name became a hallowed one in Chile and has been attached to a succession of admired vessels to the present day. Supported by Cochrane's fleet, San Martín reached Lima and at least partially liberated Peru, although the final blow, dealing what was seen at the time as a definitive end to the Spanish empire in America, would be struck by Simón Bolívar in 1824. Bolívar and General Antonio José de Sucre would go on to liberate "Upper Peru" – today's Bolivia – later that same year.

Relations between Cochrane and San Martín broke down during the campaign in Peru with a dispute over the tactics used in taking the capital and fury on Cochrane's part over the non-payment of his sailors' wages. When Cochrane returned to Valparaíso in 1822, it had been two years since his officers and men had been paid officially (they had been supported largely by what had been taken from the enemy). Now they waited a further five months in Valparaíso, still unpaid, despite constant promises from the government. Isolated acts of misconduct broke out in the town and a general mutiny was feared. A manifesto signed by officers and men threatened that they would simply take what they were owed by looting Valparaíso itself. Cochrane went to appeal personally to the supreme director O'Higgins, at the same time accusing the finance minister of using the navy's money for commercial speculation. He finally won an undertaking that the Director would himself oversee disbursement of the money.

Unwisely, the ministers concerned sought initially to pay only the crews and not the officers, and especially not Cochrane whom they accused of fomenting the mutinous atmosphere. However the men stood by their officers. The government paid up grudgingly, terrified that the port would, indeed, be pillaged.

In advance of Cochrane's return to Chile, San Martín ensured that charges against his conduct in Peru were circulating in Santiago. O'Higgins refused to condemn the English admiral and when Cochrane learned about the accusations he produced a comprehensive refutation for the governments in Santiago and London. However, getting wind of a possible assassination plot, Cochrane decided to quit. He sailed from Quintero Bay on 16 January, 1823, initially to fight the Portuguese as commander of the Brazilian navy and then to aid the Greeks in their struggle for independence from the Ottoman Empire. Cochrane

Admiral, (later) Lord Thomas Cochrane, Earl of Dundonald, the "SeaWolf".

From a painting by James Ramsay

left Chile without proper recognition of the services he had provided the country. The estate that had earlier been granted him by the Government, in the province of Concepcion, was confiscated and his personal effects taken. He left Chile owed something like $60,000 of prize money that he would never recover. On board the same ship leaving Valparaíso was the English writer and traveller, Maria Graham, who had lived in Cochrane's house in Quintero following the November 1822 earthquake and admired the admiral deeply. She also knew San Martín, and recognized his qualities, but her sympathies in the dispute were clear:

"The accusations are as frivolous as they are base; and are exactly calculated to excite and keep up that jealousy which his being a foreigner and a nobleman, and his great talents, have excited. ... Lord C. has addressed a letter to him [O'Higgins] not only exculpating himself, but exposing the baseness, cruelty and cowardice of San Martín."

Back in London, his feats in the Pacific where largely ignored. It would be 1830 before the new king, William IV, and a new Whig government granted Cochrane a pardon with respect to the 1814 stock market scandal. He was returned to the Navy List with a promotion to Rear-Admiral. Only in 1847 did Queen Victoria restore his knighthood. On the day before his funeral, in 1860, Cochrane's banner was hung again in its place in Westminster Abbey.

Other Europeans join the struggle

Cochrane was far from alone, and certainly not the first, European to join the independence wars in South America. There were Irish and Scots and English as well as French, Poles and Italians who served at a high level and mostly with distinction. They fought for a multitude of reasons, sometimes for personal gain, often because of an ideological sympathy and occasionally by pure accident. The following are some examples, but the selection is very far from complete.

One of the first was General John Mackenna, an Irishman born in County Monaghan in 1771, who trained as a military engineer in Barcelona before arriving in Chile at the age of twenty-one. Appointed by Ambrose O'Higgins as governor of Osorno, in the Lakes Region, he successfully populated the town and built its first roads. He was a royalist, like his patron. However, in 1809, Mackenna married into an influential, activist Santiago family that was supporting the cause of independence. This eventually brought him in contact with Bernardo O'Higgins and an admired commanding role in the Patriot

Army. Once described as the "warlike mentor of the great O'Higgins"[2], he was appointed to Chile's second ruling Junta and, in 1811, as governor of Valparaíso. Mackenna led a celebrated victory against the royalists, and against the odds, at Membrillar, near Chillán, in 1814. He died later the same year in Buenos Aires in a pistol duel with the brother of the then Chilean President, José Miguel Carrera, who had sent him and Bernardo O'Higgins into exile. One of his grandchildren was the celebrated patriot, historian, agitator, journalist and politician, Benjamín Vicuña Mackenna.

English doctor, James (Diego) Paroissien became Chief surgeon to San Martín's Army of the Andes. *Archivo Nacional, Santiago*

William Miller, from Kent, had fought the French in the Napoleonic Wars before – like many other unemployed officers – voyaging to Buenos Aires in 1817, and crossing the Cordillera with San Martín's 'Army of the Andes'. He was eventually put in command of the marines under Cochrane, distinguishing himself in the assault on Valdivia before suffering a devastating defeat on the island of Chiloé while commanding two hundred men. Miller led Cochrane's marines in their campaign, with San Martín's soldiers, in Peru before joining Simón Bolívar and General Antonio José de Sucre in the later stages of the Peruvian independence war. He ended up as Marshall of the Peruvian Army and, following the ceasefire, governor of the silver-rich city of Potosi in what is now Bolivia.

John Thomond O'Brien, from County Wicklow, Ireland, managed to distinguish himself in Argentina and Uruguay, as well as in Chile and Peru as *aide-de-camp* to San Martín. In Chile, he took a gallant part in the cavalry charge that decided the Battle of Chacabuco and in the Battle of Maipú. O'Brien had

2   *The South Pacific Mail*, September 17, 1925

arrived in Buenos Aires in 1811, intending to open a trading house. His subsequent efforts to make money through mining in Peru came to nothing, so it was as a soldier that he was celebrated as a hero throughout the southern cone of South America.

Another *aide-de-camp* to San Martín was James Paroissien, an Essex doctor, who also served as chief surgeon in the Army of the Andes. He rose up the ranks, surviving some of the bloodiest independence clashes. He was rewarded with a position managing the mines in Bolivia, after independence. However, the company collapsed, Paroissien was ruined and, in poor health, died during a voyage from Peru to Chile in 1827.

Cochrane establishes Chile's English naval traditions

In practice it was Admiral Cochrane, after his appointment by O'Higgins in 1818, who had responsibility for appointing senior officers in the new Chilean navy. Apart from two Americans, the commanders under Cochrane were British and, with one exception, ex-Royal Navy officers. Recruitment was easy given the wholesale redundancies that followed Napoleon's defeat. He also sought out British and North American mariners for his crews from the deserters and others – for instance from the whaling ships – who roamed the streets of Valparaíso. They merely had to be sobered up. Given the prospects of being paid for their efforts, as well as their appreciation of Cochrane's celebrated record, they generally set sail happily. The Chilean Navy was soon rooted in the traditions of the Royal Navy.

The majority of the officers responsible for the crucial capture of the Spanish warship, *Esmeralda*, off Callao, in 1820, were British. An earlier attempt to capture the *Esmeralda* had failed. On that occasion it was an Irish-born, Royal Navy veteran, George O'Brien, who impetuously but bravely led the boarding party only to be cut down in hand-to-hand fighting, thus becoming the first recognized hero of the Chilean navy.

Another celebrated British sailor who lent his skills and courage to the liberation of Chile and to the development and subsequent deployments of the Chilean navy was Robert Winthrop Simpson. It is believed he arrived with Cochrane as a midshipman. He fought in the independence campaign in Peru and was then promoted to captain in 1821. Dispatched by Cochrane to harass Spanish ships off Mexico his service record was tarnished. Leaving his ship to seek provisions, a mutiny was provoked aboard by an English boson who subsequently commandeered the vessel to pursue a campaign of piracy. Simpson had to find another vessel on which to return south.

With the departure of Cochrane from Chile, Simpson fought on, taking part both in the first, failed expedition to liberate the island of Chiloé and the second, in 1826, which definitively dislodged the royalists from the islands. He continued his Chilean naval career until 1871, eventually reaching the rank of rear-admiral, having led Chile's fleet in several major campaigns, notably the 'Confederation War' against the allied forces of Peru and Bolivia (1836-39).

As the generation of British born naval officers gradually disappeared so the commanders were increasingly of Chilean nationality, even if they had been trained in the ways of the British navy and were even the offspring of those who had fought for the nation's independence. John Williams, for instance, a Welshman who joined the Chilean navy in 1824, was another who fought in the campaign to liberate Chiloé in 1826, subsequently becoming the island's maritime governor. After participating in the Confederation War with Peru and Bolivia, he established Fuerte Bulnes, the first settlement in the Magellan Strait since the sixteenth century, to ensure a Chilean presence in Patagonia. He is remembered through Puerto Williams on the South shore of the Beagle Channel (Isla Navarino), but also because of the exploits of his son, Rear Admiral Juan Williams Rebolledo, who made his name as a hero during the 1865-66 war with Spain and again during the Pacific War against Peru and Bolivia.

Among the many British mariners to lend a hand to the independence struggle were some whose unofficial efforts were more in the piratical tradition than that of the hero of the Battle of Trafalgar, Vice-Admiral Horatio Lord Nelson. Celebrated among them, for their exploits in a few months of 1817, the year before Cochrane brought some credibility to the fledgling Chilean navy, were Captains Mackay and James and a former marine, named Budge. Mackay and James bought a launch, which they renamed *Fortuna* and set out, with letters of marque issued by Chilean leader O'Higgins, to do damage to the Spanish. With a small Chilean and British crew, the *Fortuna* quickly took a 400 ton Spanish supply ship *Minerva* off Arica. Shortly after, it was in *Minerva* that they took another Spanish vessel, *Santa Maria*, and in early 1818, sailing in a new schooner re-named *Fortuna II,* Mackay took at least two more Spanish prizes, *San Miguel* and *Gran Poder*, off Panama. Thus the basis for the Cochrane's Chilean navy was assembled.

The influence of the original commanders and crews were so strong that they have lasted until today. The Royal Navy was then, and remained, a model. Exchanges between the two navies became routine. As Admiral Jorge Martínez Busch, Commander in Chief of the Chilean navy in the 1990s, wrote:

"The discipline, the ceremonials, the daily duties on board, the meals, the

83

training and even the uniform are drawn from this origin."

Later, when it came to naval operations during the Pacific War (see Chapter 12), it was British-trained commanders using British-learned manoeuvres who often won the day. People like Patricio Lynch who had served with the Royal Navy in the 1840s and who, on his return to Chilean service, ensured that other young Chilean officers would benefit from time in Her Majesty's navy. That became a tradition, as did Britain's position as the dominant supplier of naval vessels to Chile.

French officers decide between Bonaparte and Chilean independence

Still, the French were not far behind the British in their enthusiasm to lend a hand during the independence struggles. They too, had plenty of senior army and naval officers who could no longer be paid from the public purse back home. Furthermore, there was even some complicity between the British and French officers who had fought each other for so long, but who had one common characteristic: an admiration for Napoleon Bonaparte. The Emperor was again in exile, this time on the island of St Helena in the middle of the South Atlantic Ocean. His admirers dreamed of a rescue. They included Admiral Thomas Cochrane. Napoleon had long had a soldier's respect for the British "sea wolf", and had been appalled by Cochrane's treatment during the financial scandal in the City of London. By some accounts, the disgraced British admiral considered the fallen French leader as a natural figurehead for the independence movements in South America – and especially in Chile where Bernardo O'Higgins had appointed Cochrane to build and command the navy.

In parallel with Cochrane's ambitions for Napoleon, there were several groups of French naval officers, some operating from the United States, actively plotting a rescue and a restoration. It has been suggested that among them was the much-decorated, senior infantry general, Michel Brayer – a commander whose numerous battle honours included the capture of 8000 Russian troops at the Battle of Austerlitz. Brayer arrived in Buenos Aires, on the ship *Clifton*, in February 1817, from the United States, along with José Miguel Carrera, the one-time Chilean independence leader and military dictator. They were accompanied by a small fleet with which it was hoped to reinvigorate the independence struggle. In the event, they were too late; within a few days of their arrival in Buenos Aires, San Martín had wrenched control of much of central Chile following his victory at the Battle of Chacabuco. An expedition headed by Carrera with French and American officers was no longer necessary or wanted. Carrera, in any event was quickly arrested by the Argentine authorities.

Some of the French officers would join San Martín individually. But for several months, it is widely believed that Brayer was, in reality, putting together a quite different expedition destined for St Helena and the liberation of Napoleon. Ultimately it did not happen. Instead Brayer joined San Martín's Army of the Andes. At much the same time, Thomas Cochrane also had to abandon his ambitions for the ex-Emperor of France and sail directly to Valparaíso where the demands of O'Higgins for a determined sea campaign against the Spanish had become more urgent than ever.

Michel Brayer, appointed Chief of Staff of the Army of the Andes by San Martín, had ambitions to inject the habits, discipline and unity of Napoleon's army of the Empire into the often quarrelsome and fragmented groups that the Argentine general commanded. His attempts to do so, such as they were, largely failed. He irritated and angered many of San Martín's officers. In particular, Brayer clashed with the English surgeon-general of the Army of the Andes, James Paroissien – although Paroissien was descended from French Huguenots. Having joined him early, in 1816, Paroissien was extremely close to San Martín, and not just as a medical adviser. It was not a wise move to cross him, nor others of senior rank close to San Martín.

Joining the campaign in the south, with O'Higgins and San Martín, Brayer found himself implicated in two severe defeats for the patriots. First, the assault on Talcahuano, in December 1817, led bravely by the French general George Beauchef (see below), ended in disaster and retreat. In March the following year, an attempted surprise attack on the royalist army at Cancha Rayada, near Talca, also turned to confusion. There was a bloodbath and then a chaotic flight

Benjamin Viel: from the Battle of Waterloo to the Battle of Maipú.

Archivo Nacional, Santiago

northwards by units of San Martín's forces, after the outnumbered Spanish troops had skilfully outmanoeuvred the patriots. Disillusionment among O'Higgins' followers was total, and Brayer was a handy and unpopular scapegoat. Not only was he a foreigner, but his loyalty was in question given his earlier association with Carrera. Brayer was relieved of his command of the cavalry and, returning quickly to Santiago, sought to restore his credibility through a mistaken intervention in the political machinations then rumbling among the different strands of the independence movement.

The disenchantment with O'Higgins and San Martín, because of the disasters in the South, would be very temporary. Only two months after Cancha Rayada, their overwhelming victory at the battle of Maipú transformed the prospects of the war definitively, and dampened the ambitions of internal dissenters. Belatedly, Brayer seems to have tried to ingratiate himself once more with San Martín, but by then the leader of the Army of the Andes was so unhappy with the behaviour of the French general, however celebrated, that it was too late. Brayer made his way back across the Andes, to Montevideo and eventually France, licking wounds which were both physical and reputational.

George Beauchef: a brave officer who helped overthrow O'Higgins and abandoned France
Archivo Nacional, Santiago

Brayer was not alone; in the months after Maipú, San Martín became increasingly suspicious of the loyalties of some French officers. Later in 1818, several were engaged in the conspiracy to bring down O'Higgins and San Martín in favour of José Miguel Carrera. However, they were betrayed, with two of them facing a firing squad after trial. Others may simply have been tarred by association; in any event, their service in the Army of the Andes was promptly curtailed.

Still, the other French officers continued to arrive as high-ranking refugees of the Napoleonic wars. A few months after the *Clifton* expedition docked in Buenos Aires only to be almost immediately abandoned, another vessel, the *Céleste*, arrived from Calais bringing a further band of Bonapartist officers set on a similar military intervention in Chile (or, as some in Paris believed, another attempt to liberate Napoleon Bonaparte from St Helena). Among this distinguished group was Benjamin Viel, a veteran of the Battle of Waterloo and other campaigns. Viel would fight at the Battle of Maipú and in the independence campaign in the south of Chile. He stayed on to pursue an unusual political career in Chile, eventually becoming a deputy in the Congress. In the 1830s, after a brief spell in Peru, he was reappointed to high office in the Chilean army in Santiago before taking over as military chief in Valdivia and finally becoming governor of Concepción.

Joseph Bacler d'Albe was a military engineer and surveyor who reached the rank of Lieutenant Colonel during the independence wars of Chile and Peru. He had fought through many of the bloodiest campaigns of the Napoleonic War before arriving in Chile, on the same vessel, *Clifton*, that brought Carrera and Brayer from the United States. Between 1817 and 1819 he distinguished himself in Chile, notably through his surveying and map-making in support of military manoeuvres. In 1820, he accompanied the Argentine commander in the expedition to liberate Peru. His engineering skills proved invaluable in that campaign as did his work as a cartographer both in Peru and later again in Chile.

Unwise French meddling in Chilean politics

The involvement of another Frenchman, George Beauchef, in the liberation struggle was splendid and decisive, and admired to this day. After fighting in the 4th Hussars as a young officer at the battles of Austerlitz, Iéna and other early Napoleonic victories, he was captured during the Spanish campaign in 1808. He eventually escaped – desperately diving naked from one of the prison-ships, notorious for their inhuman conditions. He passed three years in Malta before slowly crossing Europe and reaching home in France well after the Emperor's disastrous Russian campaign of 1812. Indeed, he put on a uniform again – this time in the Republican Guard – only for the "Hundred Days" in 1815, during which Napoleon met his final defeat at Waterloo and was dispatched into his second exile on St Helena.

Dispirited, Beauchef saw no future in France but was anxious to continue fighting his old enemy, this time through the independence movement in Chile. In 1817, he was named by O'Higgins as deputy-director of the Military Academy. In that role he was able to instruct young officers on French concepts of infantry and cavalry tactics, which were greatly appreciated in Chile. Although the assault on Talcahuano in December 1817 was a disaster for the patriots, Beauchef would eventually taste glory in the south. In 1820, he led a startlingly audacious attack by marines on the Spanish garrison at Valdivia, having been landed in the bay by Admiral Cochrane who was in overall command of the operation. With astute tactics – both marine and land borne – this Anglo-French pairing secured one of the greatest military achievements of the entire independence war.

Yet, three years later, it would be Beauchef who assisted in the overthrow of Bernardo O'Higgins as Supreme Director and in his replacement by General Ramón Freire Serrano. Commander of the Army of the South, and governor of Valdivia, Freire admired and sympathized with the foreign officers in the patriot army, especially the French and no one more so than Beauchef. In the early 1820s, O'Higgins' reputation and standing was already crumbling. As his administration fell apart, Freire was seen as the obvious replacement. He wrote to Beauchef, who was at that point engaged in fighting the Indians of Araucania, and instructed him to return northwards with his entire division and support "the will of the people".

On his arrival in Valparaíso, it was Beauchef who was instructed by Freire to arrest O'Higgins. There followed a Freire-led administration of more than three years (1823-1826) in which the French were especially favoured. However, while the mutual admiration did not last, the French officers, especially Beauchef, were at Freire's side for the second, and finally successful, campaign to liberate the island of Chiloé, in 1826, which set the seal on the end of Spanish rule in Chile.

However, French officers continued to meddle in the political oscillations of the country, during the 1820s, as liberals faced off conservatives under various administrations and different versions of the emergent constitution. Benjamin Viel and others supported the liberal Freire during the 1829 civil war and ended up in exile in Peru, as did their favourite. It would be a decade before they were allowed back in Chile.

Europe's military legacies

While the British Royal Navy persisted as the model for the Chilean marine, the love affair of Chile for the Bonapartist model of soldiering would not last. Certainly, the French supplied military training as late as the 1860s, but it was the German, or Prussian, model that would ultimately endure in Chile. The great-est early influence was captain of artillery, Emil Körner Henze, who had graduated from the celebrated Kriegsakademie in Berlin. He was contacted during the War of the Pacific (1879-1883) by the Chilean legation in Berlin. The government in Santiago was well aware that its army needed modernizing and reorganizing and the record of the Prussian military, after mid-cen-tury victories over both France and Austria, made it pre-eminent in Europe. Körner was appointed for the purpose in 1886 as were thirty-six Prussian officers who would put officer cadets through their paces at the Chilean Military Academy. German-made artillery and rifles were bought and everything asso-ciated with the Prussian army was copied. That included uniforms and a marching style that not only reflected the military dominance of Germany during Bismarck's time, but has lasted until today. During the Pinochet period the appearance as well as some of the practices of the army conveyed a harsh, militaristic image of the country. Körner reached the rank of commander-in-chief of the Chilean army in 1900 having backed the winning side during the 1891 civil war.

Emil Körner Henze, taught the Chilean army Prussian discipline.
Archivo Nacional, Santiago

While European armies and navies may have remained models, and pro-vided advisors and supplies to the free countries of South America, three hun-dred years of Spanish rule had left their marks. Once independent, the new nations of the region never forgot and would never again be dominated by major powers. The role of Europe in the region became economic rather than political. For better or worse, the new states governed themselves – unlike, for instance, the countries of Southeast Asia which experienced one wave of colonial repression after another, until well into the 20th century.

Independent Chile, in particular, has sustained a more or less healthy democracy almost without break since its independence. Historians certainly argue about the impact of independence; clearly, reforms had been set in motion in the eighteenth century and did not always flow smoothly in the same direction throughout the nineteenth. Democracy had its less glorious moments. There were revolutions and periods of authoritarian government. Social reform was ragged. The Araucanian people and the native tribes to their south, probably suffered as much if not more within the Republic as they had under colonial oppression. The powerful creole, land-owning, families mostly retained their domination of political and economic power, and that has continued until today.

Still, without independence, the opening up to the world that was to bring hundreds of thousands of newcomers from Europe to the shores of the west coast of South America may not have happened or, at least, not so soon nor driven by such pioneering enthusiasm. That was the real legacy of dozens of European officers and many ordinary mariners and soldiers from the old continent who chose to lend a hand to Chile and Peru as they rid themselves of three centuries of colonial domination.

Georges Beauchef would die in Santiago in 1840, embittered and disillusioned. In part, he felt inadequately recognized and unjustly criticized in Chile. Much more so, a three-year stay in France between 1831 and 1834, convinced him that the country of his birth was no longer his, he felt a stranger there. Yet his memoirs reflect the pride that lingered for his role in his adoptive country. As he bade farewell to his battalion in the south, in 1829, he wrote:

"I retire having served the cause of independence of a country, following my liberal conscience, as an enemy of tyrannies. The country that I helped with all my heart to liberate is beautiful, its men virile and its women lovely and good. Chile knows how to make itself loved and I loved it from the first instant. It was immediately my second homeland. I married there and had children there. In this second homeland, I have known more joys than adversity."

In 1970, a statue of Georges Beauchef was erected on the waterfront in the city of Valdivia, in recognition of his service to the region and the nation.

6.

The newcomers: who, why and where from?

In the roundin' of Cape Stiff¹, we had a little tiff,
With the snifters of Tierra del Fuaygo,
It blew like hell all day, carried our tops'ls all away
In that handy bandy barque, the Campanayro!

"Campañero", a traditional song on the South American saltpetre ships

As the independence struggles drew to their conclusions so the trickle of Europeans reaching the shores of Chile, Peru and Bolivia became a serious flow. There was no mass immigration of the type encouraged by Argentina, Brazil and Uruguay in the late nineteenth century. True, from the 1840s the Chilean government sought to entice German and other European farmers to populate the south, including the fertile lakes region, often over the objections of indigenous people. But the freeing of trade and the opening of the ports were more important in stimulating new arrivals, as well as relatively stable government, in Chile at least.

Most newcomers came alone, although a surprising number risked bringing their families despite an uncertain future. Some drifted across the Andes after making a disappointing start in Buenos Aires, Montevideo or Rio. Some came in style on passenger steamers with lucrative contracts as engineers, bankers and traders. Others came to pursue their investments in mines, railways or shipping. Mariners docked in Valparaíso and deserted their vessels. Many professionals took the long voyage to deliver services to their fellow countrymen: as teachers, tailors, clerks and churchmen. Sailors took their marine skills ashore, becoming bakers, carpenters, sail makers and entertainers. Some thrived and stayed, some made fortunes and some lost them. Most were remarkable people – resourceful, courageous and enterprising.

In 1811, officially just seventy foreigners of non-Spanish origin were resident in Chile. In the whole of the province of Valparaíso, for instance, according to the incomplete and idiosyncratic census of 1813, only 35 men of foreign

---

1   Sailors' jargon for Cape Horn

origin were registered who were not part of the colonial Spanish population (1,595 men and 2,190 women) and were not European Spaniards (69 men). In the province of Rancagua, south of Santiago, just two non-Spanish men were noted compared to over 30,000 men and women of Spanish descent *(Españoles Americanos)* and 27 European Spaniards. The precise figures are not reliable, but they provide an indication of Spanish dominance as the independence movement gathered momentum in a country whose overall population was then probably still below one million – though estimates of indigenous peoples either do not exist or have little foundation.

Amidst the influx of Europeans arriving after the end of Spanish rule were strands of those fleeing oppression and war – the refugees, exiles and fugitives. For instance, large numbers of Croats began arriving in the middle of the nineteenth century, in the face of wars and plague in Dalmatia. They continued to settle in the north, where they worked in the saltpetre industry, and in Punta Arenas in the far south. Today they remain a large and identifiable community. Many Greeks sought to escape hard times during the First World War while Russians were refugees from the Revolution. Armenians sought shelter in Chile from the oppression of the Ottoman Empire, as did what would become the largest Palestinian community outside the Middle East, members of which also arrived during the Crimean War (1853–56) and after the establishment of Israel in 1948. Jews arriving from Poland, Hungary, Latvia and Czechoslovakia were fleeing both communism and Nazism in the 1930s. German Jews joined their countrymen already settled in the South of Chile. Not many years later, as the Second World War ended, it was the turn of senior Nazi officers to seek shelter from prosecution in the Nuremberg war crimes tribunals and anonymity in Chile and other South American countries. Other Europeans, like the Irish, the Swiss and the Basques simply fled poverty.

Bringing the various strands of 'immigration' together – the organized settlements, the refugees, the professionals with contracts, the sailors and the individuals who arrived and stayed to seek a new life – the engagement of foreigners, especially Europeans, helped transform the region from the 1820s onwards. While some may have been escaping hardships at home, most saw opportunities and were prepared to take risks and suffer discomfort in their pursuit.

The lands of the newly free needed populating

For the most part, they were welcomed in Chile. The French explorer and diplomat, Charles Wiener, writing in the 1880s, was clear about the nation's broad philosophy, which insisted on "Chile for the Chileans" while not turning its back on foreigners who brought "their science, their skill, their capital or the strength in their arms." By the 1850s Chile was seeking immigrants and, as a virtually unknown destination, went to some lengths to present itself to potential colonists in Europe. The emigration agents, for instance, emphasized political and economic stability. In a report to President Manuel Montt, in 1857, the author states firmly: "Chile is the sole refuge of peace, order and progress in the old Spanish America..." Much the same refrain was being sung simultaneously to potential North American immigrants, coupled with the warning that US exports were losing out to British trading dominance. Thus, a plea to those in the Land of the Free from those in a land newly free could tug the heartstrings of patriotism on both sides:

"What a field there is open for the men who are brought out from the over-crowded countries of Europe to that distant but beautiful, genial and prolific

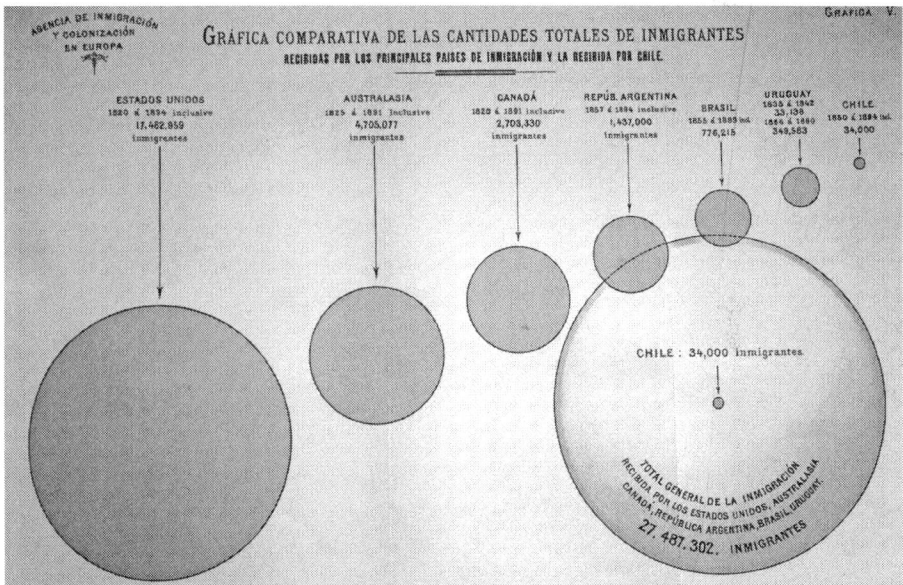

GRÁFICA COMPARATIVA DE LAS CANTIDADES TOTALES DE INMIGRANTES
RECIBIDAS POR LOS PRINCIPALES PAISES DE INMIGRACIÓN Y LA RECIBIDA POR CHILE.

CHILE : 34,000 inmigrantes

Nichloas Vega, Head of Chile's Agencia General de Colonización in Europe, tried to make clear to the authorities in Santiago just how poorly the country was doing in attracting new immigrants during the 1890s.

land, where everything is cheap, abundant, prosperous, increasing and, above all, where there is the greatest blessing of mankind – LIBERTY."

In fact, transatlantic resentment was only exacerbated in the wake of the relentless growth of European economic dominance in South America. One U.S. businessman, in 1905, aired his frustrations thus:

"… right at our very doors the trade of a great continent is slipping beyond our reach and while we are talking, Germany, England and France are engaged in a commercial invasion of American soil, and meeting with little or no opposition from us. … Now, the American is so cocksure his methods are the best in creation that, for a situation like this, he has neither patience nor tact … he is willing to hug a cherished prejudice and to look askance at South America. England and Germany, on the contrary, face the situation squarely, and meet the South American on his own footing. This is the secret of their great success. As a result of their affability, South America trusts them and believes they are sincerely interested in her welfare. But she doubts our friendship, and it seems to me not surprising that she does."

Charles Weiner, noting that Chile did not seek immigrants en masse, suggested that its emigration agents looked rather for the "malcontents". "They prefer certain races, like Basques and Swiss; they choose individuals and families with, at least, some small savings." This sounds picky, and was not entirely accurate. Yet, as the nineteenth century rolled on, there was mounting concern in Santiago at the poor showing of Chile as a destination for European emigrants.

Argentina, by the mid-1890s, was receiving each year more European immigrants than Chile had received in the previous 44 years. Between 1870 and 1890, a total of 4.4 million British citizens emigrated to numerous countries. Emigration from Germany amounted to 1.9 million, from Italy 1.1 million, with serious, but lesser, numbers leaving Sweden, Austria, Spain, Belgium, Norway and France. But of all these Europeans, parting from the lands of their birth, Chile took only 34,000. Given the hazards of reaching the Pacific coast of South America – especially when compared to the comparatively comfortable transatlantic passage to Buenos Aires or Montevideo – that ought not to have been a huge shock. Nevertheless, Nicholas Vega, the head of Chile's *Agencia General de Colonización*, based in Paris, sounded warning bells:

"The enormous mass of millions of emigrants that have abandoned Europe in this century, to create nations like the United States, Australia, the Republic of Argentina and even the little Republic of Uruguay, Chile has not wanted to take any part. … It is a real danger for the nation."

Yet, Chile had long sought to attract skilled foreigners. A law of 1824 had invited immigrants to set up factories to work Chilean materials, to use Chilean workers and not to make a secret of the technologies employed – in other words, to give easy access to any patents. For this, land would be granted freely together with an exemption from taxes for a period. In the case of a farmer, the authorities had discretion to provide land and tax exemptions on crops and livestock raised on territory regarded previously as wilderness. This gave an opening for what would become the most organized strand of European immigration, that of the Germans.

An 1845 law allowed the Chilean President to offer 6,000 cuadras[2] (over 9,000 hectares) of vacant, state-owned land to establish colonies, populated by both natives and foreigners, to pursue some useful agricultural activity. Individual immigrants could receive up to 24 cuadras (38 hectares) plus twelve more for each son over fourteen years of age. The allowance was far less (eight quadras) in the central region where Creole landowners – descended from the original Spanish settlers – had long farmed from their large traditional ranches. The newcomers were promised a twenty-year exemption from taxation and considerable financial assistance from the state. However, as an indication of their commitment to the country, they were required to take Chilean nationality.

Early efforts to attract German farming families

Initially, the government lacked the cash to provide the promised funds so the first German settlers survived only on personal savings brought with them. As a result, early colonies in the South were seeded by private enterprise. Ferdinand Flindt, a merchant as well as the Prussian consul in Valparaíso, bought more than 1000 cuadras of land between La Unión and Osorno with the intention of bringing German families to Chile to develop it. In 1846, the first eight families arrived. Among the men were two blacksmiths, a carpenter, a cabinetmaker, a millwright, a shoemaker, a gardener and a shepherd. Dispirited after a long and uncomfortable voyage, the group reached Valdivia – which, on first sight, seemed very far removed from the town of their dreams – only to find their patron had gone bankrupt. Luckily for them, another German, Franz Kindermann, bought the land and upheld the contracts of the new arrivals. Furthermore, their skills were quickly in demand. Despite their unhappy first impressions, the group thrived.

Indeed, with this limited trial an apparent success, the government in Santiago was anxious to repeat the experience on a much larger scale. In 1848, Bernhard Eunom Philippi, a German explorer and naturalist, drew up a grand plan for large-scale immigration from his home country. He was named an

---

2 One Chilean cuadra converted to 3.89 acres or 1.57 hectares.

official agent by the government and set about attracting hundreds of skilled German workers and their families. This time, however, they were to be Catholics, to offset the first group which had been composed of Protestants. The hope was to profit from the revolutionary disturbances, at the time, in the German states. Another agent went to Ireland to find three or four hundred Catholic families there.

The initiative largely failed. The German Catholic Church of the time strongly discouraged, if not forbade, the emigration of its own faithful. Philippi managed to gather only a few poor protestant families. It was evident that protestant immigration was more likely to succeed generally, even if it needed another non-official initiative. Franz Kindermann was again quick to take advantage of the situation. His father-in-law had 'purchased' large tracts of land from Indian tribes. By most accounts the purchases were at best a farce and at worst a fraud. The Indians had no ownership – apart from their limited occupation of the lands "sold" – while the purchaser handed out cheap gifts in order to secure "title" to the territory. While the government supported neither the land transfers nor the private immigration initiative, Kindermann had the

The **Pacific Steam Navigation Company's** mail steamer **"Quito"** in 1864. For a decade, during the 1880s, the PSNC had a monopoly in transporting sponsored European immigrants to Chile.   *The Illustrated London News*

confidence and audacity to press on regardless. He went to Germany and succeeded in selling 40,000 cuadras to an emigration society in Stuttgart, with an option on 40,000 more. By the time five ships carrying the first 287 immigrants had arrived in 1850, the government had declared the land purchases void. Some settlers nevertheless found their way, with local Chilean help, to establish new homesteads around Valdivia. Others headed north to central Chilean cities where they believed their skills would be more easily absorbed.

The area of southern Chile still most associated with German immigration, Llanquihue, would be the next official target for settlement. This verdant and picturesque region, a mélange of Switzerland and Ireland, lay around the shores of the lake, south of Valdivia, with the volcano, Mt. Osorno, looming majestically, and occasionally threateningly, on the eastern side of the water. The Chilean navy was sent to discover a waterway that would provide access to the sea and, therefore, trade routes. The nearest was some ten kilometers south of the Lake at a point that was to become the port of Puerto Montt. A road was quickly constructed and very soon the first settlers began to arrive. Up until 1864, when the formal settling of Llanquihue was concluded, 3,367 persons came from Germany, to whom a few hundred Catholic Germans from Bohemia[3] were added in 1873 and 1875. The newcomers, in general, refused to take Chilean nationality, and stuck with their protestant origins. However, most learned Spanish and many wore ponchos. By 1904, there were 31 German schools in the south with 2,400 pupils.

Still, the prevalence of settlers from Europe – even in the south of Chile – can be, and was often, exaggerated. An American study, in 1921, set out to examine the extent of German colonization in the south. The author, Mark Jefferson, concluded:

"The Germanization of southern Chile is simply a myth. There is no town or settlement in the country where a majority of people are of German origin or speak German."

He noted that in the 1907 census of Chile some 30,000 persons of German descent were recorded, of whom 20,000 had kept their German speech. Many of them lived in Valparaíso and Santiago and were engaged in business. Naturally, a portion of the original German colonists had returned to their native country and others had been assimilated over the fifty years or so since serious immigration had been promoted by the Chilean government. Even in Puerto Montt, though among the most German of all Chilean towns, the American observer could find little trace of a substantial German community, German language, German newspapers or German domination of the local economy.

---

3   Now part of the Czech Republic.

Jefferson accurately found these 'German' towns and provinces overwhelmingly Chilean – perhaps five-sixths of the population of Puerto Montt. Of the rural properties worth over two-thousand Chilean pesos in Valdivia province, in 1907, 64 per cent were in the hands of people of Spanish descent and 25 per cent of German descent.

However, as with the British in Valparaíso, the overall numbers may not have been overwhelming, but their local political and economic influence certainly was. Yet even that influence wavered over time. In the 1917 local elections in Valdivia, there were enough Chileans to vote out all but one of the German city councillors who were resented during the Great War in Europe. Another factor in the puzzle of the apparently diminishing German presence in the south is likely to have been the movement towards the Central regions of many original German settlers who found themselves restricted by the relatively small amounts of cultivable lands available to them.

Of course, official efforts to attract immigrants were not restricted to German farmers. Even in the colonial period there had been discussion of the potential. The Jesuit, Joaquín Villarroel had argued, in 1755, when the inhabitants of Chile probably numbered less than half a million, that the country had enough cultivatable land to support a population of twelve million. By 1863, the *Annuario estadístico* rashly raised the estimate to no less than 52 million[4]. These two projections were cited in the 1865 report of the *Comisión especial* set up by the government of President Manuel Montt to advise on the future direction of foreign immigration into the country. The report was written by the Commission's secretary and the ex-Minister of Agriculture, Benjamin Vicuña Mackenna. Mackenna, who inevitably features in any account of Chile in the nineteenth century, because of his audacious politics, copious writings and perpetual rebellion against sloppy thinking, had lived in Europe (for his education as well as, later, in exile to escape a death sentence) and in the United States. Thus he was an internationalist at heart. He was also the grandson of one of the heroes of national liberation, the Irish general John Mackenna. Such roots made it natural that he would stand firmly against those who preferred a narrow-minded, exclusively catholic, unambitious nation whose future would be safe in the hands of the old Spanish families that remained in effective control even after independence.

The Europeans were a mixed bunch as potential colonists

---

4   Within its modern borders – extended significantly northwards in the Pacific War – Chile still has a population of only about 17.5 million (est. 2013)

The report set out the case for stepping up the inflow of immigrants passing from the most evident – the need for capital, skills and manpower – to the social and moral imperatives. It cited the disturbing moral decline of towns like Valparaíso, where criminality was raging, and the desperately high death rate among children in Santiago[5]. Mackenna, however, excelled when pontificating on the innate value of specific European nationalities as immigrants. For him, the Germans came out on top, and by far. They were among the few races prepared to leave their homeland for good to make a new life among their own; they had the best character, the right skills, a superior work ethic and some savings from a more frugal lifestyle than that exhibited by other nationalities. The only issue was how to divert a few more Germans – preferably many – towards the shores of Chile.

Second in Mackenna's league table came the Italians (from Lombardy and Piedmont) and the Swiss who had the right attitudes towards establishing themselves as settlers and the right skills as farmers. Basques – from the French and Spanish sides of the Pyrenees – came next, based on their capacity for hard work. They tended to be transient emigrants, however. Belgians were also favoured mildly, but more for their artisan skills that would reinforce Chilean industry, than for agricultural talents.

When it came to English, Scottish and Irish emigrants, however, the judgment was harsh. As Mackenna put it:

"The English, properly speaking, do not emigrate, they travel. Similar to the ancient Romans, the civilization that was most comparable in its instincts and its power, the sons of old Albion explore, conquer, get rich and return home with their booty."

The English preferred to trade with and to colonize new lands, like Canada and Australia. And they did so to expand an empire. Mackenna quotes Prime Minister William Gladstone: "The great principle of England is to multiply its race by the propagation of its institutions." If that included the monarchy it would have hardly been welcome in a country that had only recently rid itself of the domination of another royal dynasty. The Scots were not much better candidates as immigrants – supposedly being more 'sedentary' than the English. The Irish, on the other hand, and given Mackenna's own forebears, might be "turbulent and wayward" but they were also "men of spirit, intelligent, enthusiastic, capable of any work, brave in war, hardworking regardless of fatigue, noble and without self-interest, perhaps like no other people on the face of the

---

5   Of 10,635 deaths recorded in Santiago in 1865, more than one-half (5608) were young children.

earth."

The French came even further down the list, with unreliability and poor character placing them outside the bounds of desirable immigrants. The Spanish character was little better, even putting aside their colonial record.

Then there was the question of the kind of settlers needed. Mackenna's group was clear that Chile did not need "proletarian" immigrants. Moreover, ordinary industrial workers from countries like England and France were far inferior to Chileans: they were "less active", "less sparing in their diet" and "less obedient and humble." What was needed were artisans.

Thus the targets were set. But how to attract the Germans, Swiss, Basques and the Italians of Lombardy? The *Comision Especial* analysed the success of Argentina in attracting large numbers of immigrants from Europe. It noted that in 1859, the Province of Buenos Aires alone was home to 25,000 French, 20,000 Basques and Spanish, 15,000 Italians and 20,000 British out of a total population of 320,000. Other statistics illustrated the flow of immigrants through the port of Buenos Aires, rising from 4,658 in 1858 to 11,682 in 1864, about half of them Italian. Impressed, the Commission drew attention to the contracts offered settlers, including the allowances and subsidies paid by the Argentine government. However, it also observed that, like the United States, Argentina was in a position to attract "spontaneous" and large scale immigration. The opportunities were so evident – notably vast areas of land that could be sold to newcomers – that little persuasion was needed at a time when much of Europe was at war and in poverty. So, if Chile wanted settlers in groups it would have to go and seek them out and offer the right incentives.

The commission made proposals to the government on the terms and administrative infrastructure that would be needed. But it also made some sensitive recommendations, calling for religious tolerance towards the German and Swiss Protestants as well as the British who had been left for decades without a recognized burial place for their citizens in towns like Valparaíso (see Chapter 14). There was also the question of Araucania and the occupation of territories that were home to indigenous people.

On the more practical side, the commission raised the problem of the sea passage facing European emigrants. The routes to the United States East Coast, Brazil and Argentina were much shorter than that to Chile – in fact, Valparaíso was four times the distance from Europe to New York. The voyage was also more dangerous and far more expensive. Thus, the fare to New York was 25-30 pesos in 1853 and those to Rio de Janeiro or Buenos Aires around 40-50 pesos. A passenger to Valparaíso would pay three times the New York fare and twice that to the East Coast of South America. The need for a direct steamer service via the Strait of Magellan, to replace the long voyage via Panama (which included an overland trek to the Pacific coast), was self-evident. Other recommendations included the need for Chile to be properly promoted at the 1867 World Exhibition in Paris and the construction of a railway across the Andes.

The steamer service and other recommendations were ultimately implemented. Yet there was no huge boost in immigration. In the 1880s, President José Manuel Balmaceda sought to encourage broad foreign immigration. In July 1887, the Chilean foreign minister informed a British diplomat that the government wanted to see more British families settling in the south. The response was rapid. By early 1888, British families were arriving in Valparaíso before travelling on to their promised new lives. Unfortunately, many of them discovered the rosy perspectives painted for them by the Chilean colonization agent in England less than accurate. They struggled, and some probably made good, but many appeals for assistance were received by the British embassy in Santiago.

The *Agencia General de Inmigración y Colonización de Chile en Europa* was created by the Chilean government in 1882 and made its base in Paris. Publicity and promotion programmes were intended to fill six to seven hundred subsidized passages to Chile each year. Sub agencies were set up around Europe. Initially, offices were established in Spain, France, Switzerland and Germany. Then the agency extended its operations to England, Belgium, Holland and Italy and, by 1895, to Russia and Scandinavia also. But it was a sensitive undertaking in many cities. Only in England was the sub-agency relatively free to pursue its promotional activities. In other capitals they were "rigorously regulated" according to the Agent-General. Usually the agencies could not even be staffed by Chilean nationals, only by locals, and frequently it proved impossible for an official representative to conduct public campaigns. Sometimes it was necessary to establish private entities to take over the work. Further, the Chilean immigration contract was often contrary to local laws and regulations. Recruitment of emigrants usually required licenses, and these had to be negotiated by the Agent-General with each government individually.

Recruiting immigrants was a sensitive business

There was often friction. The Swiss banned Chilean immigration recruitment at least twice. In 1883, the numbers of Swiss leaving their country for Chile had reached a level that created concern in Berne. Four years later, in 1887, a halt was imposed on recruitment by the agency because of reports of ill-treatment of existing colonists in Chile. One pastor from French-speaking Switzerland had travelled to Chile to discover how the disturbingly large numbers of parishioners departing the Vaud region were faring. His report, taken very seriously at the time, condemned Chilean immigration propaganda and sought to correct the vision of a new life seen through rose-tinted spectacles:

"To have no comforts, no community, no amusements, no means of education, no Sundays, no church, nothing to read nor anything that, back home, provides the charm of life, is to lead a life with little colour or interest. Is it really worth the trouble? Just as in Europe, just a few make their fortune, and by the same means: hard work and prudence."

Indeed, after 1887 immigration into Chile of Swiss nationals began to decline and, while official censuses appeared to suggest otherwise, many settlers moved on to Argentina, Peru and Paraguay. Others stayed put but with no real employment and few assets – according to the Swiss consul, they were all officially recorded as farmers nonetheless.

Similar sensitivities emerged in Germany. They were calmed only with the intervention of Chancellor Bismarck, who adeptly drew a distinction between recruitment in the towns, which was permitted, and in the country villages, which was not – in that way not draining much-needed agricultural skills and manpower. At the same time, the Chilean authorities themselves were adding to the sense of insecurity for potential immigrants by regularly suspending the recruitment process and changing the conditions for acceptance of new colonists. The Agent-General himself was bitterly critical in his 1896 report to the government.

The contracts between the Agent-General and the colonists developed over the years and, broadly, became ever more generous. The successful candidate was given an advance on his own sea passage (from Bordeaux or Liverpool), valued at 250 French francs, and that of each member of his family. Initially, in 1884, the concession offered a free grant of forty hectares in southern Chile (Araucania) which, by 1895, had been raised to seventy hectares plus thirty hectares each for the colonist's sons. On disembarking at the port of entry in Chile – normally Valparaíso – there was free board and lodging and transport for the family up to the point at which the colonist took possession of his land. The cost of medical treatment was covered for the first two years. An advance of the equivalent of 75 French francs a month was provided for the first year to cover every-day expenses. Two head of cattle were provided along with 300 wooden planks for constructing a house and farm buildings. Some forty kilos of iron nails and a collection of seeds also came in the package.

Even in the 1920s, immigrants poured into Antofagasta, mostly to work in the saltpetre industry. They came from many nations of Europe, including Croatia, Hungary, Turkey, Greece, Poland and Scandinavia. Some came by ship from other jobs in Chile and Peru, others struggled across the Andes after disappointments in Argentina or Uruguay. Among the older men were veterans of the Pacific War of 1879-81. There were engineers, accountants, teachers, miners, administrators, blacksmiths, housewives, managers, geologists, even prostitutes. They were all registered and photographed. *Archives of the Universidad Católica del Norte, Antofagasta.*

What were the colonist's obligations? Above all there was a commitment to farm the allocated land for five years. This was later increased to six. The various advances – sea passage, the first-year subsistence payments, the price of the initial cattle and materials – needed to be reimbursed over eight years with the first repayment after three years (later five and four years respectively). Title to the land was conceded by the government only when the colonist had built a house and put at least four hectares of his land into production. This was later changed to a minimum of six years' cultivation. Further, the land could neither be mortgaged nor sold for a minimum of five years.

The Pacific Steam Navigation Company (PSNC) was handed a lucrative monopoly under the immigration contracts from 1883 to 1889. The powerful British-owned shipping line was paid by the Chilean government to pick up emigrants at various points on the Continent before transferring them on to regular PSNC ships leaving from Liverpool or Bordeaux. Later, the French company Compagnie Maritime de la Pacifique gained a share of the business. When the French shipper abandoned the service after a few years, the route was taken on by two German operators: Kosmos and, later, Hamburg Pacific.

While the numbers of farmers who signed up for the officially-backed Chilean immigration contracts were the greater, there was also an effort to find skilled 'industrial immigrants.' These were sought on less generous terms than the agricultural recruits and were required to reimburse all costs. In practice, most skilled workmen found their way to the Pacific coast independently or on the basis of contracts offered by private companies. Moreover, there was always some doubt about how immigrants with any but the most sought-after 'professional' occupations – and with some capital to back them up – would thrive. One relatively down-to-earth assessment was made by a British naturalist, observing social trends in Chile at the turn of the century:

"There is no opportunity in Chile for the British workman. No European could compete in manual labour with the frugal Chileno. But a master-workman with a little capital, or indeed, any man with business enterprise, thorough knowledge of his profession, and from £500 to £1000, ought to find his opportunity. Certainly, the chances are infinitely more favourable than any which he is likely to obtain at home."

Nevertheless, such warnings did not prevent some severely ill-advised attempts at settlement in Chile, including several sponsored by the Agent General in Paris. In 1895, for instance, 320 families – many from London – were sent to the wet but fertile island of Chiloé. Little attention was paid to their skills and backgrounds. To provide space for the newcomers, industrious

104

Chilotes were expelled from their lands, without compensation. Yet, among the first 150 families to arrive there were only twenty farm workers. Many of the rest were criminals, or suffered from disabling diseases. Eventually some 28 families were expelled to the mainland for criminal acts; another 76 were driven out as useless. Others ran away. By 1899, a total of only 153 families remained on the island. They were of mixed origins and the different nationalities, far from working together, split into hostile groups.

Another troubled and troublesome group was the 280 Boers from South Africa settled, in 1903, on forcibly-vacated Chilean land south of Temuco. There were vociferous protests locally, and these eventually spread to the capital. Increasingly, Chilean citizens questioned the special advantages enjoyed by incoming colonists from Europe who were taken to be contributing little or nothing to national wellbeing and development. In 1898, the Congress approved legislation that allowed the president to grant lands to Chileans on much the same terms the European immigrants had enjoyed for decades. Implementation of the new law was, however, begrudging. While 5000 Chilean families applied, the Inspector General declared there was not sufficient land available and appeared to consider many of the applications frivolous.

So the rumblings of discontent among Chileans persisted. Although most Italian immigrants went to the cities, one official experiment sought to establish an Italian farm settlement north-west of Temuco. Again it caused trouble. Just thirty of the 100 families contracted actually arrived. Yet it was alleged that 150 Chilean families had been evicted to provide the 27,000 hectares allotted to the Italians. It became a *cause célèbre* for labour organizations and liberal newspapers. The Italians suffered menaces. Often, the immigrants found themselves trapped and resented not only because Chilean families were being evicted in their favour but because of the wider scandal of large-scale land auctions to big concession-holders linked to the government. It was these concession-holders who were profiting from the immigration promotion schemes.

Still, it has to be recognized that the problems were not one-way. Evictions sometimes hit the settlers as well. The case of Ultima Esperanza, at the turn of the century, was a stark instance. For long, the government in Santiago barely recognized the southernmost lands of Patagonia in the Magallanes region as worth the trouble of administration. It sought, without result, to settle the Magellan Strait area in 1843 – centuries after Pedro Sarmiento's tragic expedition. Ultimately, it was foreigners, especially Germans, who understood the value of the grassland for raising livestock, especially sheep, in this inhospitable, bleak landscape. They started by squatting on the land. From about 40,000 sheep in 1885, numbers grew to 500,000 in 1891 and to two million in 1916.

In 1891, Captain Hermann Eberhard, who knew the complicated waterways in the region, together with some fellow countrymen, notably his brother-in-law, Augusto Kark, went from Punta Arenas by steamer to Ultima Esperanza Fjord some 200 km northwest. The intention was to settle this rugged but beautiful stretch of country for sheep farming. The small group of Germans struggled but succeeded with no help but their own sweat. By 1906, the settlement numbered 600 and had all the necessary infrastructure, including a meat-processing plant, refrigeration sheds, wool-baling machinery and a steamship connection for exports.

It was around 1900 that the Argentine Republic woke up to the potential value of land in southern Patagonia. Without the natural frontier of the Andes in the extreme south, differences with Chile over territorial limits were inevitable. Eventually, both sides sought a mediator; in this instance the frontier dispute went to King Edward VII of Great Britain for arbitration. In 1902, King Edward sent a commission to investigate under Sir Thomas Holdich, President of the Royal Geographical Society and an expert in delineating national frontiers – notably in India. Having visited Ultima Esperanza, Holdich had little hesitation in recognizing the rights of the German settlers there. In the final award, he ruled that the area should be Chilean, commenting as follows:

"All this country of Ultima Esperanza has been occupied by enterprising colonists, who have partitioned the land between them without waiting to know to which republic it might eventually belong. They have done great things in order to improve their holdings, and it was with especial reference to their locally recognized limits of occupation that the Award was made in those few parts of the line where no natural feature was available to furnish a practical boundary."

This seemed, for a while, to safeguard the future interests of the settlers. However, the government in Santiago needed funds and its newly confirmed territory was too valuable an asset to be left financially unproductive. An auction was announced, to be conducted without the slightest concession or reservation for the very settlers whose enterprise and determination had won the land for Chile. Despite the presence of at least four other bidders, apparently with very deep pockets, the government's first attempt to auction parcels of land, in March 1905, was defeated by the ruse of one of the original settlers who was also the German consul, Rudolf Stubenrauch. The consul maneuvered to bid up the price from $5 a hectare to as much as $135 a hectare; the other bidders chose to lose their deposits and withdrew.

However, with Stubenbauch absent in Europe, a second auction was held with almost no notice that September. This time, 351,000 hectares were successfully sold to the Exploration Company of Tierra del Fuego at just $12.50 a hectare. The *Sociedad Explotadora de Tierra del Fuego* (SETF) was by far the most powerful sheep-raising and meat processing company in the region, exploiting over one million hectares of land in Argentina and Chile. Naturally, the firm was also politically influential. Eberhard and Kark were permitted to purchase their own holdings and a concession was given to the Governor in Punta Arenas who had provided the temporary licences to the settlers on the land that had become indisputably part of Chile (a service for which, ironically, he had been reprimanded by his superiors in Santiago). Most of the other settlers were driven out of the area.

The foreign communities grow and spread

By the time of the first reliable census, in 1865, there were 23,220 foreigners resident in a population of 1.82 million. Yet they were heavily concentrated in certain provinces where trade or settlements had attracted newcomers from Europe. In the Atacama region, for instance, there was one foreigner for every eight Chilean nationals (12.5 percent); in the deep South, in the agricultural settlements of Magallanes province, it was one for every seventeen. In Valparaíso province, the ratio was one to twenty-six, but in Valparaíso town itself the presence of Europeans stood at one in fourteen (7.1 per cent). Within the provinces of Llanquihue and Valdivia, where German settlement dominated, the ratios were one to twenty-nine and twenty-five respectively (though around Lake Llanquihue itself it was one to eight). In provinces which had yet to be of interest to foreigners, they were outnumbered by local people by as much as one to 900.

By the end of the century – according to the census of 1895 – the population of Chile (now inflated by the territories of Bolivia and Peru taken in the Pacific War of 1879-83) had increased by nearly a million to 2.7 million. The number of foreigners had jumped nearly four times to 80,000. France, Germany, Italy and Great Britain were the European nations most represented, each with around seven to eight thousand residents. Apart from the Spanish and Swiss, most other countries of the 'Old Continent' could count their nationals in the hundreds. Even the United States had only around 750 residents in Chile. At the same time, the newcomers were more diffusely distributed around the countryside and cities than previously. As industries developed, ports were expanded along with commercial activity and farmland became more productive and populated. Valparaíso, for instance, had some 11,300 foreigners registered in the census, although approaching 1,000 were sailors temporarily in the port. In the farming province of Llanquihue, the population had risen to over 78,000, including some 1100 foreigners, mostly German settlers.

A peak was reached sometime in the first decade of the twentieth century. In the 1907 census year the total of foreigners on Chilean soil reached 134,524 in a population, now reasonably reliably counted, of over 3.2 million. In the decades that followed, most European inflows fell back and many foreign residents went home. There were many reasons. Numerous European men took leave to fight in the First World War, often never to return – their names recorded in the Anglican and other protestant churches of Valparaíso and elsewhere. The opening of the Panama Canal in 1914 started a long process of decline for the major ports on the Pacific Coast of South America, as did the beginning of the end of the saltpetre trade. The British trading companies, shipping agents and insurers whose activities had dominated the ports for a century steadily became Chilean companies with Chilean management. Of those Europeans who stayed, many took Chilean nationality, sometimes marrying into local families. The "Europeanness" even of Valparaíso – and especially in the wake of the devastating 1906 earthquake – began to look and feel a thing of the past.

Thus, by the time of the 1930 census, the number of foreign residents had dropped to around 105,500 in a population now standing at almost 4.3 million. The counts for British, French, Swiss, Swedes and Norwegian residents had fallen back to the levels of 1885; German residents were continuing to increase as the farming communities of the South thrived. Now, the newcomers were more likely to be North Americans, Russians, Turks, Chinese, Dutch, Greeks, Palestinians, Yugoslavs, Rumanians and Serbs. The Italians continued to arrive – many crossing from Argentina – and the Spanish once more had the largest presence as foreign-born residents.

They brought with them every imaginable skill

What did the foreigners from Europe contribute? We shall see, in some detail, in later chapters. What the census figures demonstrate, in general, is the remarkably diverse range of professional, scientific and artisan skills that came with so many new foreign citizens. In the south – in and around Valdivia, Llanquihue and Osorno – the German communities were near self-sufficient. In the 1895 census, for instance, apart from farmers, the professions represented by the German communities included carpenters, blacksmiths, locksmiths, furniture makers, doctors, bakers, teachers, jewellers and watchmakers, brewers, shoemakers, priests and, as everywhere, merchants to run shops and stores and manage the all-important flows of imports and exports at the ports.

At the same time in Valparaíso 1,874 foreign merchants in; 652 of them Italian, 302 German, 201 British and 178 French. And while they looked after the essential purpose of the old port, they found around them Europeans providing every imaginable service and skill: from Italian tailors and shoemakers to French dressmakers and prostitutes; not forgetting the actors, musicians and artists from all over, the doctors, surgeons, teachers and an adequate smattering of priests – including those looking after the souls of the "dissident" English and German Protestants.

The British journalist, William Howard Russell, noted the particular presence of the French:

"As a colonizing and commercial power France has ceased to exercise any considerable influence in this part of the world. She still asserts herself in her own way. Her

PSNC sailing schedule, in the "South Pacific Mail," 1925

language is the common vehicle of intercourse among civilised Chilians in all the large towns. French modistes, tailors, shoemakers, perruquiers, hair cutters, French musicians and dancing masters, French restaurants are in the van, but as merchants and bankers Frenchmen are in the rear. There are some great French commercial houses in the copper and nitrate trades, and in all that decorates life Frenchmen are potent agents, but they have relinquished their grip on the West Coast. For one French there are three German, and as far as I can judge there are more Germans than there are English; all other nationalities, Italians, Spanish American together, do not equal, perhaps, either the German or the English."

Not that the Europeans were all people of fine qualities. Such a view is encouraged by the idea that the newcomers were largely professionals, farmers and capitalists. Evidently, that was not the case. In reality, most were the 'proletarians' that Vicuña Mackenna wished to keep out, as well as deserting sailors[6] and a few debtors on the run. The predicted improvement to national moral fibre that Mackenna vaunted as secretary to the *Comisión Especial* on immigration, if it ever happened, certainly was not a reflection of the overall behaviour of European immigrants. Police reports from the main cities suggest quite the contrary. For instance, during 1872 and up to March 1873, the *Guardia Municipal* of Valparaíso arrested, on a broad variety of charges, 200 English, 50 French, 65 Germans, 26 Spanish, 56 Italians, 22 Russians as well as 80 North Americans. Numerous mariners were undoubtedly part of the harvest. And if they were not in jail, many Europeans were to be found jobless, begging in the streets.

Indeed, by the turn of the century the level of overt xenophobia directed explicitly at what were portrayed as useless and undesirable European residents had become acute. Newspapers railed at the 'abject dregs' of European cities placed on Chile's doorstep while politicians attacked the recruitment policies of the *Agencia General de Inmigración* in Paris.

And yet, the official sentiment in favour of large-scale immigration remained prevalent. It had been asserted succinctly and unambiguously in 1885 by Nicholas Vega, in his report to the Foreign Minister in Santiago on the first twelve years of operations of the *Agencia General de Emigración* in Europe:

"...that exclusively because of this feeble immigration, the majority of Chile's political problems are unresolved. ... And if this is not the case, to what other cause must one ascribe this marvellous success of the United States, Argentina and Australia? ... Think for an instant on each of these problems and you will see that all have a simple and sure solution in the rapid augmentation of the European population of Chile."

In reality, the days of significant state-sponsored immigration were coming to a close. Newcomers would continue to arrive; Chile would remain open and inviting while establishing its own character, its own solid institutions and its own force of independence and patriotism.

---

6   Few precise figures exist, but one diplomatic note addressed to the US Minister in Santiago, dated 19 December 1861, reported a total of 1484 desertions from American ships in the ports of Valparaiso and Talcahuano alone, for a period between 1857 and the end of 1860. This was very much the tip of the iceberg. (Bucher 2001)

7.

A home from home

She came, a ship from Valparaiso,
She furled her sails close by the strand,
Her name was a kingdom of the sun
Her game was a promised land.
"Go," said she, "far far away
With me from clouds and from fog;
There lies on slopes of Andean blue
A shaded city, bright as a jewelled box."

From *Tháinig Long ó Valparaiso[1]* by Monsignor Pádraig de Brún

Having withstood some of the worst conditions that nature can inflict during their passage, those Europeans who finally found themselves safely in port on the west coast of South America, might not have blinked at further discomfort. But it was rather the contrary. Many of them, especially the better-off, expected most if not all the creature comforts of home. It was as if the terrors, illnesses, sea-sickness, mutinies, attacks by native tribes, bad food or starvation that many encountered during three months at sea somehow qualified them, once back on land, for the sweetness of comfortable beds, fine meals and wines, good beer and the most fashionable clothes. Having stood the test of the voyage they anticipated compensation in the form of a lifestyle that measured up to high expectations.

From the earliest times, Europeans went about creating their little Englands, little Bavarias, little Croatias and little Italys wherever they settled. What they could not find locally, the Europeans ensured arrived soon enough on those distant shores, and principally through the port of Valparaíso. The necessities of life and their much-missed luxuries were shipped out seemingly regardless of cost. Mid-century import data demonstrate just how far the new arrivals went to ensure continuing access to the comforts of lives left behind. In 1851, for instance, imports into Chile included: brass beds worth a total of US$17,785; cotton handkerchiefs to the tune of US$66,542; stockings worth about the same

---

1   Translation from Gaelic by Barry Tobin

amount; books valued at US$35,500; US$50,000 of tea; US$32,000 of pickles and pianos worth some US$25,000. Indeed, piano shipments were severely depleted that year; in 1846 they had been worth double that sum.

If the colonial power had created some basic imitation of Spain in Latin America, from the sixteenth century onwards, it was London, Paris, Rome, Saint Petersburg and Berlin that became the models as the nineteen hundreds progressed. The great trading houses, banks, mining companies and ranches grew to commercial maturity in the seventy-five years that followed Chile's independence, in the process generating much wealth. By 1900, photographs of Valparaíso, Antofagasta, Iquique and Concepción, as well as Santiago and other large towns, displayed fine buildings, elegant boulevards, advanced transport services, fashionable citizens walking the streets or riding in carriages, busy cultural institutions and much else that would have brought no shame to the capitals of Europe.

Not, of course, that the wealth was equally shared; no more so than was the case in Britain, France and Germany at the time. Some of the original Spanish family dynasties of Chile and Peru held on to the reins of economic power as well as the near totality of political power. Still, the new Europeans established their own communities while promoting and protecting their growing assets. Lifestyles that were relatively lavish, if not ostentatious, confirmed a communal status and national identity. After all, these countries were not colonies. The British could not behave as though they were living in some outpost of Empire. The lifestyles of the Europeans were broadly acceptable so long as they reflected not merely self-interest and oversized profit from natural resources, but a solid contribution to the development of independent nations.

A great lady's reminiscences

Many travellers wrote diaries recording the life and habits of Valparaíso and other Pacific-coast cities they visited or lived in, and many of these eventually emerged as books. None did so with more flair, style and perception than Maria Graham. Her "Journal of a Residence in Chile" is probably the finest account of Chilean society – both foreign-born and indigenous – to emerge from the nineteenth century in English, or Spanish. Even today, Chilean historians lean heavily on Graham's observational skills, regarded as not merely remarkably accurate but just about at the peak of descriptive travel writing.

Maria Graham's was a tragic story, however. She left England in 1821 when her husband, Thomas Graham, a Royal Navy officer, was ordered to South America with his ship *HMS Doris* to protect British trade interests. After passing Cape Horn, Commander Graham suddenly died, reportedly of a fever. His wife, arriving alone in Valparaíso, decided to stay, rented a cottage and devoted herself to the travels and observations of South America that would be published to acclaim in 1824. She came to know people at every level of Chilean society and was only pushed to leave a few months after the devastating earthquake of November 1822. She returned to Britain via Brazil where she stayed long enough to witness the end of colonial rule, as she had in Chile. She later married again; this time to an artist, Augustus Wall Callcott, making her Maria Dundas, Lady Callcott. However, she was struck by chronic tuberculosis from which she died in November 1842, at the age of fifty-seven.

Graham's writings could be harsh and uncompromising; equally, like many Victorian travel writers, she could be condescending and imperious about societies that did not match up to the supposedly high standards of the one from which she came. At the same time, she recognized fine human qualities among the poor and the powerful alike and could respond with warmth and compassion when she felt they were earned. And, for all her finicky complaints about customs and lifestyles, her writings always revealed a sense for accuracy and objectivity which might have made her a great newspaper reporter had that profession been open to women at the time. Certainly, her words speak for themselves and need little introduction or explanation. The following quoted passages provide some perspective of the contrast between Chilean traditions and the privileged lifestyles available to

Maria Graham in 1819

Portrait by Sir Thomas Lawrence.

the European communities.

A day of her arrival in Valparaíso, Maria Graham was examining the shops:

"Today...I rode to the port; and had the leisure to observe the shops, markets and wharf... The native shops, though very small, appear to me generally cleaner than those of Portuguese America. The silks of China, France and Italy; the printed cottons of Britain; rosaries and amulets and glass from Germany – generally furnish them. ... The French shops contain a richer variety of the same sort of goods; and there is a very tolerable French milliner... The English shops are more numerous than any. Hardware, pottery, and cotton and woollen cloths, form of course the staple articles.

"The only articles of dress publicly sold are shoes, or rather slippers, and hats. I do not, of course, mean that no stuffs from Europe or dresses for the higher classes are to be bought; because, since the opening of the port, retail shops for all sorts of European goods are nearly as common at Valparaíso as in any town of the same size in England. But the people of the country are still in the habit of spinning, weaving, dying, and making every article for themselves in their own houses, except hats and shoes..."

"The Germans furnish most of the glass in common use: it is of bad quality to be sure... Toys, beads, combs and coarse perfumes are likewise found in the German shops... The English tailors, shoemakers, saddlers, and inn-keepers, hang out their signs in every street; and the preponderance of the English language over every other spoken in the chief streets, would make one fancy Valparaíso a coast town in Britain. ... The more elegant Parisian or London furniture is generally despatched unopened to Santiago, where the demand for luxury is of course greater."

She was impressed by the European luxuries in the most affluent Chilean homes. After visiting the house of the governor of Valparaíso, Graham comments:

"[He] seemed delighted to display the English comforts of the apartment I was received in. An English carpet, and English grate, and even English coals, were all very agreeable on this cold raw day."

Maria Graham was particular about food. Yet she was impressed by the fresh fruit available in the old port city, and in raptures about the vegetables:

"As to the kitchen vegetables, the first and best are the potatoes, natives of the soil, of the very first quality. Cabbages of every kind; lettuces, inferior only to those of Lambeth; a few turnips and carrots, just beginning to be cultivated here; every kind of pumpkin and melon; onions in perfection; and I am promised in the season cauliflower, green peas, French beans, celery and asparagus; the latter grows wild on the hills. The French beans are, of course, the very best..."

She was less keen on the local cooking and dining habits. While condescending to eat a meal with a Chilean neighbour, after a walk into the country surrounding her rented cottage, she had little patience with the local customs on display:

"The first dish that appeared was a small platter of melted marrow, into which we were invited to dip the bread that had been presented to each, the old lady setting the example, and even presenting bits thoroughly sopped, with her fingers, to Miss H., who contrived to pass them on to a puppy who sat behind her. I, not being so near, escaped better; besides as I really did not dislike the marrow, though I wished in vain for the addition of pepper and salt, I dipped my bread most diligently and ate heartily. The bread in Chile is not good after the first day. The native bakers usually put suet or lard into it; so that it tastes like a cake; a few French bakers, however, make excellent bread; but that we had today was of the country, and assimilated well with the melted marrow. After this appetizer, as my countrymen would call it, a large plate of *char-qui-can* was placed before us. It consists of fresh beef very much boiled, with pieces of charqui or dried beef, slices of dried tongue, and pumpkin, cabbage, potatoes and other vegetables in the same dish. Our hostess immediately began eating from the dish with her fingers, and invited us to do the same; but one of the daughters brought us each a plate and fork, saying she knew that such was our custom. The dish was good, and well cooked. It was succeeded by a fowl which was torn to pieces with the hands; and then came another fowl cut up, and laid on sippets strewed with chopped herbs; and then giblets; and then soup; and, lastly, a bowl of milk, and a plate of *harina de yalli*, that is, flour made from a small and delicate kind of maize. ... Our drink was the wine of the country; and on going to the veranda after dinner, apples and oranges were offered to us."

Despite her fussiness, Graham evidently ate heartily and continued to accept dinner invitations. On another occasion:

"The dinner was larger than would be thought consistent with good taste; but every thing was well dressed, though with a good deal of oil and garlic. Fish came among the last things. All the dishes are carved on the table, and it is difficult to resist the pressing invitations of every moment to eat of everything. The greatest kindness is shown by taking things from your own plate and putting it on that of your friend; and no scruple is made of helping any dish with the spoon or knife you have been eating with, or even tasting or eating from the general dish without the intervention of a plate. In the intervals between the courses, bread and butter and olives were presented. Judging from what I saw today, I should say the Chilenos are great eaters, especially of sweet things; but that they drink very little."

In all, Maria Graham found plenty to praise and even more to criticize. She had her good days and her bad days in Valparaíso. Ultimately, however, it was all a little too grubby for a true lady. At one point she groans:

"'England, with all thy faults, I love thee still,' Cowper said at home, and Lord Byron at Calais. For my part I believe if they had either of them been to Valparaíso, they would have forgotten that there were any faults at all in England. It is very pretty and very charming to read of delicious climates, and myrtle groves, and innocent and simple people who have few wants; but as a man is born a social and improvable, if not a perfectible animal, it is really very disagreeable to perform the retrograde steps to a state that counteracts the blessings of climate, and places less comfort in a palace in Chile than in a labourer's hut in Scotland."

By the end of the same century, Maria Graham would probably have made a kinder assessment of Chile. The country, and especially the port towns, had taken on many of the features of their counterparts in Europe. Most travellers seemed perpetually to be pinching themselves to be certain they really were half a world away from their cities of origin. One such was William Howard Russell, the renowned, globe-trotting reporter for *The Times* of London.

Keeping themselves to themselves

Russell had been invited by the self-described "Nitrate King", Colonel John Thomas North, to join his party visiting Chile and touring the nitrate fields of Tarapacá in the North. Russell's commentaries on the industry, British investments and the politics of the country are recounted in Chapter 13, but he made many observations of the manner in which Europeans were living in Chile at the time of his visit in 1889 and 1890. He was especially sensitive to the compartmentalization of life among the European communities.

"It is only natural that the foreign communities in the large towns should generally keep very much to themselves. It is certain they do so in Valparaíso. There is a German life quite distinct from the English life. The Italians stand apart from them both. Perhaps the French do the same. The English Club is not frequented by any but English, and the German Club is used only by Germans. There are English, German, Italian and American doctors with their national

116

clientèle. There is a Chilian Club very hospitable to strangers. But strangers visit it as rarely as natives visit the clubs of aliens in their midst."

Russell was also struck by the houses the Europeans were then building themselves in Valparaíso, notably those on the hills of Cerro Alegre and Cerro Concepción.

"Nothing can be prettier in their way than some of the little *maisons de campagne* of the merchants, built chalet-wise in the midst of gardens which are bevelled out of the side of the rising ground, girdled in with trees, the trellis-work and veranda bright with flowers, haunted by twittering humming-birds, hammocks and easy-chairs outside, and the comforts of home within, a rivulet

Well-heeled 19th century travellers usually headed for the thermal baths at Cauquenes, south of Santiago. From an 1872 engraving.

The British Library, London

babbling at the foot of the hill by the boundary hedge, lawn-tennis ground, conservatories. Such I saw at Las Sorres[2], Mr Berry's "The Foxes" (they actually had a pack of hounds and hunted the Chilian reynards over the worst-looking country that ever lamed horse or dog), and at Mr Raby's."

In Valparaíso, whose climate resembles that of the Côte d'Azur in the summer and England in the winter, the grafting on of European habits and comforts might have seemed natural. But when he reached the north and stayed in the nitrate port of Iquique, Russell began to take account of the "artificiality" and precariousness of life for the European commercial adventurers in Chile.

"With money in your purse there is very little you can desire which you

2   Probably a misspelling of *Los Zorros* – the foxes

cannot buy in Iquique. Day after day the wonder of this artificial existence was at work under our eyes, but it was only on reflection that its strangeness struck you, and that you were led in a vague way to think what would happen if water and food failed, if the condensers and steamers ceased to work owing to want of coal, and if the provision stores gave out; and to recognize that this town has literally struggled on through flood and fire, for it has been nearly swept away by tidal waves, shaken down by earthquakes, and converted into blackened ashes by conflagrations."

Still, Russell found in Iquique much more than just the basis for survival:

"For those not occupied by business there are not many resources, but in comparison with an average European town of the same size, Iquique has no reason to be ashamed of itself. It is provided with banks, shops, hospitals, public schools, barracks, prisons. It supports two or three newspapers... There are excellent saddle horses and carriages, open and shut, for hire; there are tramway cars, there are three clubs and many restaurants, and at the corners of the streets are popular 'bars' and exchanges, and there is a theatre for any itinerant troupe that may visit the coast; there is a well patronised racecourse and a cricket ground. ... The telegraph and the telephone are in full play; the houses are provided with electric bells. ... There is an excellent and vigilant police, and there is a large and well-proved fire service, mostly supported by the merchants of different nationalities. But strange to say there is no English or British section, and Colonel North, who brought out the prize Exhibition fire-engine from England to present to the town, had no British *Bomberos* to whose charge he could consign it."

Reginald Enock, a pompous American traveller who, in 1910, described the entire western coast of the Americas from Alaska southwards, was overwhelmed by the extent of the saltpetre industry of Tarapacá. In particular, he paid a well embroidered tribute to the manner in which the British had made Iquique their own:

"... the main facts impressed upon you, both before and after your visit, will be first, the matter of nitrate export, and second, the matter of cocktail consumption.

"At the British Club in that enterprising town, both matters (the latter possibly with exaggeration) are awarded the honour of the world's record! It is commonly stated (again I trust with exaggeration) that ten to twelve cocktails before 'breakfast' – which meal in Spanish-American countries is partaken at twelve o'clock – is about the average of the regular Iquique man. Of this club, however, let us speak no evil. We have enjoyed its hospitality; it is an admirable

118

institution provided with all the leading magazines and periodicals of Britain by every mail, and upon its library walls hangs a portrait of Edward VII Rex."

The national clubs were the epicentre of daily life for many Europeans. Sometimes several nationalities might be represented in these important local institutions. The Club Iquique, for instance, initially had a French chairman with an Italian, a German, a Spanish, a North American, an Englishman and an Austro-Hungarian as officers. It was necessarily the social, but also the business focus not merely of the city but of much of the region.

Up and down the length of Chile German clubs could be found; that in Valparaíso – believed to be the first in South America – was formed in 1838. Many *clubes Alemanes* thrive today and some are still capable of serving as good a plate of *sauerkraut* or *apfelstrudel* as can be found anywhere. English or British clubs, while seldom named as such (for that would have suggested the British community was something less than the natural dominating foreign presence in the country), were omnipresent. However, the Italians, French, Scandinavians and eventually the Asian communities all opened gathering posts where old times and traditions could be remembered and practised. Above all, national identities could be cherished and asserted.

The Union Club was the focus of the British community in Valparaíso and received praise from one grateful traveller in the 1870s:

"It had newspapers from home (at least three months old), billiards in all-male company. I am bound to say that the draught beer was admirable, and the cold roast beef was as good as could be found in London itself."

Indeed, beer would always be a vital beverage, especially for the newly-arrived Europeans. Initially, casks of beer were imported. But local producers quickly began to meet the needs of immigrants and visitors. Andrew Blest was probably the first to set up a brewery, in 1827, in Valparaíso. By 1850, Karl Andwanter began producing in Valdivia. While his drinks initially quenched the thirsts of successive waves of German farmers arriving in the area, ales from that region have long since been adopted by the Chilean population in general. Andwater's operation was significant. With an investment of $200,000 he was able to produce 1,440,000 litres per year with 54 workers. His products were seen as eminently comparable with the bottled beer that was imported in vast quantities from England at that time. Even so, new brewers sprang up regularly in Valparaíso. By the 1870s, one of the main streets, Chacabuco, alone boasted no less than four beer makers: P S McKellar, Mauricio Mena, Haertel & Cie., and Plageman & Cie.

Naturally, the necessary pubs, or taverns, were opening their doors in much the same period. In 1864, for instance, William Harvey kept The Eagle Tavern in Valparaíso; George Leach, The Shakespeare Bowling Saloon; and 'Jack' Pilcher, The Right and Left-Bower hotel. The English Tearoom did not start serving a "large and select clientele" until 1922. The proprietors, the Vogels, sound to have been of German origin rather than hailing from the country most associated with teatime. Still, advertisements of the time assured the bankers and traders around Calle Arturo Prat that not only would they be served by true English ladies but that no music was permitted in the establishment.

First with the news – in whatever language

Newspapers would certainly have been available in the cafés, as they had been from the earliest days after independence. *El Mercurio de Valparaíso* remains the world's oldest surviving Spanish-language daily newspaper, having started its long life in 1827. For much of the nineteenth century the paper had regular columns in English to ensure the local business community was able to keep up with politics in the capital as well as shipping movements through the port, notably the regular mail steamer. The paper also kept them in touch belatedly with the latest company incorporations and flotations in the city of London and other European bourses, in some of which locals would have had a personal stake.

The European communities in Chile soon began producing their own daily papers and periodicals. Most did not last long, but they met a European craving for printed news that looked and

The first issue of "El Mercurio," dated 12 September 1827, reported disturbances in Valparaiso following aggressive behaviour by a British naval officer.

read a little like the publications they had been used to in London, Liverpool, Paris and Hamburg. Above all, they probably believed that newspapers produced in their own languages would necessarily reflect a quality of journalism and accuracy on which they could rely. Valparaíso was especially well served by these publications. *The Chilean Times*, for instance, lasted from 1876 to 1907. More impressively, *The South Pacific Mail* delivered English-language news the length of the Pacific coast, from 1909 to 1965, though during its early years it was in competition with *The West Coast Leader,* a weekly published in Lima, Peru. Among the truly local efforts was *The Valparaíso Echo,* "The Organ of the Foreign Population of Chile," which took over from *The Diario* in August 1853. Even earlier, the celebrated American Congregationalist minister and educator, David Trumbull, launched and edited *The Neighbor* in Valparaíso. The weekly newspaper survived just four years, from 1847 to 1851, and, while focusing principally on the activities of the port and earthly, mercantile priorities, it adopted a predictably high-moral stance. As the editor marked out in the very first issue:

"As to principles, we shall practice and try to promote good feeling, good humor, good sense, and good manners. And error shall be handled in a spirit of kindness. Of sobriety, manliness, good nature, charity, good behaviour, with stainless honesty towards all men, and towards God also; this paper shall be a continual advocate. In a word to sum up all, we shall strive to act, in its best and widest meaning the part of a good Neighbor".

Trumbull may not have made a complete success on this first attempt, but a later effort, *The Record,* stayed on the streets of the port from 1869 to 1889. While the English-language publications may have outnumbered all but those in Spanish, newspapers and magazines were also produced in several cities for the French, German and other European communities.

A pleasant life on the hill

Nowhere did the Europeans pay more care, or lavish more money in recreating their traditional lifestyles than in the hills above the port of Valparaíso. Cerro Alegre (sometimes called 'Happy Hill' or 'Pleasant Hill') and Cerro Concepción provided the delightful climate and geology on which large houses and mansions of every description – culminating, in the 1930s, with the magnificent Palacio Barburizza – would be lovingly constructed. The bankers, entrepreneurs, traders and professional people from the old continent wanted comfort, space, healthy air and familiarity – and they had the money to buy it. The soft breezes from the ocean, the tranquillity and the flowered gardens all provided a relief from the hullabaloo of the quayside streets below. It is the case now, and it would have been so much more so in the heyday of Valparaíso's commercial glory, in the mid-nineteenth century, when bustling crowds, dirt, noise, violence and robbery were the trademarks of the port. And by the end of that century when the lucky owners and tenants on the two hills could take funiculars from the busy commercial area to their residences above, the sensation of living in some form of earthbound paradise must have been complete.

Much of the land on the two hills had long been in the hands of the church; namely the Augustinian friars whose monastery was initially the only significant structure on Cerro Alegre. Joshua Waddington, the most powerful man in Valparaíso bought Cerro Concepción (he also owned most of Valparaíso's

Advertising for European businesses in Valparaiso around 1860

Playa Ancha quarter at the time). Later in the 1820s, another of the partners of the trading house, Waddington, Templeman and Co., Henry Cood, purchased a large swathe of Cerro Alegre from the monastic brothers – a purchase that would be the subject of legal disputes for many years. In the decades after, these huge areas of prime real estate were parcelled up into ever smaller lots and sold on to other investors, mainly British. Only in the final two decades of the century did substantial sections of Cerro Alegre become home to affluent German families also.

Outwardly, the fine residences looked much like their European equivalents. Yet these houses were not constructed with bricks and mortar. Rather, full adobe construction was common – thick walls held together only by drying out a mixture of straw and mud. Later, the adobe was contained within a timber skeleton. On the outside, a covering of corrugated zinc protected the adobe from the winter rains and wind and, today, provides the surface for the multi-coloured decoration of the dwellings that survive.

Inside, these homes were remarkably reminiscent of their European equivalents built in the eras of Queen Victoria and Chancellor Bismarck. High ceilings, fine wood-panelled doors, wide curving staircases, elaborate chandeliers, Oregon pine wood flooring and sash windows helped make these residences as comfortable and familiar as could reasonably – and, given the expense incurred, sometimes unreasonably – be imagined. Kitchens would often be situated in basements, with the same serving shafts and hatches for the dining rooms above as would have been found in nineteenth-century Chelsea or Kensington in London. Servants' quarters were often to be found on the same level or in small outhouses.

Windowed galleries were popular too: places in which residents on the hills could take their tea or morning coffee and watch the life of the port below and the vast bay stretching out into the far distance, with the Cordillera de los Andes behind. In summer, the terraced gardens had all the blooms and scents of home with a good many additional tropical plants to provide yet more colour and fruits. A deck-chair, a cigar, a glass of fine wine and a book, these were the accessories that would have made a Valparaíso evening in December such a joy to those whose days were spent making money down below in the port.

Such dwellings were also to be found in other large port towns up and down the coast of Chile and Peru, in Santiago and in the rich estancias of the rural Central Valley. Next door to Valparaíso, Viña del Mar was, by the end of the nineteenth century, establishing itself as a place for the wealthy to build luxurious seaside residences. Burton Holmes, who wrote a celebrated series of travelogues in the early twentieth century, was ecstatic about the classy homes of the rich he found there:

"It is our privilege to be received in one of these splendid private palaces. Lordly simplicity, combined with simple elegance – a ballroom of exquisite design – a picture gallery rich in old masters, but these merely as incidental features of an ideal home where French is spoken as in Paris – where English, when there are English-speaking guests, seems to be the mother tongue of the delightful hostess and her sons and daughters. Yet this is a Chilean home of an old Chilean family – a family blessed with great wealth and endowed with refinement into which enter the elements of all that is most admirable in the

English, French and Spanish civilizations. One was not sure, on leaving the estate, whether the carriage would turn into Pall Mall, the Champs-Elysées, or the Puerta del Sol."

Keeping up a sporting life

Familiarity was also invoked by sport. A glance at any issue of the *South Pacific Mail* would make the point vividly. Pride of place on the sports pages of the very first issue, in November 1909, went to a cricket match. The Old Residents had played the New Comers in Viña del Mar a few days earlier. Presumably to encourage those many readers not completely riveted by the world's slowest sport to keep reading, the introductory sentence read: "This interesting fixture resulted in a match far more interesting than the score actually indicated." The score showed that the New Comers won easily. This report was followed by a story on a second cricket match, again in Viña del Mar, in which the staff (present and past) of the English firm Williamson, Balfour & Co were thrashed to defeat by the Valparaíso Cricket Club. A further issue of the paper, a few days later, reported on a match between a Ladies XI and a Gentleman's XI. Quite who the "Gentlemen" were, their ages or state of health, is not recounted but they managed to lose severely, with one feminine star notching up 120 runs and taking four wickets in the process.

The *South Pacific Mail* tended to follow its cricket coverage with news of lawn tennis competitions. Reported in one 1909 edition, the Valparaíso club had played the tennis enthusiasts of Viña del Mar. The commentator was less than enthusiastic, noting: "Play on the whole was slack, principally no doubt on account of the little practice the players have had this early in the season." After tennis coverage came horse racing news. As well as a "Copa El Mercurio" – presumably with a prize offered by the newspaper – and other locally-named races, the season in Viña del Mar had a 'Derby', a 'Grand National' and a 'St Leger' just as racing devotees in Britain would have enjoyed at the time, and still do. Other reports covered rugby, athletics, hockey and badminton, the participants in which were largely, but not exclusively, British.

Hunting was especially attractive for the new arrivals. Fox hunts were established in many towns, including Valparaíso in the hills above the port. As always, the British community got the sport organized and financed and English was the predominant language to be heard as the "unspeakable" pursued the "uneatable" – as Oscar Wilde supposedly put it – across the largely barren slopes and gullies. But hunting had been a long-standing pastime of the Spanish. The large haciendas of the south of Chile offered many choices of game, even condors since it was long believed that these giant birds attacked live domestic animals, and a price was offered by farmers for killing them. In 1880, one French traveller, Count Eugène de Robiano, visited the hacienda of an aged Spanish nobleman, the Marquis de Huidobro, and witnessed a condor hunt. He noted that preparations were elaborate since the challenge of downing these giant birds was well recognized. Precision was the only approach because if the birds' "wings were of steel, then their bodies were of iron" and they would only be defeated by a shot through the neck or head. The party did manage to hit two condors after several hours of exhausting pursuit, but the birds fell onto cliffs, completely out of reach.

These pursuits of the affluent omit one celebrated English game: football, or soccer. Although British sailors had kicked around makeshift balls, to the bemusement of the local population, from the late nineteenth century, it was a decidedly working-class game which received little attention in the English language newspapers of the time, and even less in the Spanish press. Not that it was avoided by the worthier foreign citizens of Valparaíso and other Chilean and Peruvian towns; but soccer games were staged in the context of broader athletics competitions. It was the day of the "all-rounder". As one modern enthusiast for the game has commented:

"The port's residents watched in astonishment, not knowing whether to laugh or admire the crazy British, who ran around trying to shoot the ball, in trousers that – to the great shock of the women present – were too short to cover their knees, so that it was possible to see how white their legs were."

Sporting clubs became football clubs and, by 1895, the Football Association of Chile was established. Local English schools began turning out soccer teams as did particular localities, like Cerro Alegre, Aduana (around the customs house) and Playa Ancha in Valparaíso. Eventually, however, the shoots of what was to become the most gifted continent of world football broke through the barren wastes of makeshift pitches. In Chile, two teams whose names reverberate with the thunderous cheers of the finest days of English soccer were set up within a few years of each other and remain, today, among the most successful national clubs: Santiago Wanderers and Everton.

The "Wanderers" were not English but a group of young Chilean teenagers who probably began playing together around 1892 and who had to scrape or beg their parents to raise even the price of a new ball. They played wherever they could find sufficient space and often enough to harbour some ambition that, one day, they would be good enough to take on one of the British teams. They struggled not merely with equipment and pitches, but with language too, since most competitions were run by the British and spoken, or shouted, English ruled the games, as it did in London, Manchester and Liverpool. Nevertheless, with a smattering of British players, the Wanderers survived and eventually thrived. They owed supplies of their first green-coloured strip to a sailor paying off a Valparaíso hotel debt in kind on his return to England. Green has remained the prevalent colour of the team until now.

If Santiago Wanderers was the team of Valparaíso (and never the capital, Santiago, as might be assumed), Viña del Mar, next door, is home to Everton. The two teams have long been among the biggest rivals in Chilean football. Yet Everton started out in Valparaíso town – with a few school friends knocking about a ball in what is now Plaza Bismarck, above the port. They were a mixed bag of English and Chileans who seem to have taken inspiration from the success of the original Everton FC at an international tournament in Buenos Aires in 1909. They have been described as a group dominated by Victorian, protestant values, and a strong devotion to the amateur game. Several lost their lives as volunteers in the First World War. Professional status for the team was adopted only in 1944, at about the time it made its permanent home in Viña del Mar and ceased to be Valparaíso's second club.

Long before the days of organized soccer, the European mariners who found themselves ashore in Valparaíso and other Pacific coast ports were able to indulge their longings for other "sports" that reminded them of home. Various forms of bowling and skittles were practised, often in tandem with illegal betting. Sailors could also easily rid themselves of their wages by putting money down in cockfighting and bullfighting arenas. And if those spectacles began to pall, they could fight each other to a drunken, prostrate standstill on the street. Yet, such delights were only a small part of the multiplicity of familiar, even nostalgic, entertainment that awaited seamen, immigrants and visitors as they set foot on the quaysides after so many months on the high seas.

The entertainers

Captain Basil Hall, of the Royal Navy, and his crew, arriving for Christmas 1820, were impressed by the free-wheeling drinking and bawdy entertainment on easy tap in the port of Valparaíso:

"In the course of the first evening of these festivities, while I was rambling about the streets with one of the officers of the ship, our attention was attracted by the sound of music, to a crowded *pulpería*, or drinking house. We accordingly entered, and the people immediately made way, and gave us seats at the upper end of the apartment. We had not sat long before we were startled by the loud clatter of horses' feet, and in the next instant, a mounted peasant dashed into the company, followed by another horseman, who, as soon as he reached the centre of the room, adroitly wheeled his horse round, and the two strangers remained side by side, with their horses' heads in opposite directions. Neither the people of the house, nor the guests, nor the musicians, appeared in the least surprised by the visit; the lady who was playing the harp merely stopped for a moment, to remove the end of the instrument a few inches further from the horses' feet, and the music and conversation went on as before. The visitors called for a glass of spirits, and having chatted with their friends around them for two minutes, stooped their heads to avoid the cross piece of the doorway, and, putting spurs to their horses' sides, shot into the street as rapidly as they entered; the whole being done without discomposing the company in the smallest degree."

Elitist entertainment, on the other hand, was often paraded as a mark of social standing, and audiences reflected as much. In 1844, the Victoria Theatre opened its doors for the first time not far from the wharf in Valparaíso. While the bars, brothels, cockfighting rings and street music groups throbbed with excitement all around, the Victoria Theatre's stage brought a supposedly enlightened culture to an affluent portion of the town's population. The first opera performed there was Donizetti's *Lucia de Lammermoor*. There were similar institutions opening in Santiago and other large cities at the time. By the time it was destroyed by fire in 1878, the original Victoria Theatre of Valparaíso was attracting more inclusive audiences. Its replacement was opened in 1886 but collapsed during the 1906 earthquake. Reconstructed a second time, the new theatre opened in 1910 with Pietro Mascagni, in person, conducting his opera *Cavalleria Rusticana* and other works at a series of concerts the following year.

Much earlier, the celebrated Irish soprano, Catherine Hayes, had sung at concerts in Valparaíso and Santiago in October 1853, part of her long tour of the American continent, which included Washington, New York and Californian recitals for the gold prospectors. The report of the *Valparaíso Echo* was ecstatic:

"That talented artiste, MISS CATHERINE HAYES, after plunging the Valparaíso public in a wilderness of delight during a series of most brilliant concerts, after enchanting our oral organs with the deep pathos of her magnificent voice, the thrilling tones of which will be ever present in our memory; is now laying Santiago under that contribution of enthusiastic applause which is the just meed of her unrivalled powers. According to all accounts, the discriminating and non-discriminating public of our Capital has been thrown into transports of delight at Miss Hayes' splendid performances, and people there are perfectly frantic in their efforts to obtain admittance to her concerts."

It was much the opposite for Sarah Bernhardt in 1886. The famed French actress, who had travelled the world entrancing audiences with her interpretations of everything from vaudeville melodrama to Shakespeare's King Lear somehow failed to melt the hearts of theatregoers in the several Chilean towns where she presented her troupe. Even the commentator in the *Album de la Colonie Française*, noted nervously a "cold reception in Santiago … I will not hide that Mme. Sarah Bernhardt was not understood in Chile."

For the great lady herself, it was worse. Getting to the country had been a trial: her ship had come close to being wrecked in the Strait of Magellan. In Lota, in the south, she was received enthusiastically by crowds chanting *La Marseillaise*, before sailing on to Talcahuano and Valparaíso. She tirelessly travelled the length of the country, presenting dramas in Iquique, Coquimbo, Valparaíso, Santiago and Talca. Only in the last town, did she have an unqualified success. For the rest – whether it was the social conservatism of old Spanish Chile, the stuffiness of the clergy, or even the disapproval of some ex-patriots – she provoked huge enthusiasm outside the theatres and sullen disapproval inside. She commented afterwards, from the safety of Washington DC that she had adored Buenos Aires, Rio and Mexico, but had hated Chile: "… there they are brutes, so cold, so lacking intelligence, so disagreeable! They are atrocious."

El Mercurio de Valparaíso fired back indignantly:

"We can be very gross we Chileans, but at least we have some dignity, and we also distinguish between the merit of the artist and the merit of the woman. We do not treat, in the same way, a lady like La Ristori [the actress Adelaide Ristori, who was a favourite in the country in those years] and a bag of bad manners and bones like La Bernhardt."

Others tried to put a more positive light on what seems to have been a debacle; French commentators in particular. Charles Wiener glowed with admiration of French productions staged in Chile. He claimed to have seen *Carmen* eighteen times in Santiago, as well as his fellow countrymen performing *Faust, William Tell* and *Romeo and Juliet*. He especially appreciated an 1886 production of *A Midsummer Night's Dream*. On the other hand, Wiener noted that French operatic singers had to "defend themselves" against the "raucous, full-throat force of the Italians".

As for 'La Bernhardt', he reported "extravagant" seat prices but theatres always filled to the point of bursting. Wiener admired the actress's energy: over the space of one month she performed twenty-five times while – as he claimed – organizing hunting and riding parties during her periods of rest. He considered Bernhardt had boosted the prestige of France in the country, especially its literature and its fashions; with many Chilean ladies frantically seeking out copies of her dresses in Santiago stores. That view would certainly have applied to her stay in Peru where students supposedly lay down in her path, such that she would use them as a carpet.

Sarah Bernhardt was scheduled to try once more in 1906, but before she could fulfil the engagement the earthquake destroyed Valparaíso, and with it the theatre. Far more appreciated in Chile was the renowned Italian soprano, Carlotta Patti, who performed in Santiago in December 1870 and in Valparaíso a month later. Although slightly less celebrated a singer than her sister, Adelina Patti, she could nevertheless set fire to theatres, sometimes literally. Her Santiago recital had only just ended when the Teatro Municipal almost burned to the ground. When she appeared in a grand event in Valparaíso's Odeón Theatre, it was to raise money for the wounded of the Franco-Prussian War which had not yet concluded its bloody course. The local French community was ecstatic: the diva was a well-known admirer of France, where she had studied music and where she would die twenty years later.

As well as presenting drama and opera the Odeon Theatre would later have a place in the development of Chilean cinema, screening the very first home-produced film – a three-minute long record of a parade of Valparaíso's mostly foreign-born firefighters. In the nitrate mines of the North, cinema would eventually provide a welcome form of relaxation to the thousands of men labouring there, an alternative amusement to the bars and brothels. Many of the *oficinas salitreras* had theatres of greater or lesser quality, with travelling music hall groups and some more refined artistes circulating among them.

Take the Oficina Chacabuco, north-east of Antofagasta, a plant owned by The Lautaro Nitrate Co. Ltd, of London and opened in the 1920s. The Teatro Officina Chacabuco[3] had a busy programme. In October 1933, for instance, according to the company's accounts, its theatrical offerings included the well-known Argentinian comedy troupe of Martres-Valicelli. A few days after, the managers and workers were treated to the 1931 Boris Karloff silent horror movie, *Frankenstein.* And if they missed that masterpiece, there was *Las Luces de Buenos Aires* (The lights of Buenos Aires), a Chilean-made classic

---

3   This particular oficina would later play an inglorious role in Chilean history; in 1973, it was expropriated by the army as an internment camp for political prisoners of the Pinochet regime. Many of those held there were tortured and murdered, their bodies presumed interred somewhere in the surrounding desert.

to enjoy the same month. In February 1934, the cinema programme included *A Sangre y Fuego* (Of Blood and Fire) and *Héroes del Progreso* in a double bill for Sunday which, no doubt, was intended by the mine managers to be

The theatre at the Oficina Chacabuco in 1932.   *Collection Guillermo Burgos*

inspirational. It is worth noting, however, that these shows were in no sense an incentive or extra benefit offered the workers. Quite the contrary: seats had to be paid for and the company turned a good profit. Like the company stores at the oficinas, what was given in wages or benefits was soon taken back in the form of employees' spending on goods and services.

Amusements at home

In the cities, there was a tradition of local music-making, at all levels of society, and especially among the foreign communities. As Maria Graham noted:

"The number of piano-fortes brought from England is astonishing. There is scarcely a house without one, as the fondness for music is excessive: and many of the young ladies play with skill and taste, though few take the trouble to learn the gamut, but trust entirely to the ear."

Young women were taught piano in most middle-class European and Chilean families, some to a high standard. One Valparaiso newspaper was quoted by The London Illustrated News as claiming: "A bed, a piano and a lamp are the first requisites for a Chileno household." Numerous fine young singers also emerged often modelling themselves on the foreign artistes heard at the Opera de Santiago or the Victoria Theatre in Valparaíso. Naturally, the tradition of home-produced and community-based entertainment was not restricted to the British. The German communities, for instance, enjoyed their own music and theatre which sometimes spiced up their rigorously devout religious lives. The Lakes and Magellanes regions became known for their German choirs. Croatians established their cultural clubs and societies from as far south as Punta Arenas to Iquique in the north. Italians sang their operatic arias in their front-rooms as loudly and energetically as in any piazza napoletana.

The musical and theatrical entertainment as well as the sporting activities pursued by the various European communities was part and parcel of the assertion of national identities. Needless to say, no national identity was asserted as energetically or consistently as that of the British. And, without there being a suggestion of any colonial status associated with their presence in Chile, Her Majesty's subjects, as they did the world over, ensured that the spirit of Empire and monarchy were properly celebrated. Queen Victoria's golden and diamond jubilees – recognizing fifty (1887) and sixty (1897) years on the throne respectively – were the excuse for parties, official banquets, theatrical reviews and special horse races throughout Chile and especially in Valparaíso.

The glamorous figure of the Prince of Wales – later to become King Edward VIII for less than a year before his abdication in 1936 – wowed crowds in Chile during his tour in 1925. The entire British community, but also copious ranks of diplomats as well as the Chilean political and business classes, turned out massively for a series of military, state, sporting and social events the equal of which the country had seldom witnessed. These were not occasions to be noted as absent. The *South Pacific Mail* newspaper maintained weeks of near-blanket coverage, before, during and after the visit. Undoubtedly, local British residents lived and dined proudly off the experience for months, if not years, afterwards.

Middle class families from the Old Continent kept in touch with even the most banal activities through social columns in the newspapers and magazines. As a random example, the *South Pacific Mail* of November 20, 1909, had the following titbits aimed largely at the English and German residents of Valparaíso and Viña del Mar: the marriage of Mr Percy Compton and Miss Dora Nicholls at Viña del Mar, prior to their taking up residence on Cerro Alegre; the engagement of Mr Clementz Arnolds and Ms Spoerer of Concepçión; the departure for several weeks in Italy of Mrs Compton, Mrs Edmund White, Miss Martindale and the Misses Fell; the arrival on *RMS Oriana* of Mrs Price and Mrs Brownjohn after an absence of seven years; a performance of "On a

Summer's Day" at the Viña theatre, featuring various members of the British community; news of a "subscription dance" in support of the 11th company of *Bomberos* (a fire station manned by English residents) in the German Hall; two concerts by pupils of Mr Hucke, with Miss Schultz distinguishing herself along with Miss Caraccioli who made an "able rendering of Beethoven's Sonata Op. 31"; the last of four concerts arranged by Herr van Dooren in which, among others, Miss Hagnauer "sang charmingly"; a cable from home announcing that Archdeacon Hobson – presumably of the English church – would not be in Valparaíso for Christmas; and the departure of Mr. S D Price on *RMS Oronsa* to take over the Iquique business of Gibbs & Co. Ltd. And if any local Scots felt neglected, they would have spotted, across the page, an advertisement for the Annual St Andrews Day Dinner and Dance to be held a few days later.

Britain's Prince of Wales visits Viña del Mar for a polo game in 1925.

The sense of creating a home from home in Chile was deliberate, marked and welcome to the travellers who landed in the country for the first time after months at sea. Many aspects of the life that awaited them on the Pacific coast could hardly have been more foreign. The compensation of a familiar, non-threatening, lifestyle was probably necessary. One important business figure, John William Hardy, who established himself in Valparaíso in the 1870s, wrote to his fiancée, in 1881, just prior to her and her mother setting out from Britain for their new lives on the other side of the world:

"If your mother is still complaining she will find the voyage do her a lot of good. If she will just try to put away all care and anxiety from her mind and feel convinced that she is coming to her son's home, the journey will be made much easier and pleasure and benefit will be derived from it. Above all, do not come with an opinion already formed to the disadvantage of Chile. Be inclined to like it and you will find it in time a pleasant and comfortable place to live in. It is not a foreign country in the sense home folk are so ready to view it in, because between your house and the houses of the many Scotch and English here you need never realize how far you are from home. And take my word for it, you will endorse every word I say before you live long in it."

Valparaiso Bound!

8.

Nature's challenges: earthquakes, fire, drought and disease

When I arrived in Curacautin it was rain-
ing ash because the volcanoes willed it.

I had to detour to Talca where they had grown so wide, those tran-
quil rivers of Maule, that I fell asleep on a boat and went to Valparaíso.

In Valparaíso the houses were falling around me and I ate
breakfast in the wreckage of my lost library between a sur-
viving Baudelaire and a dismantled Cervantes.

... I made my bed next to a river that carried more stones than water,
next to some serene oaks, far from every city, next to stones that were
singing, and finally I was able to sleep in peace in certain terror of a star
that was watching me and winking with a certain malignant insistence.

But the gentle morning painted the black night blue
and the enemy stars were swallowed by light while I sang
peacefully with no catastrophe and no guitar.

From *Desastres* by Pablo Neruda[1]

They may often have thought that the voyage was the worst they would face, that nature could have nothing more extreme to throw at them than the conditions already faced and survived rounding Cape Horn. The newcomers from Europe were back on dry land. They probably had a bed to sleep in, fresh food and, for some, most of the comforts of home. Certainly, the new arrivals were aware that they had arrived in a region that was renowned for climatic extremes unequalled elsewhere. If they were heading southwards, perhaps to a sheep farm in the Magallanes region, they would experience rain of an intensity and duration that even England could

---

1   From *The Yellow Heart* by Pablo Neruda, translated by William O'Daly. With kind permission of Copper Canyon Press.

seldom match. If moving on northwards, maybe to take up a position in the nitrate industry, they would have heard of the world's driest desert, the Atacama – receiving no rain at all for years and with temperatures capable of swinging from some 30 degrees centigrade by day to below zero at night.

Yes, they were aware of all that, but still unprepared for the reality. The entire region was, and remains, disaster prone. Wildfires, floods, droughts, volcanic eruptions, the ubiquitous and destructive earthquakes and the risks from epidemics provoked by poor sanitation and sparse health services were the true challenges. These were hazards against which human beings were often defenceless. Stamina, fortitude, sometimes courage and a smattering of humour were the characteristics most needed.

The 1868 earthquake and sunami that hit Arica and the surrounding pampa.
The Illustrated London News

As with the frontiersmen pressing westwards in North America, the challenges of nature and isolation in Chile, Bolivia and Peru were there to be overcome as resolutely as possible, and, for the most part, they were overcome. Nature in these countries is unforgiving and relentless; it had to be recognized and accepted.

For a start, there were earthquakes, along the fault-line that runs along the

Pacific coast and all the way north to California. Looking solely at the period in which we are taking most interest, Chile experienced severe earthquakes in 1730, 1822, 1839, 1851 and 1906. Severe meant significant losses of life and devastation. Yet between these years which mark truly catastrophic events, there were also dozens of significant earthquakes – of a kind that today make headline news around the world and are measured at 6 or more on the Richter scale. One estimate suggests that since 1570, some 125 earthquakes above 6.5 have been registered in Chile. The strongest of all – and a record anywhere – was in Valdivia in 1960, when the shock measured 9.5[2]. As for tremors, if anyone had bothered to count, they would have numbered in the tens of thousands.

Earthquakes that rumble for weeks

The sense of terror felt during the most cataclysmic earthquakes was well described by European and North American travellers. Among the very best accounts was that of Maria Graham who, in the night of 19 November 1822, was staying in Quintero, thirty kilometres north of Valparaíso, at the house of Admiral Lord Thomas Cochrane, the British commander of the Chilean Navy:

"...we were sitting quietly conversing when, at a quarter past ten, the house received a violent shock, with a noise like the explosion of a mine; and Mr Bennet starting up, ran out, exclaiming. 'An earthquake! For God's sake follow me!' I... sat still... until, the vibration still increasing, the chimney fell, and I saw the walls of the house open. Mr Bennet again cried from without, "For God's sake, come away from the house!' So we rose and went to the veranda, meaning of course to go by the steps; but the vibration increased with such violence, that hearing the fall of a wall behind us, we jumped down from the little platform to the ground; and we were scarcely there, when the motion of the earth changed from a quick vibration to a rolling like that of a ship at sea... The shock lasted three minutes; and by the time it was over, everybody in and about the house had collected on the lawn, excepting two persons; one the wife of a mason, who was shut up in a small room which she could not open; the other Carillo, who, in escaping from the room by the wall which fell, was buried in the ruins, but happily preserved by the lintel falling across him.

"Never shall I forget the horrible sensation of that night. In all other convulsions of nature we feel or fancy that some exertion may be made to avert or mitigate danger; but from an earthquake there is neither shelter nor escape: the

---

2   For comparison, the strongest earthquake measured ever in France had an intensity of 6.2 and was centred in the Provencal town of Lambesc in 1909. Greece and Turkey have both experienced record shocks of 7.6.

"mad disquietude" (Byron 'Darkness') that agitates every heart, and looks out in every eye, seems to me as awful as the last judgement can be.... Amid the noise and destruction before and around us, I heard the lowing of cattle all the night through; and I heard too the screaming of the sea fowl, which ceased not till morning. There was not a breath of air, yet the trees were so agitated, that their topmost branches seemed on the point of touching the ground."

Tremors continued through November and December with a "tremendous shock" at 8.00 am on Christmas Day. Another graphic account was recorded by the British engineer, John Miers, who was staying at Concón, between Valparaíso and Quintero:

"It was very sudden and violent; we were all alarmed and paused for an instant, when the falling of the glasses from the sideboard, the cracking of the timbers of the roof, and the rattling of the falling tiles, caused us to rush out of the house. The earth was violently convulsed, heaving up and down in a manner hardly conceivable, and as little capable of being accurately described as our feelings. The timbers of a large corridor were breaking in all directions, and flying off in fragments, while the air was filled with dust from the falling roof. The situation of our two children instantaneously occurred to us. I rushed into the falling building, snatched one boy from one of the front rooms and, carrying him in my arms, ran to the back of the house, where the other boy was in bed; my sensation in this painful situation cannot be imagined.

"... On the Saturday and Sunday following the earthquake, I visited Valparaíso: on my way, I found the houses at Viña del Mar levelled to the ground. On entering Valparaíso I was astonished at the extent of the ruin, and dismayed at the miserable appearance of the place, as well as at the forlorn and wretched condition of the people. The houses were nearly all unroofed; many had been thrown to the ground, while the thick walls of sundried bricks which remained were split in all directions. The desolation was horrible ... about one hundred and fifty people were killed, and many were wounded or bruised. ... No bombardment could have produced such complete ruin as the earthquake affected. The desolate condition of the people was lamentable in the extreme, and this was dreadfully increased on the night of the 27th when, to their surprise and astonishment, it rained heavily. If any one thing more than another could add to their wretchedness, it was this unseasonable and unexpected fall of rain."

While he missed the catastrophe of 1822, Commander Basil Hall of the Royal Navy spent some time in Valparaíso in 1820 and 1821. His observations on life and customs are among the most colourful of the period but include a dismissive attitude towards earthquakes:

"I went in the evening to visit a family in the Almendral. The ladies were ranged, as usual, along the wall in a compact line, with their shawls drawn over the head and across the chin, so as nearly to conceal the face. One young lady was playing the harp and one the guitar; while others occasionally joined, with their shrill voices, in singing the patriotic songs of the day. Some were chatting, some working, and the evening was passing away pleasantly enough, till suddenly, and without any apparent cause, the whole party jumped up, cast away their music and work, and flew in the most frantic manner out of the house, screaming 'misericordia! misericordia!' all beating their breasts and looking terrified beyond description. I was astonished... It was a bright moonlight evening, and the street, from end to end, was filled with people; some only half-dressed, having just leaped from their beds...

"On returning to the room, I begged to know the cause of this amazing commotion, having a vague idea of its forming some part of a religious ceremony, when, to my surprise, I learned that it had been produced by an earthquake so severe that the people had been afraid of the houses tumbling about their ears... for my part, I was totally unconscious of any motion... I was assured that, for a considerable period after the arrival of foreigners, they are generally insensitive to shocks, which a native or an old resident can at once distinguish. It may also be mentioned, as an unusual effect of experience, that the sensation of alarm caused by feeling an earthquake, unlike that caused by other kinds of danger, goes on augmenting instead of diminishing in amount; and that one who at first ridicules the terrors of inhabitants, comes eventually to be even more frightened than they are."

The 1906 quake from which Valparaíso never fully recovered

While the 1822 earthquake was as severe as any, Chile's coastal towns at the time – including Valparaíso – were little more than villages with huddles of wood and adobe brick cottages and few large public buildings. When an earthquake struck Valparaíso, at 8.00 pm on 16 August 1906, it destroyed a heavily-populated, bustling, elegant European-style city. Together with the opening of the Panama Canal seven years later, the 1906 quake ultimately helped spell the end of Valparaíso's commercial and maritime dominance in the region. The arsenal, railway station, custom-house, hospitals, convents, banks, restaurants, hotels, the Victoria Theatre were all for the most part levelled to the ground. The fire services struggled to control fires while the military stepped in to control looting. Summary execution of looters was common, and officially encouraged with newspapers carrying graphic photographs of the pathetic results as if to provide due warning.

Some accounts insist that the first tremor lasted at least four minutes and, just after, the second, more violent, another two minutes. The strength of the earthquake was around 8.2, compared with that which devastated San Francisco in the same year and measured 7.8. Destruction was widespread in towns and villages throughout the centre of the country, including in Santiago. While fatalities have been put at anything between 1000 and 20,000, the authoritative US Geological Survey regards the 3882 estimate produced by the University of Chile as the most accurate assessment. Some 60,000 people camped out in the hills above Valparaíso for weeks afterwards, often without food or water.

Many accounts were dispatched back to Europe and North America, all of them dramatic and tragic while largely failing to communicate the full extent of a catastrophe which only those present at the time could conceive. One Englishman, William Robinson, who had arrived in the town to work as an

The ruins of the Victoria Theatre in Valparaiso after the 1906 earthquake

accountant for the Chilean Trading Company, wrote to his fiancée back home from the deck of a German cargo boat of the Kosmos Line on which he had taken refuge:

"The noise was awful, the whole earth seemed to be growling and masonry falling and people shrieking, and to add to the effect there was a terrible flash of lightning and all the electric cables fused, so that the whole place was instantly in darkness."

There were lighter moments. Robinson decided to retreat quickly from the restaurant in the town, where he was at dinner, to "the English Hill". Yet he found Cerro Alegre rife with fires and its population in the streets. He went in search of a friend, John Hardy, a well-known importer and storekeeper:

"He had been dressing for dinner at the time of the first shock, and had been caught minus his trousers. He had hurried into a pair and cleared out of the house as quickly as possible, leaving the question of braces for future consideration. ... The rest of the family were down at the tennis court. They had just been sitting down when it came on, and of course they had not stopped to finish it. We warmed the soup up about midnight and I helped them eat it."

The *British Isles*, the troubled ship (see Chapter 1) of the young apprentice William Jones, arrived in Valparaíso Bay from Australia nearly four months after the earthquake. The crew had read of the disaster while loading a cargo of coal in Newcastle, New South Wales. Yet the shock of witnessing the reality of the disaster was severe:

"[We] saw that the city on the foreshores was reduced practically to heaps of rubble and charred beams. A fire had raged unchecked after the earthquake. The city was still under martial law, with a curfew imposed by the military and naval patrols, to prevent roving bands of escaped convicts from looting in the debris."

Their cargo was unusually welcome; rather than the crew struggling to get the coal ashore, the ship was greeted by teams of willing workers who did the work urgently and enthusiastically. Relieved of that burden, the crew could not enjoy the traditional delights of the town: they no longer existed. But the captain was required to go ashore, and the young Jones found himself detailed to row to the mole. He and his mates took the opportunity to look around the ruined town:

"[It] was an appalling sight. Some streets were obliterated under heaps of rubble, and the roofless shells of buildings were leaning over at crazy angles. A deathly silence prevailed, broken only by the occasional shouts of men working at salvage operations in the ruins, or by the roar of an explosion, followed by a crash of rubble, as a ruined building was dynamited by military engineers. ... After dark, Valparaíso was like a tomb. Not a glimmer of light shone from the streets which once had been famous for their gay night-life. No sound of animals or human beings broke the deathly silence. The roar and bustle of a beautiful and pleasant city had been stilled by this dreadful disaster."

Valparaiso Bound!

The ship stayed just long enough to unload and take on ballast. As they sailed out of the Bay, they looked back at the fires still burning near the sea shore as dead animals and parts of human bodies were being cremated, in efforts to avoid the risk of typhoid and other diseases.

"When the wind was blowing from this part of the shore, the smell of burning flesh and bones reached the ships with a horrible stench, which made us only too anxious to clear away from such a place of death and destruction, with the least possible delay".

Charles Darwin, during his voyage round the world in *HMS Beagle*, in the years 1833-1836, had a ringside seat as an earthquake struck and volcanoes erupted on the Pacific coast. On 19 January 1835, anchored off the island of Chiloé he was amazed by a spectacular eruption of the Osorno volcano, almost opposite on the mainland. Thirty of Chile's active volcanoes have erupted at least once since the year 1800. And, since 26 of them are within thirty kilometres of towns and villages with populations of between 1000 and 10,000[3], evacuations were, and are, frequent.

Just a month after this experience – with nature seeming to want to show the great scientist what it was capable of – Darwin witnessed a violent earthquake in Valdivia that also destroyed the city of Concepción and the port of Talcahuano. A few days afterwards he landed in Talcahuano itself and observed the desolate scene: "… the whole coast being strewed over with timber and furniture as if a thousand ships had been wrecked." A tsunami had followed the initial shock with breakers up to 23 feet (7 metres) high hitting the port head on. "Their force must have been prodigious; for at the fort a cannon with its carriage, estimated at four tons in weight, was moved 15 feet inwards. A schooner was left in the midst of the ruins, 200 yards from the beach."

Darwin noted a cheerful stoicism among the inhabitants, including the foreigners. The British consul, Henry William Rouse, who for many years would later occupy the same post in Valparaíso, had taken in a large party under his protection, living for the first week in a garden beneath some apple trees. "At first they were merry as if it had been a picnic; but soon afterwards heavy rain caused much discomfort, for they were absolutely without shelter."

From the extremes of drought to violent floods

Particularly severe periods of abundant rain and the contrary are reckoned to be closely tied to the phenomenon of *El Niño-Southern Oscillation (ENSO)* – unusually warm ocean temperatures in the Eastern Pacific Ocean and their

3   According to the Smithsonian Institution's Global Volcanism Program

atmospheric equivalents. It is reckoned that in over 100 of the past 450 years, Chile has suffered some degree of drought. The duration of those droughts has been between one and six years and they have extended for a thousand kilometres or more up and down the country. For the pioneer farmers from Europe, the capricious climate made livelihoods all the more precarious.

Early episodes of drought in the eighteenth century had inspired plans for the construction of the first major canal project joining the Mapocho and Maipo rivers south-west of Santiago. The project – the San Carlos canal – was not completed for many decades and ultimately served little purpose. In autumn 1877, a serious and lengthy period without rain was testing communities in the Central Valley, in a manner well described by one of Chile's most prolific elder statesman, Benjamín Vicuña Mackenna. So great was the fear of a climatic and economic catastrophe at the time that he was moved to rush out a 500-page "essay" on the historical antecedents as a means of calming any overreaction in the streets. This followed his assurances at a public meeting that all droughts eventually end, and history proved it.

"'The desert is invading us' was the call during this moral panic that was starting to take the consistency and tenacity of an obsession. 'How can we fight against the desert' was the refrain of this panic and the theme of public and private preoccupations in that and all kinds of meetings."

His confidence was rewarded: even before the 'essay' was printed, the rains arrived. As he inferred in his preface, Mackenna might well have been recognized as a prophet had the book appeared just a few weeks earlier.

But regular and persistent chronic shortages of water still haunted the agricultural communities. The year 1924 was especially disastrous. Farms from Coquimbo in the north to Curicó in the Maule Region towards the south were hit by severe losses in the wheat harvest while the only means to protect livestock was to transport animals south by train to the more humid regions. Nevertheless, in the Coquimbo region alone, two-hundred thousand sheep were lost, along with two-hundred-and-fifty thousand goats and twenty thousand head of cattle. Misery in the rural population was absolute.

While droughts can strike long, hard and over a wide area, floods generate short, sharp punishment on a more localized scale. Whether it is swollen rivers in springtime caused by the swift melting of higher-than-normal snowfalls in the Andes, or deluges direct from the skies, seemingly often driven by events related to *El Niño*, Chile is well experienced. Had Mackenna waited a few weeks before publishing his essay on the climate he would have been able to record that after the debilitating drought, 1877 was to be remembered as one of the most devastatingly rainy years on record. Floods were experienced the length of the country. "A truly phenomenal year" was Mackenna's conclusion, with the like having been seen only two or three times in the previous century. Even the provinces of Coquimbo and Atacama – where serious rain is normally expected only twice in a century – experienced torrential downpours that July and August.

The winter of 1899 was even worse. Storms hit the country and inflicted damage from as far north as Iquique to Osorno in the south, hardly abating from May to August. One weather front created huge storm waves which hit Iquique and Antofagasta while Santiago, Viña del Mar and San Felipe were flooded. Going further back, 1783 was the "Year of the Great Flood", considered the severest inundation suffered in the capital since its foundation. Its nearest equivalent in the nineteenth century was the year 1845; it rained for only 21 days but that included a continuous downpour lasting some 417 hours, or just short of 18 days.

Like most towns in Chile, Valparaíso was seldom prepared for these episodes of prolonged and torrential rain, and was particularly susceptible to the damage and havoc they caused. The city's unique topography of hills and ravines ensured that massive amounts of water would always be channelled in a manner that maximised loss and danger. The year 1888 provides a sad example, even if the losses – 75 dead and around 300 injured – could be said to have been provoked as much by men as by nature. "The Tragedy of the Mena dam" was a disaster that had been foreseen by *El Mercurio* and civil works officials but, given the powerful interests involved, the warnings were pushed aside. How did it happen?

Don Nicholás Mena owned some 66 hectares of land, making up almost the whole of Cerro Florida, one of the larger hills behind the port. In an effort to ensure the irrigation of his land as well as providing drinking water and supplying an ice factory, Mena closed off a rocky ravine between the neighbouring hills of Cerro San Juan de Dios and Cerro Yungay. The dam was constructed 277 metres above sea level and at the time of the tragedy was holding back some 61,000 cubic metres of water.

On August 10, it had rained heavily on Valparaíso. The following morning at 8 o'clock, the dam could no longer withstand the pressure; it gave way with a thunderous roar, sending an estimated 90,000 cubic metres of water, stone, earth and garbage hurtling down towards the centre of the town. Everything collapsed in the path of the avalanche with local residents barely having the time to realize what was happening. Many had no chance to escape its devastating

144

path. In a few minutes, debris, sludge, uprooted trees, doors and windows and other remnants of buildings taken in the mudslide were deposited in the main streets below, from Aníbal Pinto Square to Victoria Square.

Forty years later, the son of Nicholás Mena died leaving almost his entire fortune to establish a foundation intended for the construction of a children's hospital (which still exists, in his name, today). Much of the rest of his wealth also went to charitable causes.

Foreigners prepare for the perpetual curse of fire

Throughout the history of Chile, fire has been a continual purveyor of tragedy. Whether it has flared in the forests behind the coast as a consequence of the parched conditions of summer or in the cities where wood construction,

Fire destroys large areas of Valparaiso in 1858   *The Illustrated London News*

incestuous living conditions and near-impossible access for rescue services turn minor accidents into infernos, there is a sad and unending register of disaster. Valparaíso suffered the worst fire in its history, as recently as 2014.

Even before the Spanish arrived, the indigenous tribes living around the area which is now Greater Valparaíso, were conscious of the risks. Supposedly, they knew the place as "Aliamapu", or *tierra quemada* – meaning "scorched earth". Later, the city was ironically referred to as "Pirópolis", by local inhabitants.

It had mushroomed without even a minimum of urban planning during the first half of the nineteenth century; spontaneous and precarious development which allowed neither time nor space for the infrastructure that a modern town requires. The city was unprepared for emergencies, like fire. At the same time, it had taken root in a place where fire, when it came – and it came often – would inevitably be spread by the habitual strong winds and the prevailing arid conditions.

Yet, the foreign citizens of Valparaíso in the mid-1900s were aware of the need to prepare and defend themselves. It took a catastrophe for them to act. A large blaze destroyed houses, shops, stores and offices in the centre of the city on 15 December 1850. Within days, with the prompting of *El Mercurio*, a group of influential local figures met and decided to form a fire service. The *Primera Compañía de Bombas* of Valparaíso[4] – consisting mainly of British and North American men – was established on 6 June 1851 at a ceremony in the stock exchange. By the end of that month, 151 volunteer firefighters had been registered and were soon receiving their uniforms. On 8 July, the company had its first serious emergency to deal with: a fire aboard a stranded steamship.

The second company – this time of German citizens – was created only one day after the first while the third, backed by the powerful Cousiño family, was formed after another major fire in the town, in 1854. That same year the fourth company was set up by the Spanish community. In their turn, 120 French inhabitants of Valparaíso set up their own fire service, in 1856, and the Italians launched the seventh brigade in 1858. Other companies followed, with the 11th, *Compañia George Garland* being formed in 1901 following a meeting at the Anglican Church – and named after the founder of the original *Cuerpo de Bomberos de Valparaíso*, under which all 16 brigades in the region are now grouped.

The first organized fire service in Santiago did not emerge until 1863, twelve years after that of Valparaíso. The *Cuerpo de Bomberos de Santiago* was set up in four brigades by mainly Chilean volunteers just days after one of the most infamous tragedies the country has known. On 8 December, 1863, some two thousand worshippers died in a fire in the Jesuit Church. Starting, probably, in one of the chandeliers the fire spread rapidly causing a panic among the dense congregation, and especially the women and children. No firefighting or rescue services existed in the city which had mushroomed into a large urban centre within a few decades. Little could be done in the burned-out church other than remove the corpses of the victims. Local newspapers were scandalized

---

4 Now the *Primera Compañia Bomba Americana*

and influential citizens, including the American entrepreneur and railway constructor, Henry Meiggs, soon got together to launch the fire service.

Foreigners also set up fire brigades in other cities. Iquique boasts companies that were originated by the local German, Italian, Spanish, Austrian and Croatian communities. The fast-growing town had experienced continual blazes, many of them serious. It was inevitable given the arid conditions, strong winds combined with the inflammable building materials common in the narrow, busy streets. The risks were aggravated by the industrial units, gas production plants and electrical generators which sprang up, even within

The desolate scene after the horrendous Jesuit Church fire in Santiago in 1863. With nearly 3000 people trapped inside, only a few hundred escaped. The New York Times reported that US diplomats and the engineer Henry Meiggs were among those who ran to help in the largely hopeless rescue efforts.

Picture: The Illustrated London News

residential and commercial quarters, to feed the saltpetre industry. Apart from the damage done during the 1879 Battle of Iquique, which was a turning point in the Pacific War between Chile, Peru and Bolivia, the centre of the town was regularly and severely damaged by one blaze after another.

147

In the south, Valdivia is the home to the second fire service established in the country, naturally supported heavily by the town's German citizens. One of their most celebrated combats was a conflagration that destroyed the historic, wood-built centre of the city in December 1909. Eighteen blocks, with one hundred houses and 98 commercial premises were lost in the flames, making it one of the nation's most destructive blazes.

Fire remains one of Chile's most ferocious and unrelenting threats, a perpetual generator of destruction. The "thin red line" of the *Bomberos,* many of whose units were founded by the new arrivals from Europe in the mid-1800s, are the highly professional and courageous force on whom the country's modern-day citizens depend.

Absent healthcare and imported disease

In examining the risks facing European immigrants there is a danger of seeing everything from the perspective of the pioneers while ignoring the fortunes and tragedies of the indigenous population. While climate and geology tend to dish out their anger without much discrimination disease can be choosy. Chileans, Peruvians and Bolivians, whether from the original native peoples or of mixed 'mestizo' blood, frequently suffered the exploitation, slavery, land confiscation and wars brought or imposed by foreigners. And they did so in very large numbers. They also suffered the maladies of Europe.

The story of the end of the Inca civilization – military defeat by the conquistadors then depletion through diseases, especially smallpox, imported by the Spanish – is well known. The successful but costly struggle of the Araucanian Mapuche to repulse the Spanish invaders from occupying their lands in the Central Southern forests of Chile is a matter of legend. Yet the social decline of the Mapuche people is a continuing tragedy, to this day. The eventual near eradication of the Chonos tribes of Southern Chile and the Ona, Yaghan, Aush and Alacaloof peoples of Tierra del Fuego, is one of the most shameful episodes for which immigrants must stand accused. Illnesses like measles and smallpox brought by Europeans, especially missionaries, and the occupation of native lands for cattle and sheep rearing, all contributed to this decimation. Other tribes like the desert Atacameños in the north, the Changos fishermen and the Aymaras of the Andean *antiplano* are now vanished, assimilated or severely depleted in numbers.

Perhaps the most moving, and impressive, attempt to bring some harmony to the always troubled relationship between settlers and indigenous people was that of the Bridges family whose head, Thomas Bridges, arrived in Tierra del

Fuego in 1871. While financed to spread the gospel, Bridges understood two things: he needed to know and speak the language of the local inhabitants – initially the peaceful Yahgans near Ushuaia and later the more aggressive Onas from the mountains behind – and to provide some sustainable farm development in which the tribal peoples could participate and advance. He did both. He eventually produced a unique dictionary of Yahgan words and phrases. The

Yahgan mother and child outside their dwelling, around 1905.

From "Chile" by G.F. Scott Elliot

family established three different ranches and employed dozens of Indians with whom they reached such a level of understanding and confidence that one son was almost raised as an Ona, only returning to England to fight in the First World War.

That son, Stephen Lucas Bridges eventually wrote a book, *'Uttermost Part of the Earth'*, on his life and experiences in Tierra del Fuego where he was born in 1874. It is an extraordinary and inspiring tale. However, by 1947 he could only note sadly that the population of pure-bred Indians on 'Fireland' had declined from an estimate of seven to nine thousand when the family first arrived to less than one hundred and fifty. Seventy per cent of the Onas had died

149

with successive measles epidemics – including most of his childhood friends. The white population, on the other hand, had grown to 9,560 in the Chilean and Argentinean territories together. The struggle to maintain the viability of the tribes in the face of the encroachment of ranching interests ultimately failed. Ironically, Bridges notes also that cattle and sheep raising in the southern territories of Tierra del Fuego, where the Yahgan and Ona were originally concentrated, did not prosper either.

Yet death from disease and untreated illness was always present, with or without the newcomers. From the sixteenth century on, outbreaks of bubonic plague and smallpox occurred regularly. In the mid-nineteenth century, infant mortality in Chile was above 300 per 1000 live births and male life expectancy was a mere 28 years. Imported diseases continued regularly to decimate the population. In 1885, the government sought to suspend immigration from Europe where a cholera outbreak had been reported. It was too late. In the following two years the disease wiped out some five per cent of the populations of urban centres in Chile. In all, more than 28,000 people died. During the same period, in the North, some 11,000 people perished from smallpox. That disease killed nearly 25,000 people in the years 1890 to 1895 and another 14,000 in 1905-6. During the 1905 outbreak of smallpox in Valparaíso and Viña del Mar, some ninety to one hundred fresh cases were reported every day and total fatalities approached six thousand.

Certainly, the Europeans arriving in the first half of the nineteenth century made a contribution to improving the appalling state of medicine and health care on the Pacific Coast. In large part they did so in their own interests – or those of their countrymen – but some had a deep and significant impact on the fight against disease and the improvement of sanitary conditions in the region generally. One of the most celebrated was William Cunningham Blest, from County Sligo in Ireland, who sailed to Chile, for reasons of his own health, in 1823. A doctor and surgeon, within three years of his arrival he would write influential papers for the Chilean government on the fundamental causes of the desperate state of medicine in Chile and the means of improving it. Taking Chilean nationality in 1833, he was appointed director of the independent nation's first school of medicine and would later hold political office. One of his sons, by his Chilean wife, became a famous diplomat and novelist while another was an admired poet.

As we have seen, British and French doctors served in the independence armies. One such was Nathan Miers Cox, the first surgeon in O'Higgins's Patriot Army. Born in Monmouth, the Welshman studied for the priesthood at

Oxford University before turning to medicine and qualifying as a surgeon following spells at Guy's and St. Thomas's hospitals in London. After a few years as surgeon in the Russian navy he took a similar post aboard *HMS Phoebe*, under the command of Captain James Hillyar, who is remembered as the victor in the 1814 Battle of Valparaíso in which *Phoebe* outgunned and captured the US frigate *USS Essex*. Cox took no part in that action, having been granted leave from the navy after the ship's arrival in Montevideo in 1813. However, he crossed the Andes to Santiago set on re-joining Hillyar. Instead, on arrival, he was advised to assist O'Higgins. He did so with honours, sharing exile in Mendoza with O'Higgins, before taking various senior medical posts in the military and staying on in Chile until his death in Valparaíso in 1869.

In the wake of the revolutionary uprisings in Germany in 1848, numerous medical men and their families made their way to South America, including to Chile. Among the most important, in the early years, was Dr Jerman Schneider. He practised in Valdivia, initially, before moving to Valparaíso and befriending Federico Errázuriz, who would shortly become the country's president. Errázuriz used his influence to secure senior academic posts for Schneider whose discourse to the Faculty of Medicine of the University of Chile in 1868 concerned the diagnosis and treatment of Diphtheria, Typhus and Smallpox. Not only did other German doctors teach in the new medical schools, but many of their Chilean students would leave to study in Germany before practising in their own country.

German doctors also meant German hospitals. The first to be established in Chile, and the best known, was that in Valparaíso. Although it was founded in 1875 to meet the needs of the 71-strong German community of the time, its superior services were put to work to support other nationalities. In 1910, it was boasted that German patients accounted for just 26 per cent of the annual total treated by the hospital, Chileans for a further 30 per cent with the rest accounted for by other nationalities. With the Valparaíso experience in mind, a second German hospital was built in the more obvious location of Valdivia. Opening its doors in 1897, it was granted permission to use the empress's name some ten years later. Thus it became the *Kaiserin Auguste-Victoria Krankenhaus* caring for twice as large a proportion of Chileans as Germans. The *Clínica Alemana* of Santiago was opened in 1918.

It should not be imagined, however, that hospital care and doctors were unheard of during the colonial period. On the contrary, the Spanish monarchy had set out domestic rules for medicine and surgery as early as the thirteenth century and by 1535, the regulations in force in Castile were applied in the colonies. Those who wished to practise were required to qualify in much the same manner as applied in Spain and to be examined by the royal physicians sent to America by the King especially for the purpose. This was a demanding obstacle course. So, while standards were enforced, the availability of adequate healthcare for any but the powerful, the rich and the indispensable was hard to find, and harder still to afford. While some naval doctors arriving in Pacific coast ports would treat patients onshore while their ships were anchored, few stayed on.

The need for new hospitals in the nineteenth century, to cope with the steep growth in population, was more than evident. In 1850, the charity hospital in Valparaíso's central Almendral quarter was described by an American naval observer, Lt James Gilliss. The institution could accommodate two hundred patients. Advice and medicine was available freely to all, but in-patient treatment was rationed and difficult to obtain. Any foreigner needed a note from his consul; a native needed one from his last employer. But the hospital catered to the poor and, for this observer, did a better job than counterparts in Santiago, with death rates among in-patients rather lower than in the capital. Private hospitals also existed, catering for those with the means to pay their way personally and for visitors whose consuls had instructions to meet the costs of their nationals falling ill.

In 1832, a scarlet-fever outbreak, which had spread from Brazil and Argentina, is believed to have killed several thousand people, especially children, in Santiago alone. Only nine doctors in the capital were initially prepared to treat those struck down by the illness (and just four in Valparaíso). The government eventually issued a decree penalizing doctors who refused to attend the sick without good reason. Poor hygiene made dysentery, typhoid and syphilis common.

That many Europeans also succumbed to these illnesses and conditions, can therefore hardly be a surprise. Of course, mid-nineteenth century life in England, France and Germany was far from healthy. Nevertheless, average life expectancies on the Old Continent (around 40 years) were higher than on the west coast of South America and rapidly improving. It took decades for improvements to show in Chile where, as late as 1910, the average citizen could still expect no more than 29 years on this earth.

And the risks were as real for those in the most cossetted situations as those exposed to the rough life of the streets and mining camps. Take the family of James ('Santiago') Humberstone, the Kentish-born chemical engineer whose revolutionary techniques were to transform the saltpetre nitrate industry in the second half of the nineteenth century. In 1877, Humberstone – whose story is told in Chapter 11 – took his new wife Irene, whom he had just married at the British consulate in Arica, to live in the *oficina salitre* San Antonio above Iquique in the province of Tarapacá, then still part of Peru. They would later move to the Oficina Agua Santa, further north. They lived in spacious conditions, fine ranch-style houses. They were comforted by imported luxuries, clothing, food and drink, and with servants to look after them. Superficially, as a senior manager, Humberstone and his kin lacked very little. True, they were socially isolated, but there was much to compensate.

Like most young couples they wanted a family and their first child, Louise Elizabeth, was born at San Antonio, in January 1878. A sister was born in September 1879 and named Amy Agnes. She died in February 1881 while a third daughter, Irene Cecilia, was born in August of that year but passed away just sixteen months later. Irene Humberstone gave birth to the couple's first son, Horace James Lewis, in August 1883, and he was followed by Arthur Edward in December 1884. However, Horace was dead five months later and Arthur in April 1886. Irene Mary was born in 1887 but another sister, named Inez Sophia, seems to have died at birth in May 1888. Four more sons, Francis, Ernest, Harry and Charles, were born between 1889 and 1896, though Charles survived little more than a year. Jessie Rose was the Humberstone's last daughter, born in April 1897. In summary, of twelve children only six survived early childhood on the Pampa.

The grave of four of the Humberstone children at Tiliviche, north of Iquique. Their father lies close by.

Such was the cost to families in the most prestigious positions, those at the top of the tree. Down below, the regular workers in the *salitreras* – and by 1870 there were dozens of *oficinas* scattered the length and breadth of the Atacama Desert with many thousands of employees – may have been strong young men, more resistant to the most common illnesses, but they had to face the hazards that went with their exhausting and usually unpleasant duties. The work was fraught with danger, from the vats of boiling liquids to the perpetual movement of carts, conveyor belts and locomotives. Injuries were common. Fingers, toes and feet were crushed, twisted, cut and burnt. Arms and legs were amputated. Men were left maimed and without the potential to work again.

One of the largest producers and biggest employers in the Antofagasta region was the Oficina Aníbal Pinto. Its record books of workplace accidents were perfectly ordered and conscientiously filled out with every incident that required even a day's absence or meant some minimal medical intervention. Indeed, the books would have done credit to any British or French coal mine of the time. Medical certificates proliferated, hospitalizations recorded, costs and compensation payments were assiduously noted. Accidents in the plant were many but mostly the injuries were minor. Every month or so, however, a tragedy occurred. December 1928 saw such a case. Twenty-six year old Adolfo Guzmán Faundez, a married man, was working on the railway system in the *oficina*, as a *carrilano*[5]. The precise nature of the accident was not recorded, but he was severely crushed. Injuries to the back, chest and upper left arm left him incapable of work and, ultimately, needing a hospital stay, including over four months the following year at the nearby Chacabuco plant, which was better equipped for such cases than Aníbal Pinto. A day after finally leaving hospital, in November 1929, Señor Faundez was paid off by the company, evidently he would be a permanent invalid. Quite how far he and his family got with the 3000 pesos (UK£75 or US$350 at the time) handed him, is not known.

Nature threatened everyone, irrespective of nationality, rank and wealth. The exploitation by foreigners of the natural resources of these countries can be, and often still is criticized. What cannot be denied, however, is that the men and women who journeyed so far to take part in the post-independence development of Chile, Peru and Bolivia needed a heady mixture of ambition, foolhardiness, courage and stamina to defy the natural odds stacked against them.

---

5   Railway track maintenance worker

9.

Farmers and fishermen: a new start in fertile lands and waters

And such thy strength-inspiring aid that bore
The hardy Byron to his native shore.
In horrid climes, where Chiloe's tempests sweep
Tumultuous murmurs o'er the troubled deep,
'Twas his to mourn misfortune's rudest shock,
Scourg'd by the winds, and cradled on the rock,
To wake each joyless morn, and search again
The famish'd haunts of solitary men,
Whose race, unyielding as their native storm,
Knows not a trace of Nature but the form;
Yet, at thy call, the hardy tar pursued,
Pale, but intrepid, sad, but unsubdued...

From *The Pleasures of Hope* by Thomas Campbell, 1777-1844

If minerals were the foundation of Chile's wealth, and remain so today, Europeans know the country for other products of its earth and its seas: particularly wines, out-of-season fruit and salmon. Farming and fisheries have been among the nation's great success stories. Yet, for centuries, they were developed and financed by Europeans. Like mining, it was the story of sometimes shameless exploitation of resources and people, much enterprise, great risk-taking, ingenuity, a pioneering spirit and stamina.

"I think that no one who knows Chile today will dispute the suggestion that her fertile soil has chiefly contributed to her social well-being.... There is a spring of life about the farming region of Chile, a sense of energy, health and freshness that is extraordinarily exhilarating. Much of this land is still but newly opened: one may pass through hundreds of miles of land where the tree-stumps of the primeval forest still stand among the vigorous corn, where the farmhouse is but an impermanent thatched hut. But the dark rich earth, the lusty crops, the blossoming orchards and hedges, the green pastures with their sleek cattle, create a scene of genuine content. The holdings may be new, yet they are plainly homes."

It was not always so. This euphoric view from the 1920s by the traveller and writer Lilian Elliot reflects the relatively happy end-point of a millennium of change and four hundred years in which mostly foreigners decided how the land, the lakes and the ocean would be farmed. There were centuries of Spanish rule in which hunger was common and the exploitation and near-slavery of Indian peoples the norm. Another form of land appropriation was put in place after independence as a lure for rural immigrants from the poverty-stricken farms of Bavaria, Ireland, the Basque region and Eastern Europe.

The story begins well before the arrival of Pedro de Valdivia and the conquistadors. Various forms of subsistence farming had thrived and met the needs of the indigenous Indian tribes and the Incas as they encroached southwards from Peru. The Chinchas of Southern Peru had brought elements of organized farming to the coastal and desert lands as far as the Maipo River, which flowed through the great fertile valley a little south of what is now Santiago. These northern people raised llamas to provide wool for clothing as well as cultivating potatoes, corn, peas and fruit. They also dug canals for irrigation. Their skills were adopted and extended to other crops, like squash and beans, by the fierce Quechuas who conquered the Chinchas and would later themselves be dominated by the Incas. The Vitacura Canal, meant to water farmland near Santiago, is one waterway built in the Inca period whose traces can still be seen today. As well as the llama, the similar-looking vicuna and guanaco were also raised for wool by the Quechuas.

Deeper into the Central Valley and the Lakes region, and inhabiting some of Chile's most fertile territory, were the Araucanian peoples. This strong and resilient race were not farmers, but hunters. Their meals were basic, whatever meat and fish could be caught being supplemented by vegetables found growing wild, including potatoes and beans. Nevertheless, their diet was rich in comparison to the tribes living further south: the Chonos of Chiloé and its archipelago as well as the Yaghans of Magallanes and Tierra del Fuego lived largely on shellfish found on the shore along with any seabirds that could be trapped and the occasional seal or sea lion. The Onas from the mountainous interior of Tierra del Fuego, hunted guanaco for skins and meat. Among other indigenous tribes, the Changos in the North were fishermen while the Atacameños farmed in the oases dotted around the desert.

Evidently, with or without the Incas, the tribes were diverse and largely isolated, often nomadic, indigenous communities. Their rudimentary farming

Farmers and fishermen: a new start in fertile lands and waters

could hardly meet the demands for sustenance from the Spanish invaders. From 1540 onwards, as Pedro de Valdivia and his expedition moved steadily south from Cuzco, founding new cities as they went, they also sought to establish viable colonial infrastructure in the countryside. That meant organized, productive agriculture. There was no shortage of fertile land in the central and southern regions of Chile, so the potential for profitable farming was large.

But first the captured territories were to be shared out among the most favoured or most powerful conquistadors. This was called *'repartimiento'*. There was plenty of land and few soldiers; thus, some Spaniards ended up with unmanageable swathes of the country, in some cases stretching all the way from the sea to the cordillera. In 1544, Pedro de Valdivia made his first division

A harvest in Chile at the turn of the 20th century

From "Chile" by G.F. Scott Elliot

of a tract of land, some 450 kilometres north to south, between the Aconcagua and Biobío rivers. This generated sixty vast parcels which he later reduced to thirty-two, the Spanish commander himself taking a parcel that included rich mines and the coast between Valparaíso and Quillota.

All that was missing was labour. This was the motivation for introducing the *encomienda* system, an arrangement bordering on slavery but sometimes practiced with a few scruples. For three hundred years, until its final abolition at the end of the eighteenth century, the efficiency and severity of this arrangement for ensuring a constant supply of manpower in the fields, lurched regularly between the extremes of human cruelty and something bordering decency. It was a system imposed throughout the colonies by the King of Spain. In essence it ruled that not only were the conquered territories assigned by the monarch to individual Spanish army officers, but the Indians living on them also. In principle, the rights reverted to the Crown after just two generations. In practice, it was usually much more. In the meantime, there was good land and unwilling labour to be exploited at will and without challenge. Even if the exploitation of gold and silver mines was a priority, farming was vital for sustaining the colonial presence. Very quickly new crops were introduced – like wheat and grapes for winemaking – and new livestock imported from Spain including fowls, pigs, sheep, goats, horses and cattle.

Church, monarchy and encomenderos always at odds

The operation of the *encomienda* system was marked by even greater inhumanity in Chile than in most other Spanish colonies since large parts of the territory were never at peace. The twists and turns in military policy towards finally overcoming the rebel Araucanian tribes often occurred in tandem with efforts – mostly by the church, and especially the Jesuits – to force reform of social conditions. There were always underlying tensions between the monarchy, the church and the *encomenderos* – the Spaniards with *encomienda* rights.

It was an inhuman system, subjecting captive families to exhausting toil, the sparsest sustenance and every imaginable abuse. Ultimately, even the King and his court in Madrid were sufficiently embarrassed by the reports of the bestial treatment of the indigenous peoples of Latin America – and no doubt by the potential reduction in gold shipments if such ill-treatment were to damage mining output – that it was decided to act. Certainly, the condition and treatment of natives in the colonies had been a matter of intense political, doctrinal and philosophical debate in Spain. While a constant supply of gold was a royal priority and prerogative, the King was subject to many pressures, not least, that of the church which gave precedence to adding and saving souls. So, calls for reforms were taken seriously, at least in Spain. As early as 1512, the 'Laws of Burgos' set out the first of many sets of reasonably humane conditions – a kind of labour code – to be observed by the *encomenderos*. Later measures – for instance the Ordinances of Toledo in 1528 and the New Laws of 1542 – defined Indians as free people and forbade their enslavement. However, these reforms were ignored on the ground. One simple reality always remained: rigid enforcement of reformist decrees from Madrid would deny access to the already-limited supply of cheap labour and spell the end of the *encomienda* system on which the prosperity of the colonial empire depended.

In 1559, a new regulation was announced. Hernando de Santillán, a judge of the *audiencia* of Lima – the highest court under the viceroy – had spent enough time in Chile to recognize the iniquities of the *encomienda* system and the extent to which it was abused. He had also observed that even the most eminent personalities – the wife of Pedro de Valdivia included – were ignoring the reforms under which the system was supposed to be operating.

Santillán petitioned the supreme body overseeing the colonies, the Council of the Indies, in Madrid, which eventually endorsed his proposed legislation to force the Governor's hand towards reform. In this way, the requirement that all those entrapped by the system were obligated to provide their 'personal service' to the *encomenderos* was abandoned. In its place was a supposedly lesser condition that the local chief *(cacique)* offer one in every six of his tribe for work in the mines and one in every five to work the land. There would be modest remuneration and food (including meat three times each week). Women, youths and the elderly would be excused from such work. Other obligations placed on the *encomenderos* required them to sow crops to feed their enslaved workers, look after them when sick, instruct them in being good Catholics, treat them decently and protect them when necessary. Broadly, they were to be treated like human beings rather than animals as had been the practice.

Santillán's measures have been described as the most significant social and political experiment attempted in Chile during the sixteenth century. They were certainly well-intentioned, if self-interested. But they did not square with the needs or priorities of the *encomenderos*, who saw their labour force being severely depleted. Further, the native workers did not feel much better about their supposedly improved lot. Many continued to escape whenever and wherever possible. The sugar-coated system was never properly tested.

Very much at the same time as Santillán was pushing Chile's governor, García Hurtado de Mendoza, towards a serious softening of the terms of 'personal service', the governor was being pressed on another, but closely related, policy front. A Dominican friar named Gil González de San Nicolás, also one of Mendoza's advisers, set out to steer the Spaniards away from another violent attempt finally to tame the Araucanian rebels. He lambasted the authorities for armed incursions into Araucanian territory, for forced conversion to Catholicism and for the taking of prisoners as slaves. Naturally, it was the last of these on which the *encomienda* system increasingly depended. Gonzalez sought to ensure that the views of the church and the edicts of the King, which were broadly sympathetic to the plight of the natives, were observed in practice as well as in word. This first attempt to support a sustained policy of 'defensive warfare' ultimately failed. With his return to Peru in 1563, Gonzalez composed a searing written condemnation of the suffering of the *mapuches*, concluding: "In a word, the Indians experience no relief whatsoever from the time they are born until the day they die."

A further half century of cruel, forced labour for the tribal peoples in the fields and the mines would pass before another attempt was made to provide for humane and decent treatment. This time it was the Jesuits, and, notably, a priest called Luis de Valdivia, who set the tone for reform and pressured the King to change the system once and for all. Earlier, the Jesuits had put an end to personal service in their own institutions. That created resentment and fear among the *encomenderos*. Nevertheless, travelling to Madrid, the determined and forceful priest was able to bring all the influence of the Catholic Church to bear on to the monarch, Philip II, who ultimately conceded. Native peoples would no longer be forced to work, but where they did so they had to be paid and cared for. This time there would be little choice about the enforcement of the reforms since Luis de Valdivia returned from Spain, in 1611, with what amounted to a royal warrant to exert authority and override the governor.

The immediate outcome was a near collapse of agricultural output. Moreover, the gold mines almost ceased to operate as well. The *encomenderos* found themselves with virtually no labour force. Without compulsion the workers were not persuaded to make any effort, while the absence of any viable currency made the now obligatory payment of wages complicated. Moreover, given the much more favourable conditions, there was competition to work on the Jesuit farms. An answer needed to be found quickly which would satisfy the *encomenderos*, the indigenous labour force and the church all at once.

What finally emerged was the ingenious *inquilino* system. A subtle mixture of slavery, tenant farming and feudalism, the arrangement allowed for each native to have a patch of land to do with what he wished, including growing crops and raising animals for his family's account. Seeds could also be provided. However there was a price to be paid; the *inquilino* was required to work for the proprietor whenever called on, although for such work he was required to be paid a small wage and fed. It was not a revolution and the new system was as subject to abuse as the old one, but it did spell the beginning of a better future for at least some of the indigenous peoples of Chile.

Naturally, plenty of the *encomenderos* held out and continued with their old habits of ill-treatment and forced labour. Valdivia's policy of 'defensive warfare' against the Araucanians was overturned on his departure for Spain

160

in 1619, with natives once more being captured and transported towards slave-like conditions on the haciendas. The South of Chile, in particular, was just too remote whatever the wishes and decrees of the monarch in Madrid, his advisers or the best-intentioned church leaders. It would take until General Don Ambrosio O'Higgins – father of the founder of independent Chile – was presented with the royal seal of office as governor in 1788 for *encomienda* exploitation finally to be outlawed and those remaining slaves set free. The *inquilino* system was confirmed; the imprisonment and torture of natives who escaped from rapacious masters was no longer tolerated. O'Higgins, a great reformer, improved irrigation and sought to establish fisheries, sugar-cane and cotton cultivation and much else that would stimulate agricultural development. In a sense, he completed the work initiated by the Jesuit activists over a century and a half earlier. It is perhaps an irony that the Jesuits, who had become major land-owners and successful farmers, were expelled from Chile – and all other Spanish colonies on orders of the King – just twenty years before Ambrosio O'Higgins took office.

Still, the system of huge haciendas and increasingly productive tenant farming in the Central Valley was now the dominating feature of Chilean agriculture and lasted, in one form or another, until partial land reform in the 1960s and 1970s. The old Spanish families, with their roots among the conquistadores, intermarried with the gradually enriched *inquilinos*, forming a vast strata of mixed-blood, middle class Chileans many of whose descendants work and profit from the land today.

Potential for farming is finally fully recognized

Yet, if the structure of Chilean farming in the Central Valley had stabilized by the time of Independence, huge regions of potentially fertile and productive land to the south remained unfarmed. John Miers, the English traveller and engineer, toured the area in the 1820s. Viewing the fertile lands around Chillán and Concepción, Miers noted that there had once existed great haciendas producing corn and wine. He saw potential for raising wheat there also. But the war of independence had brought disturbance to commerce and then desolation:

"The haciendas, which were numerous and well peopled, are now in great measure deserted by the peasants; the miserable beings who remain live almost without restraint and cultivate such portions of the ground as they require for their subsistence: while nearly all the vineyards, so long neglected, have become ruined; and the buildings and bodegas for the preparation of wines and spirits, are either destroyed or fallen to decay. The present government of Chile is so unable to afford protection either to property or person that the *hacendados* dare not return to their farms, but remain chiefly at Santiago employing what they have been able to save from the wreck of their fortunes in commercial pursuits."

The story of the German and other immigrants who arrived from the 1850s onwards to populate and farm the Lakes Region – sponsored initially by the administration of President Manuel Bulnes – was told in Chapter 6. The effort to reinstall productive farming in the south ultimately paid off, though at a cost to the indigenous peoples, especially in Araucania. Equally, there was a cost to

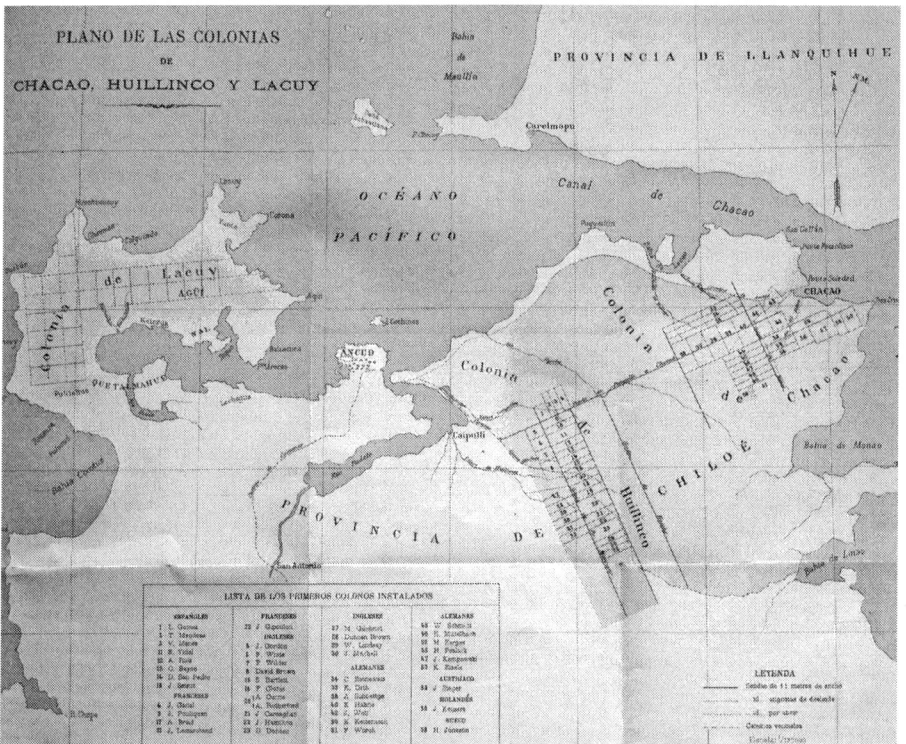

A map of northern Chiloé marked out with plots for potential colonists, published by the Agencia General de Colonización in 1896.

the immigrants themselves who withstood perpetual hardship. During the harsh 1853-54 winter many colonists came close to death from starvation. A plague of small birds devoured the 1855 crop, but a few years later the newcomers had succeeded in putting much of their allotted land under successful cultivation.

We have also recounted some of the story of settlement in the far south of Chile, in Magallanes and Tierra del Fuego, but not that of the sheep farmers. Colonists had tried and failed to settle the region from the sixteenth century onwards. They were worn down by attacks by local tribesmen and the harshness of the climate. Yet it was obvious that the region was ideal for raising sheep. The cold climate means the animals grow long and dense wool. Quite who brought the first flocks to the region is in question. Often, the Spaniard José Menéndez, who secured vast land concessions from the Argentine government and assembled a consortium of Buenos Aires businessmen for his enterprise, is credited with bringing animals from the Falkland Islands and establishing what quickly grew into a powerful wool-farming, frozen meat and fat-rendering enterprise stretching across Patagonia and Tierra del Fuego. Another view[1] is that two Frenchmen, M. Francois Roig and a 'M. Marius' brought Merino sheep down from Montevideo in 1874, some years before Mr. Menendez went into business on the northern shore of the Strait of Magellan. A third version[2] suggests that it was an Englishman, with a suspiciously French-sounding name, Henry Reynard, who had landed that same year and quickly recognized the potential. He supposedly brought 300 sheep from the Falklands, first to an island off Punta Arenas and then to the mainland.

Whoever takes the honours, the growth in sheep farming and meat processing was exponential. In 1878 there were 185 sheep in the entire territory. By 1894 that figure had jumped to 700,000 and rising. In addition, 60,000 head of cattle were also grazing the pampas. With the first deep-freeze plant opening in 1905, a few kilometres from Punta Arenas, any constraints on the continued development of a vast global business were removed. In 1925, the *South Pacific Mail* reported that the Sociedad Explotadora de Tierra del Fuego (SETF), of which Menendez was a major shareholder, controlled two and a half million acres of pasture on the continental side of the Strait and another three million acres leased from the Chilean state on Tierra del Fuego. By that point there were something around two million sheep within the company's territory producing some 600,000 lambs every year. Ten million pounds of wool were clipped annually.

Punta Arenas, where shipments of wool, frozen meat and hides were

---

1   South Pacific Mail Thursday, 17 September, 1925
2   "Foreigners and Religious Liberty in 19th Century Chile", David Pytches, Thesis May 1984.

concentrated[3], had been founded in 1849, at which point it was known as Sandy Point. The little town then had 700 inhabitants of which 300 were convicts or political prisoners. It was hardly a stable population on which to base any nascent industry: trouble was inevitable. In 1851 a mutiny broke out. It was quelled relatively easily and its leader was taken to Valparaíso and shot. The rest of the convicts were shunted elsewhere. From then on sheep farming thrived, originally managed largely by Australians and New Zealanders, but often with Scottish-born shepherds. While there were ruinous speculative bubbles as world wool prices boomed and then crashed, fortunes were made on both sides of the Andes. By 1905 Britain was taking seven-eighths of exports from Punta Arenas and supplying one-third of its imports.

French show the way as wine starts to improve

In modern times, Chile is less well-known in Europe for its sheep than for its wines. While grapes had been introduced by the Spanish in the early colonial period, it was not until the middle of the nineteenth century that European influence, especially that of French experts, initiated grape growing and wine production that would ultimately satisfy refined and everyday thirsts the world over.

The English traveller and writer, Maria Graham, provided some of the most perceptive observations on the state of Chilean alcohol production and consumption in the 1820s.

"The liquor is contained in skins and brought from the interior on mules. It is not uncommon to see a hundred and fifty of these under the guidance of ten or a dozen peons, with the *guaso* or farmer at their head, encamping in some open spot near a farm-house in the neighbourhood of the town. Many of these houses keep spare buildings, in which their itinerant friends secure their liquor while they go to the farms around, or even into town, to seek customers, not choosing to pay the heavy toll for going into port, unless certain of sale for the wine. I bought a quantity for common use: it is rich, strong, and sweetish white wine, capable, with good management, of great improvement. … I gave six dollars for two *arobas* of it, so it comes to about 3½d. per bottle."

Among her many acquaintances were senior politicians. One of the most important had retired to his vineyards after serving as 'supreme director' of the nation.

"This gentleman, Don Henriques Lastra, the ex-director of Chile, is at

---

3   The frozen meat and fat-rendering plant constructed near Puerto Natales is today a museum.

present entirely removed from public life and devotes himself to the cultivation of his farm or hacienda, and to making various experiments for the improvement of the wines of the country. He has succeeded in making a wine little if at all inferior to champagne; and his ordinary wine, in which he has pursued the Madeira method, is like the best *vino tinto* of Teneriffe. In general the wines here are sweet and heavy. His fields appear to me to be in excellent order; and all about the farm looks more like European farming than anything I had seen in this country."

It seems likely that the first vines were introduced into South America soon after the territories from Mexico southwards were progressively subjugated by

Mechanized farming techniques were imported quickly from Europe. This threshing machine, which was devised by Ransome's of England, began to replace the use of horses in Chile during the 1860   *The Illustrated London News*

the Spanish. Columbus appears to have transported Spanish vines on his second voyage and the practice of transporting at least some plants on each ship heading west from Spain became a requirement under royal ordinance from 1522. Perhaps to ensure adequate supplies of sacramental wine, the first arrivals of vines to Chile and Peru seem to have been ensured by monks. It is likely that Brother Francisco de Carabantes brought plants by sea to what is now the port of Talcahuano in 1548. Not long afterwards, cuttings were planted in the hills around the southern port town of Concepción from where the Spaniards were struggling to conquer the Mapuche territories of Araucania. The very first successful wine production was probably in the area of Santiago in 1555. Not that the quality would have been anything but rough: the first vine varieties were rustic yet robust in difficult climates and soils. The two most common types brought by the conquistadors were *País*, producing red grapes, and *Moscatel de Alejandría*, which was vinified into a white wine.

John Miers who, like Maria Graham, wrote copiously on all aspects of Chilean culture but also of its industries in the 1820s, had a poor view of the wines being produced at that time. He considered that "the quantity of grapes, and not the quality, is the main object". He criticized the failure to weed and hoe between the lines of vines as well as over-watering; practices he found likely to be the cause of the low sugar content of white grapes. The fact that Graham could appreciate a rather sweet white wine was down to another practice much frowned upon by Europeans. This entailed boiling down, in copper pans, a portion of must to a concentrated liquor *(cocido)* which was then added to the rest of the grape juice during fermentation. Not that fermentation necessarily was allowed to go to finality. Much of the wine drunk in the *pulperias* was a still-fermenting drink called *sancochada* which was especially appreciated as being more intoxicating than the finished product. Miers himself claimed that he could produce a wine "in no way inferior to the best Teneriffe" by adding sugar to the *sancochada* and then allowing fermentation to proceed.

Even officialdom recognized the shortcomings. In 1857, a report to President Manuel Montt on the state of the country and its economy was scathing about winemaking in the Valley of Colchagua, now a leading source of fine wines in Chile:

"The wine that they send to Valparaíso, almost immediately after the completion of its tumultuous fermentation, is only a *moût* to which is often added, at the point of its despatch, a quantity of grape juice which has carefully been concentrated by boiling after leaving the press. This molasses, when it is not too concentrated, is known in the business as '*cocido*', and as '*arrope*' when it is more consistent. The spirit that is produced in the province is made from the *marc* (the residue left after grapes are pressed) and wine which is turning bitter; it has a corrosive taste and an empyreumatic (tar and burnt wood) odour."

The increasingly sophisticated palates of the Spanish landowners and aristocracy – who travelled sufficiently often to Europe to understand that their local wines were of the poorest class – would have to await the arrival of the French at the beginning of the nineteenth century for some relief. The French brought technical expertise. They also brought new varieties. Those, like the *Cabernets, Malbec, Merlot, Carmenère* and the white grapes of *Sauvignon Blanc, Chardonnay, Semillon, Reisling* and *Gewürztraminer* began to appear through the efforts of wine pioneers like M. Nourrichet, a French resident of Chile, in the 1840s. However, the fifteen years spent studying Chile by the

French geographer, naturalist and botanist, Claude Gay, would have provided much of the basic geological, botanical and climatic understanding, necessary for the foundation of what would become a thriving wine industry.

Then there was the 'great escape'. In fact, two escapes. The minor threat, in the mid-1850s, was a new form of the fungal disease, odium, which had migrated back to Europe from North America and reduced wine production on the Old Continent, in 1854, from 29 million to 11 million hectolitres. Chile's Central Valley climate, being extremely arid in spring, summer and the harvest season, is unfriendly for fungal growths, and the country escaped the damage experienced in France and the other big wine producers.

However, the wine growers faced a potential disaster fifteen years later when French vines started dying, inexplicably at first, from a disease that spread rapidly to Portugal in the west and as far east as Turkey. By the time the culprit was named – an insect called *Phylloxera vastatrix*, again with its origins in North America – it was too late. Throughout Europe from 1860, the root systems of vines were attacked fatally. Within a few years, *Phylloxera* had struck in Australia, Argentina, Brazil and the rest of South America. But not Chile. Why Chilean vines escaped – and have continued to avoid the disease to this day – was the subject of much theorizing. Most likely it was simply the geographical isolation of the country – the Andes, the desert and the ocean – aided by some fast-footed administrative action when the Chilean authorities, on hearing the plant disorder had reached Buenos Aires, in 1869, slapped an import ban on all vines and shrubs. This close shave with disaster, explains, in part, the particularity of Chilean wines today, still the product of the only vines cultivated without the need for grafting.

From that time on, the partnership between French wine expertise and the ambition of powerful Chilean landowners to develop the finest labels remained solid. So close was the Franco-Chilean relationship that, in 1906, a commentator in the *Album de la Colonie Francaise au Chile,* could boast, without a touch of modesty, that:

"If the winemaking industry in Chile has reached its present level of development, it is due without contest and almost exclusively to the French vine growers who planted the first vines here; to the French cellar masters who learned to elaborate their wines; to the French teachers who, from the old land of the Gauls – through their books – or as expatriates in these hospitable valleys, gave, and continue giving, to the Chileans their prolific learning."

As related by Rodrigo Alvarado, one of the country's foremost oenologists, the list includes the Bordeaux winemaker, Labouchere, who steered the first output of the *Concha y Toro* winery; oenologist Pierre Godefroy Durand, who was hired in 1878 to manage the *Cousiño Macul* vineyard; Fernand Saligne who was installed to develop what would become the giant *Santa Rita* winery, founded by Domingo Fernández-Concha; and M. Pressac and George Henri Dubois who respectively managed the initial plantation and landscaped much of the *Undurraga* vineyard and gardens. Responsibility for systematically passing on the skills and science of good winemaking to oncoming generations fell eventually to another Frenchman, René F Le Fleuvre. Le Fleuve served for many years as Director of the *Quinta Normal*[4] of the Agricultural Institute of Santiago.

Chilean wines soon became eminently tradable assets; the first exports were despatched to Europe around 1887 and the *Undurraga* winery began to ship to the United States in 1903. As the popularity of these products grew so the merchants moved in. Initially, among the best known and most successful were the *Vicuña Mackenna Catalonians*. With their wineries lining the Avenida Vicuña Mackenna in Santiago, and with rail connections and other infrastructure geared up to meet the ever-growing demand, the group of Spaniards made their fortunes trading bulk quantities of not necessarily the highest quality Chilean wines. From there on, however, there was little to block the progression of the industry into a dominant force in world wine production and commerce.

How the first salmon travelled from Germany to Chile

Even the development of the Chilean fishing industry – at least with respect to its most familiar product, salmon – owed something to European influence. Not that the record was all positive. The English naturalist G F Scott Elliot observed in 1907:

"The government, every now and then, imports specialists under contract to carry out some scheme or other, which has, too often, not been thoroughly studied beforehand. Thus, for example, Grimsby fishermen were brought over at great expense. They had not, of course, a swift trawler and a steamer to carry their fish, and there is no London market, so that, eventually, the government took undoubtedly the least expensive course, and shipped them back to England again."

The story of the introduction of salmon into Chilean waters also had a share of accidents. According to an official government report of 1907, the first person accredited with having brought salmon eggs to Chile from Europe, in the

---

4   Named after the Ecole Normal of Paris which specialized in developing plant varieties.

nineteenth century was Señora Isidora Goyenechea de Cousiño. A remarkable and resourceful woman, Señora Goyenechea de Cousiño found herself managing the coal mines of Lota, in the South of Chile, after the death of her powerful entrepreneur husband. Her efforts to introduce salmon to the region failed when the eggs, albeit successfully transported from Europe, died because of the stark difference between winter river temperatures in Europe and those in the year-round freezing waters off Chile.

Serious work restarted in 1901 when the President commissioned a feasibility study by the much respected, German-born, naturalist and conservationist, Federico Albert. The conclusion was positive: salmon could be acclimatized in Chilean waters. Albert was charged with developing an establishment for the incubation of eggs and their development on the Río Blanco (near Los Andes, north of Santiago). He was then sent to Europe to seek out the best breeding techniques. This led him to an important German pisciculturalist, Rudolfo Wilde, who was quickly contracted to plan and manage the transfer of eggs from one continent to the other. By February 1905, the eggs and the necessary equipment to protect and eventually hatch them had been purchased in Germany and shipped, first to England. Some 400,000 eggs of four different species started the journey. Special facilities, including a refrigerator, were installed on the steamer that eventually left Liverpool on 2 March. The accompanying team tenderly monitored the water temperature and changed the water every week throughout the voyage.

Arriving on the northern coast of Brazil, it was evident that the eggs were developing too quickly and the planned voyage time through the Strait of Magellan might be too long. It was decided to take some eggs overland, across the Cordillera, while the rest would continue, in the care of the German entrepreneur who was responsible for the shipment, by sea. The first party travelling overland, mainly by train, encountering temperatures as high as 40 degrees centigrade as well as a freezing snowstorm crossing the Cordillera. Ingenious means had to be found to protect the eggs. The cart rumbling over the pass was constantly threatened by potholes, ruts and boulders and a bridge was frozen from higher-than-normal river levels below the Aconcagua mountain. When they wearily arrived at the Río Blanco base they found the incubator room unfinished and had to spend twenty-four hours working non-stop to prepare it for the eggs. The journey had taken 38 days in all. Yet within two hours of the eggs being placed in the incubation waters, the tiny salmon began to appear. Twelve days later, the second shipment arrived by sea in Valparaíso. Although some eggs were subsequently lost in a burning train wagon, most of that batch also found its final home safely by the Río Blanco.

Lagoons were created beside the river and the breeding process continued over many weeks. By October 1905, the population of the lagoons had reached around 200,000 fish measuring between four and five centimetres. Most of the new salmon population was transported in wooden barrels and set free in rivers around the country: notably the Aconcagua, Paine, Tinguiririca, Liguimo, Maule, Cautín and Tolten. The suitability of Chilean rivers for the raising of four types of salmon had been proven and, though in recent times it has generated criticism for polluting some of the southern fjords through industrial breeding techniques, the industry never looked back. Salmon are among Chile's key export products.

Whaling in the 18th century. An engraving from "Voyages autour du monde" by Francois de Pagès (1782)

Fondation Laurent-Vibert, Lourmarin, France

Whaling has its day on the Pacific coast

In earlier times, the products of whaling were also traded heavily from Chile. The initial attempts to launch an industry, provides an example of free-wheeling speculation by the British doggedly thwarted by the Chilean authorities. As recounted by John Miers, the British engineer and writer, a scheme to export whale oil to Europe was dreamt up, around 1820, by an English merchant called

William Henderson and an American rear-admiral, William Wooster, who had recently ended his service with the Chilean navy. This was the first attempt at serious industrial whaling rather than the small-scale 'artisanal' fishing that had long existed. The intention was to hunt and then refine sperm-oil. Initially, the Chilean government welcomed the initiative, promising to waive duties on equipment imports and not to tax the exported oil either. The enterprising pair raised some US$60,000 allowing vessels to be leased, equipped, crewed and sent to sea from Valparaíso.

The refining was to be done in Coquimbo. A large quantity of wood barrels was needed and was duly assembled. However, with the whaling fleet already at sea, the governor of Valparaíso realized that Chile's navy lacked water barrels (hogsheads). His answer was to send word to authorities in Coquimbo to appropriate all the barrels collected for the whale oil enterprise. Protests from the whaling managers proved useless. Panicked by the prospect of the imminent arrival of their fleet they were left with no alternative but to scrape together whatever barrels they could find locally. To add insult to injury, when the whalers arrived the governor of Coquimbo announced that he would levy heavy duties on the blubber. Again, protest to the Supreme Government in Santiago had no effect. The enterprise might still have thrived, but there was yet more official obstruction to come. With the problem of the shortage of casks unresolved, it was decided to place the blubber temporarily in reservoir pits dug into the hills above the port. Although several miles from the town, the governor then ruled that the storage of the whale product would be a threat to public health. Left with no answer, as the whalers crowded into the port, the enterprise collapsed with the investors' money lost.

While two or three whaling ventures were launched from the 1870s, it was only after the First World War that a significant industry was established. With global whale stocks being plundered in less remote seas, serious industrial whaling was a long time arriving in the south-east Pacific region, within reach of the coasts of Chile and Peru. The two principal figures who engaged themselves in the new enterprise were, predictably, Norwegian and hailed from the same town, Sandefjord. Equipped with the latest harpoon gun, Adolf Andresen, started whaling operations from Punta Arenas in 1903. Later he established the Sociedad Ballenera de Magallanes with several Chilean partners and expanded the business steadily. By the end of the 1914-1918 War, struggling with falling international prices for whale products, Andresen sold up and returned to Norway. When he returned, in 1933, he set up a new company, Comunidad Chileno-Noruega de Pesca. For several years his ships hunted successfully as far south as the Antarctic. However, the company's debts finally overwhelmed the business and Andresen died alone and poor in Punta Arenas in 1940.

The other Norwegian, August Christensen, together with his brothers, pioneered whaling based in Valdivia and the island of Chiloé. Their activities largely mirrored those of Andresen in the South. From the 1930s the whaling industry thrived mainly under Chilean ownership and management, before being abandoned in the 1980s.

In 2013, Chile was the world's fourth most important wine exporter, after France, Italy and Spain[5]. In 2014, salmon exports from Chile were second only to those of Norway[6] and were the nation's second biggest export after copper. The production of salmon had tripled in a decade, but the industrial farming practices used have been the subject of much criticism for their ecological impact. As for the export of table grapes, Chile is now the world leader[7] and by far.

---

5   International Trade Centre, Geneva
6   Industry sources
7   U.S. Department of Agriculture (for 2013)

10.

Miners: risk, ruin and (a few) fortunes

Now. miners, if you'll listen, I'll tell you quite a tale,

About the voyage around Cape Horn, they call a pleasant sail;

We bought a ship, and had her stowed with houses, tools and grub,

But cursed the day we ever sailed in the poor old rotten tub,

Oh, I remember well, the lies they used to tell,

Of gold so bright, it hurt the sight, and made the miners yell.

From *Coming Around the Horn* in

Put's Original California Songster (1868)

In 1903, some 11,746 mines were in operation, pulling from Chile's earth minerals of every kind: gold, of course, but also silver, copper, lead, iron, cobalt and manganese. Add to those the nitrates, borates, iodine and coal and there was enough work underground and in quarries for over 30,000 miners. And these were just the officially registered excavations on which dues were being paid; unofficial, uncounted workings would have added many more.

George Scott Elliott, an American naturalist, made this assessment almost eighty years after the English engineer, John Miers, had provided his unequivocally damning judgment of the prospects for foreigners making money in Chilean mines.

"Yet persons in this country, the best informed of the real state of Chile, and the utter impossibility of employing any considerable sum of money in mining with the least chance of it being productive of any profit whatever, put forth proposals for raising immense sums from the credulity of persons less informed than themselves, for the purpose, as it was pretended, of working mines of gold, silver, and copper, which were to produce immense profits."

In other words, the City of London was being taken for a ride, again. To do him credit, Miers regarded what mining activity there was as old-fashioned but reasonably efficient despite the habit of the Chilean miners of only "working from dawn to dusk". But foreign fortunes would never prosper.

"If there had existed any great indication of metallic wealth in places where mining could be carried on with any chance of success in Chile, it would unquestionably have been undertaken by the Spaniards… The fact is, no single great mine has ever been known in Chile, not any one of sufficient importance to call together any of the principal Spanish capitalists, who have risked their fortunes in the more productive mines of Peru…"

Certainly, Chile never became an *El Dorado* nor did it conceal immense silver deposits comparable with those of Potosi in Bolivia. On the other hand, in the decades following Miers' dismissive comments, the country would experience a gold rush of its own and a bubble of speculative investment in silver. As for copper, multinational corporations were founded on the promise of Chile's vast reserves and today underpin the development of Chile's economy. Miers was wrong!

It was true that most of the miners were Chilean – or Bolivian and Peruvian, since much of their countries' richest territories had been lost during the Pacific War of 1879-83 (see Chapter 12). Of those performing the heavy and hazardous work, only a few thousand were Europeans. And, as Miers had to admit, the locals were knowledgeable and skilled. However, in the wake of independence, when it came to managers and owners, the British in particular occupied the plum positions. They understood commerce, controlled the largest proportion of the global freight fleet and had easy access to international markets. Even in 1930, when much of the sector had become thoroughly Chilean, of the 1,677 mining patrons recorded in that year's census, more than 400 were foreign. Moreover, controlling many of the richest and most productive properties were the descendants of the British capitalists who had first made Chilean mining such a profitable investment in the nineteenth century.

Experience with gold, silver, copper, coal and other minerals – as well as the accompanying capacity to reach distant markets – made the Chilean mining sector a world leader by the mid-nineteenth century. Valparaíso, as the major port on the west coast of South America, was the focal point, a kind of global economic hub of its era. It was the extraction of metals that helped make modern Chile, and that is a story that goes back a long way.

No El Dorado… but Chileans lead the gold rush in California

Indeed, it all started with that so seductive yet treacherous of commodities: gold. Well before the arrival of the Spanish and their subsequent obsessional interest in amassing it, tribal peoples in Peru, Bolivia and Chile prospected, mined and worked the precious metal and left jewellery and other gold artefacts.

The Incas used gold as the basis for cult objects in their worship of the sun. It was not a token of monetary exchange, but Inca settlements were required to send gold tributes back to their capital, Cuzco. They extracted the raw material by panning alluvial deposits and some superficial rock mining. For a brief period, the Incas mined and smelted at least as far south as Coquimbo and Quillota in Chile.

While Pedro de Valdivia's premier remit had been to conquer Chile, he nevertheless set about resuscitating what remained of the Inca gold exploitations. Between Santiago and Valparaíso, he restarted workings at Marga Marga with

The silver mines of Potosi. Engraving by John Ogibly/Arnoldus Montanus, 1671
Fondation Laurent-Vibert, Lourmarin, France

the recruitment of 1700 young native men and women, donated by the local tribal chiefs. While the first two shipments to Lima were lost, Marga Marga gold, and the output from other sources in the Central Valley and North, was soon providing a worthwhile tribute to the Spanish monarchy and fortunes for the conquistadors. Later, the Spanish began refining gold in the south, around

Valdivia and Osorno, with particularly abundant reserves being found at the famous Madre de Dios and Ponzuelos workings.

As with the farming activities on the haciendas, the mines needed cheap – preferably free – labour. So the slave-like conditions of the *encomienda* system were applied in the goldfields as they were in the cornfields. If anything, given the harsh conditions that had to be endured even without the innate cruelty of the system of forced-labour, the aboriginal miners suffered more than the enslaved farmhands. In 1553, a Dominican friar, Francisco de Vitoria, made the point graphically in a letter sent to the Council of the Indies in Madrid:

"All the *encomenderos* send their Indians – men, women and children – to the mines to work without giving them any opportunity to rest, or any more food than a daily ration of maize during the eight months of the year that they labour there. The Indian who fails to produce the required amount of gold is beaten with clubs and whips. And if any Indian conceals a single grain of gold, he is punished by having his ears and nose cut off."

The only reason they could not be pressed to produce gold for more than eight months a year was not down to any softness on the part of the *encomenderos;* in fact, the streams dried up for four months making panning impossible.

One of Valdivia's officers and the eventual husband of his formidable mistress Inés Suárez, Rodrigo de Quiroga, appointed by King Philip II as the governor of the province of Chile in 1573, was probably no worse than many other *encomenderos.* He is reported to have put to work in his mines no less than six hundred native peoples from his *encomienda*, half of them women and all between the ages of fifteen and twenty-five. Naturally, Rodrigo de Quiroga made sure the modest efforts that had been made to improve the conditions of the Indians caught up in the *encomienda* system – notably those of Hernando de Santillán and the Dominican Fray Gil González de San Nicholás – were stripped of their effect. Appointed commander in chief of the Chilean forces, in 1574, he was explicitly permitted to transport six or seven hundred Mapuche prisoners of war from Araucanía to the mines in Coquimbo. Allegedly, this arrangement was agreed in order to help pay his soldiers. Quiroga had earlier instituted a legal case against the Indians for insurrection; they were found guilty in absentia, and condemned to death. Servitude in the mines, following some form of physical mutilation, was the lesser sentence imposed after that of death was commuted. When the prisoners arrived in La Serena, according to the commissioner charged with their transfer, their ill-treatment reached grievous and self-defeating limits:

"When the deportees arrived at this city some of them tried to escape, but they were recaptured and six or seven of them were hanged while the feet of about five hundred others were cut off; and although some people are of the opinion that these mutilated creatures can be of use in the mines they are actually good for nothing except work in gardens and on farms."

The subsequent campaign of the Jesuit, Luis de Valdivia, to end the *encomienda* system had some impact on the extreme levels of cruelty in the gold mines and especially the forced transfer of prisoners from the south. The labour shortage hit production hard. Moreover, by the end of the sixteenth century the rich sources in the south had to be abandoned as the Spanish were pushed out by the Mapuche tribes of Araucania.

It would not be until the eighteenth century that gold production could pick up again in Chile, largely through mining activities in the area of Copiapó and as a result of the foundation of the national mint in Santiago. By 1810, on the eve of independence, estimates suggest that Chile was producing as much gold as Peru and Mexico combined. However, output declined steadily over the following century – although the discovery of modest reserves in Chilean Patagonia and Tierra del Fuego attracted European adventurers, notably Yugoslavian immigrants.

Still, the Chilean and Peruvian expertise in gold mining and panning remained, with thousands of men looking for worthwhile outlets for their skills, their dreams of making fortunes still intact. Their big chance came with the Californian gold rush[1].

Some accounts have Chileans indirectly responsible for setting off the gold fever on the west coast of the United States. James Wilson Marshall, a carpenter originally from New Jersey, had found the first gold in the Sierra Nevada mountains on 24 January 1848. In May 1848, the Chilean brig *JRS*, owned by a Valparaíso entrepreneur, José Ramón Sánchez, and captained by Alfred Andrews, was docked in San Francisco harbour. A trader aboard the vessel generated excitement in the town – then home to no more than 1000 men and women – when he offered $12 an ounce cash for local gold rather than the standard $8-10 rate. When Andrews set sail for Valparaíso again, having sold the hides and tallows his ship had brought from the south, he had a valuable consignment of gold in his hold. Most of all, when JRS arrived back in its home port on 19 August, it brought the first news to the outside world that something was stirring in California.

Almost simultaneously, the *New York Times* was publishing initial reports

---

1   See Jay Monaghan's book, "Chile, Peru and the California Gold Rush of 1849" for a full account.

on the discoveries. But for potential gold prospectors to raise funds and set out on the long journey westwards it required more than just press speculation. Only in early December 1848 did President James Polk confirm publicly that discoveries had indeed been made. The "rush" started. Yet rushing was hardly the word: there were neither railways nor roads heading westwards. The sea route – whether round Cape Horn or to Panama and then overland to the Pacific coast – was long, two months at best.

Not only was Valparaíso, at that time, far closer logistically to California than was the East Coast of the United States, but the 'Jewel of the Pacific' was a natural place in which to do gold business. The sailing distance to San Francisco was 6,700 miles compared to the 19,300 miles from New York. Miners and traders in Peru and Chile therefore had a considerable advantage over North Americans. This was the basis for an enterprise that reaped fortunes for a few and ruin or tragedy for others. The resentment in the United States over what happened next was deep and long-lasting.

When Captain Andrews had anchored in Valparaíso Bay he went with the ship's trader to the offices of Hobson & Cie. The two received US$17.50 an ounce for their gold – meaning a handsome profit, even if they had paid over the prevailing odds. Initially there was no great fuss locally and the newspapers ignored the deal. But rumours began circulating in the port, nonetheless, and merchants responded. Within a few days, two ships had been chartered for passages to San Francisco – *Undine* for Hobsons and *Virginia* for the powerful trading house Waddington, Templeman and Co. The *Virginia* quickly booked 45 gold-seekers as passengers – many with British names, like O'Neill, Ellis, Ware and Crocker – and left port on 12 September with mining equipment and a hold full of supplies to be sold in San Francisco. *Undine*, under Captain Andrews, left eleven days later. While many Chilean merchants remained sceptical, they had little choice but to follow suit. Several other vessels were chartered and departed northwards in hot pursuit.

Valparaíso's principal newspaper, *El Mercurio*, woke up to the sensational story after the arrival of a mail steamer on 3 November, 1848. Passengers were full of well-embellished tales from California, backed up by the gold stowed in the vessel. Once it became apparent that ordinary working men might gain a fortune with a prospecting pan and the fare to San Francisco, trading houses and agents began quickly chartering vessels, loading them up with cargoes to sell in 'Frisco and offering passage to would-be gold seekers.

From then on each new vessel arriving from the North brought more enticing reports of the riches awaiting those who cared to set forth. Such was the fever swilling round the port, as *El Comercio* put it, that a ship offering passage to California in the morning could sell all its available berths by two o'clock in the afternoon. Within a few days in December, seven new ships were chartered and filled with prospectors set on beating the impending influx from the US East coast. Men from the haciendas came from the countryside to clog the streets of Valparaíso, though seldom with the cash to purchase what had become an expensive passage north.

The first signs of stress between Chilean enthusiasm and North American resentment, were not long coming. The American paddle-steamer *USS California* had cruised up the Pacific Coast of South America, taking on a few passengers in Valparaíso and, under pressure, a considerable number in Callao. As a result, when the ship arrived in Panama there was little space left

An attack on a very Mexican-looking miner during an 1849 anti-Chilean riot in San Francisco. *Century Magazine, February 1892*

for crowds of Americans who expected passages onwards to San Francisco. Protest meetings were held in Panama City. The ship's captain was pressured to the point where he had to stretch the accommodation on his ship beyond the permitted limits: he sailed on with 400 on board, twice the normal.

At that point there were already proposals in Washington for new regulations to stop to Latin American encroachments on North American mineral assets. However, by June 1849, most of the celebrated 'forty-niners', as they became known, had yet to arrive on the West Coast. They were still on the high seas. Over two hundred ships had left New York alone, for a passage via Cape Horn. San Francisco harbour was still crowded with Chilean ships, or European ships hailing from Chilean and Peruvian ports, all doing a roaring business.

By the end of June 1849, some 1,350 Chileans had arrived by sea in addition to numerous sailors who had deserted from their merchant vessels to join the stampede. And the new arrivals were already sending gold southwards. One unverifiable estimate suggests they took the equivalent of US$15 million south from California by September 1849 when the East Coast '49ers were finally getting established. And the Chilean miners were not alone: the services of traders, artisans, engineers and even doctors and teachers who had sailed from Valparaíso and other South American ports were in heavy demand.

Yet for many, while profitable, the stay was to be short. The initial, organized assaults on Chileans by 'patriots' in San Francisco, Sacramento and other Californian gold towns took place around the 4 July, Independence Day, celebrations of 1849.

Sensing an increasingly threatening mood, many of the first groups of Chilean prospectors to arrive were already returning home in the summer of 1849. But others kept arriving. Apart from squabbles over prospecting rights, fights also developed over women – especially over Chilean prostitutes who were much sought-after. Local gangs attacked groups of Chileans who were injured, robbed and threatened. As news of ill-treatment arrived back home there was public outrage and uproar in the National Assembly in Santiago. There were demands for a warship to be sent despite the risk of upsetting Washington. Eventually, a British naval vessel sailed in August 1849 with a remit to rescue Chileans wanting to return. When it docked again four months later, *HMS Inconstant* had just six homesick miners aboard. The political indignation in Chile was mirrored in Washington where the Congress was being pressed to act firmly in favour of its compatriots.

Nevertheless, the Valparaíso-based trading houses, like Gibbs, Alsop and Waddingtons, were stepping up their operations to make a killing. The economy of the port city was in shock. Normal trading was demoted as merchant ships were diverted towards whatever services might be profitable in California. That included supplying food, notably flour. Chilean wheat output was stepped up to meet the surging export demand, sending domestic prices skywards. Shortages developed, including coal and Chile's favourite alcoholic beverage, pisco. When, in January and February 1849, the US '49ers, on their way to California from the East Coast, had docked in Valparaíso, the visitors had spent freely. That too pushed up local prices. With more and more able-bodied men going north the poor were left to suffer.

Yet the ships kept departing and the gold continued arriving in Valparaíso. During the whole of 1849, some 303 cargo vessels sailed from the port destined for San Francisco. In one six-day period, the equivalent of US$60,000 of the precious metal arrived in three ships. And fortunes continued to be made in supplying the prospectors as well as from the gold. For example, 5,250 gallons of Chilean wine were shipped in the first three years of the gold rush.

But the window of opportunity for Chilean miners was inevitably short-lived. They were soon being pushed off their prospects by fair means and (mostly) foul. There was talk of 'wars'. Encouraged by populist politicians, the American miners began asserting their rights to reserves on US territory. In December 1849, there was one especially unpleasant clash over claims worked by Chileans some 50 miles from Stockton on the Calaveras River. The Chileans, despite being supported by the authorities in Stockton, were attacked, defended themselves, and were then subjected to some rough local justice. There were at least two lynchings and other violent punishments.

The Chileans crowded back into San Francisco. There, living conditions were appalling, so the one-time miners jumped at any chance of a cheap passage back home. In one ill-equipped and under-supplied tramp schooner on its way to Talcahuano, the captain refused to call in at Valparaíso to get medical help and supplies, and six such passengers died of starvation and thirst. Most of the rest were left ill and exhausted.

For the Valparaíso trading houses, money was still to be made. However, the great fire consumed the centre of San Francisco in December 1849 reducing the offices of several Chilean businesses to ashes. The merchants began to lose interest and the newly developing nitrate business in Chile and Peru was looking promising.

The Chileans were never fully forgiven for winning the race to grab the first slices of the glistening treasures of California. By the same token, their ill-treatment was not forgotten in Chile, and remained a source of anti-Yankee sentiment for decades after. Nevertheless, the Californian gold rush added to Chile's early economic success. Some 50,000 South Americans are said to have arrived in California between 1848 and 1852 – the majority from Chile. Some fortunes were indeed made, though true rags-to-riches successes were rare. The gold served in the construction of grand houses, fine public buildings and

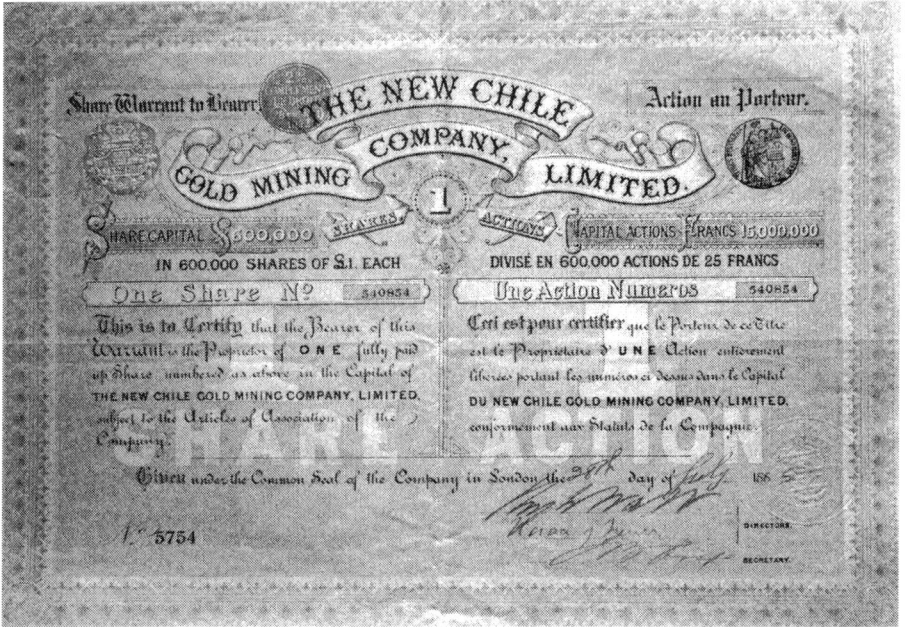

Long after the best days of Chilean gold mining, speculative share issues were common on the European stock markets. This one, launched in 1885 in London and Paris, was already being wound up just three years later. *Authors collection*

much else that now makes up Valparaíso's cultural heritage.

Silver, and a French adventurer

Chile had nothing to rival the vast silver deposits of Potosi in Bolivia where travellers in the early sixteenth century described seeing six thousand smelting furnaces glowing in the night sky. True, there were once rich silver mines operating near the Uspallata Pass which has for centuries been the principal Andean crossing between Santiago, Mendoza and eventually Buenos Aires. These were largely spent by the 1820s. But enthusiasts continued to believe. Alexander Caldcleugh, travelling around that time wrote:

"If Chile were to become so settled in its government as to afford perfect security of property, the application of capital to the mines would return a large profit. The quantity of metal still remaining in the Andes must be stupendous; but there is this to be considered, that if all the mines were properly worked, it is more than probable, that silver would fall in Europe to a very low price."

The fact is that silver prices did, indeed, fall in the latter part of the nineteenth century and did not recover, in dollar terms, until the 1960s. However, this was not because Chile had become more settled. Rather, it was the discovery of major seams in California and the introduction of new techniques to exploit them, together with large-scale sales of silver reserves by Germany and other European powers. The US share of world production jumped from around 20 per cent in the 1860s to 52 per cent in 1874, just when Chilean production peaked.

However, there was a 'silver rush' in the region and the settlement on which it was centred, Caracoles, became legendary. Initially on Bolivian territory, some 3100 metres up in the pre-Andes, north-east of Antofagasta, it fell to Chilean military occupation in the Pacific War, just nine years after the first discovery of silver was made in the locality.

The development of the saltpetre nitrate industry, together with the exploitation of gold and copper deposits near Antofagasta, had already drawn thousands of Chileans north from Copiapó. Bolivian territory or not – and the Chilean and Bolivian governments were already deeply in dispute over their frontier – the temptations were too great. But was the discovery of silver at what would become Caracoles down to a Chilean … or was it a Frenchman?

The credit usually goes to a Valparaíso-born Chilean prospector named José Díaz Gana. While searching for copper around the port town of Mejillones, he came across the stories and imprecise maps of an Indian named Garabito who had reported finding silver in the Sierra Gorda area, and had samples of ore to prove it. Díaz Gana initially tried to get backers for an expedition. His excited proposition was rejected; undoubtedly there was a profusion of potentially profitable pitches at the time for those with the means to back them. Attempting to go it alone, he had neither the finance nor the technical capacities necessary and the project quickly collapsed. It was then that Díaz Gana met Baron Henri Arnous de Rivière.

De Rivière was one of many adventurous characters, with colourful pasts they preferred to forget, who found their way – or fled – to South America in the nineteenth century. Born in 1828, he served as an officer in the French Foreign Legion from 1853, fighting in the Crimean War and taking part in the siege of Sebastopol. Despite being cited for exemplary service and promoted, he deserted and lived for five years in America. While in New Orleans he was involved in a duel. Given shelter in the house of a local army officer he subsequently absconded with the wife and daughter, allegedly to marry and live in Cuba. Already having been prosecuted in an embezzlement case in Paris, the Baron was pursued by the angry husband in the New Jersey Supreme Court[2]. Quite what happened to the two ladies in question is not recorded but de Rivière never appeared in court and certainly did not serve time in jail.

We next find the baron in Bolivia seeking out guano and silver prospects. He also represented a French trading house, Armand of Bordeaux, arranging shipments to and from France. A French account of the discovery suggests that the proposal for an expedition to the supposed area of the silver reserves came from de Rivière himself. Whoever thought of it first, Díaz Gana and de Rivière got together to form a company. They added several prospectors including the celebrated José Ramón Méndez. He had made many discoveries though, as the new expedition was launched, he had also just served time in the prison at Copiapó for the theft of minerals. Nevertheless, finance was raised and respective shares in any potential discoveries were agreed.

However, just as the group was getting underway, de Rivière decided to return to France to fight in the bloody Franco-Prussian War. Given a command, he was quickly taken prisoner along with the rest of the French army of the Rhine. Escaping equally quickly he resumed his service before, in January 1871, taking his wife and children to safety in London. There he learned that a discovery had been made in what was now known as Caracoles, nearly a year earlier. Although accounts differ, the initial reaction of Díaz Gana had been to cut de Rivière out of the shares in the new mine, pretending to believe his partner was dead. Thus, on his return to Bolivia, the Frenchman had to secure his rights through a court action, which he won.

The two principle shareholders made their fortune. And the silver rush started. Encouraged by over-excited press reports, hundreds of miners set out for the remote and treacherous desert in which the silver had been found. Indeed, so intense was the enthusiasm to get moving towards the Cordillera that many of the mines around Antofagasta and as far south as Copiapó in Chile were drained of their workers. Oddly, few of the men who set out towards the new discoveries were Bolivian: the locals were largely indifferent. The Chileans, however, could not be restrained, even when the newspapers began to suggest not only that the silver reserves might not be so widespread but that the hazards

2   Various accounts in The New York Times

to be faced in venturing into the bleak and unmerciful desert were very real. Even for the mining companies in place and seeking to exploit the finds, the difficulties were endless; the distances were large and the communications too meagre to get provisions and equipment in place easily.

Nevertheless by the middle of 1872, the population of Caracoles had reached 2000. Two years later, a school had been opened and other facilities and services for over 5000 people inhabiting a piece of arid desert where previously not even plants and animals were to be found. Yet, the future of the remote site of Caracoles was undermined not merely by its geographic and climatic extremes but by the unstable political environment which, ultimately, would lead to war between Bolivia and Chile. One of the casualties in the 1870s was the plan to construct a railway to the silver mines from the coast.

From 1871 to 1873 a 'silver bubble' centred on Caracoles inflated prices. New commercial banks opened up in Santiago and Valparaíso to provide the easy loans on which speculative silver mining companies were launched in the same two cities. The forty-eight companies formed in the years from 1870 until 1875 revitalized the local stock markets, at least temporarily. Investors in the City of London dived in. Chileans and foreigners rubbed shoulders in these silver enterprises, each bringing some valued commercial or mining expertise, or simply the security for finance. Once funded, the supplies were purchased and the prospectors set out for the desert to secure their share of the bonanza. In the booming mining town itself the local authorities worked from early in the morning until late in the evening to issue licences on thousands of prospects, each of which had to be measured out.

Inevitably, the bubble burst even while new companies were still being constituted. By early 1874 their share prices were crashing as it became evident that many had been formed without serious intent to explore or develop mines, but as purely speculative vehicles. Share values plummeted by as much as 95 per cent in just a few months. And it was not just the usual ranks of wealthy capitalists who were hit. Many modest citizens had raised loans and committed savings without the least understanding of the nature of the enterprises they were backing. The Chilean economy was rocked.

There had been earlier silver discoveries than that in Caracoles. That at Chañarcillo, fifty kilometres south of Copiapó, in 1832, attracted miners and speculators from afar and also the attention of one of Chile's most celebrated essayists and social commentators, José Joaquín Vallejo, better known in the newspapers of the time as 'Jotabeche'. While he did not disdain the extraordinary fortunes being made at the time, he felt the need to comment on the conditions suffered by the miners themselves. Visiting the famously rich Descubridora mine, he wrote:

"To see a half-naked man appear at the mouth of the mine, carrying on his back two or even three hundred pounds of rocks after having climbed with such an enormous weight through that long succession of galleries, pits and chambers, and then to hear the painful howl he makes when he finally gets a breath of fresh air, we conclude that the miner belongs to a more accursed race than man, that he's like a creature emerging from another world less fortunate than ours, and that the deep sigh he emits when he finds himself among us is a bitter reproach directed at heaven for having excluded him from the human species."

The copper port of Coquimbo in 1909.   *Library of Congress, Washington*

No account of silver mining on the west coast of South America would be complete without reference to one of Britain's finest engineers, and the inventor of the high-pressure steam engine, Richard Trevithick. Born into the mining traditions of Cornwall in 1771, Trevithick experimented with engines and boilers using high-pressure steam before constructing his first locomotive, *Puffing Devil*, which took passengers along the main street. He continued developing better locomotives, and stationary pumping engines which were designed, among other things, to evacuate water from mines and for under-water tunnel construction. He also began to build rudimentary steam vessels.

However, in 1816 Trevithick set sail for Peru. He had met a mine manager, Francisco Uville, who had responsibility for exploiting the giant Cerro de Pasco mine, at an altitude of over 4000 metres in the Peruvian Andes. Uville had described the problems of draining water from the mine with the low-pressure pumping engines constructed on the designs of Trevithick's great competitor,

James Watt, and Matthew Boulton. The Cornish inventor was confident that his engine would produce the necessary power at a high altitude. He agreed to provide a large quantity of the necessary equipment in return for shares in the mining company; these he sold on to investors in the City of London.

Trevithick's confidence was quickly justified and the mine development looked promising, especially for its financial backers. Unfortunately, shortly after arriving, Trevithick's fell out with Uville. According to the account by John Miers, there was a clash of interests and professional jealousies among the engineers. That led to delays which, according to other accounts, may have been exacerbated by the disturbances of the local independence struggle and the behaviour of the Simon Bolivar administration. In any event, Trevithick became disgusted and walked off the project.

The inventor continued to travel in South and Central America, interesting himself in various mining projects, notably in Costa Rica. Eventually his money ran out. He only made it home to England through the fortuitous chance of meeting a young man named Robert Stephenson who paid for Trevithick's passage. Robert was the son of great civil engineer, George Stephenson, who was in the process of taking Trevithick's steam engine concepts to new heights, namely the construction of the world's first railways. Trevithick himself continued to pursue new inventions on his return but died a poor man a few years later. As for the Pasco mines, despite all the challenges associated with mining at such high altitudes, Pasco remains today Peru's largest silver producing area and one of the most important in the world.

Copper, the foundation of modern Chile's economy

There is a largely misplaced sense of romantic adventure attached to the stories of gold and silver prospecting two centuries ago. As was the case in California and Australia, the men and women who were fired up with the prospects of a bonanza lying just beneath the surface of the earth faced, for the most part, only the cruellest conditions, endless labour and little, if any, pay-off. A few became rich, of course, but most of the profit, where there were sustained rewards to be banked, flowed back to the wealthy investors in the cities and abroad. The stamina and courage of those pioneers who set out with their mules into the Atacama Desert on the basis of little more than bar-room chatter and over-excited newspaper reports cannot be denied.

But neither gold nor silver created modern Chile. Copper was different. So great is the dependence of the country on this single mineral that fluctuations in its world price reflect directly and dramatically on the Chilean peso and almost every aspect of the economy. For nearly a century some of the world's largest multinational companies and some of the most admired, or notorious, capitalist barons have developed an industry that is a global leader. Chile's reserves of some 190,000 million tonnes (according to the US Geological Survey) account for nearly thirty per cent of the world's total and its 2012 mine production of 5.4 million metric tonnes confirmed the nation's control over at least one-third of the global market. The next biggest producer that year was China with 1.5 million tonnes and then Peru with 1.2 million tonnes. No other country – not even Russia and Australia – produces more than one million tonnes.

Inevitably the industry and, principally, the largest corporation, the state-owned Codelco, has extreme political importance and influence. The nationalization ("chileanization") of the foreign shares of the largest mines by the administration of President Salvador Allende in 1971 brought confrontation with the United States, notably over the lack of compensation for the American firms involved, and certainly played a part in Allende's subsequent overthrow by the army. Nevertheless, General Pinochet, despite his admiration for the private sector, did not reverse the expropriation – though his government did belatedly pay compensation

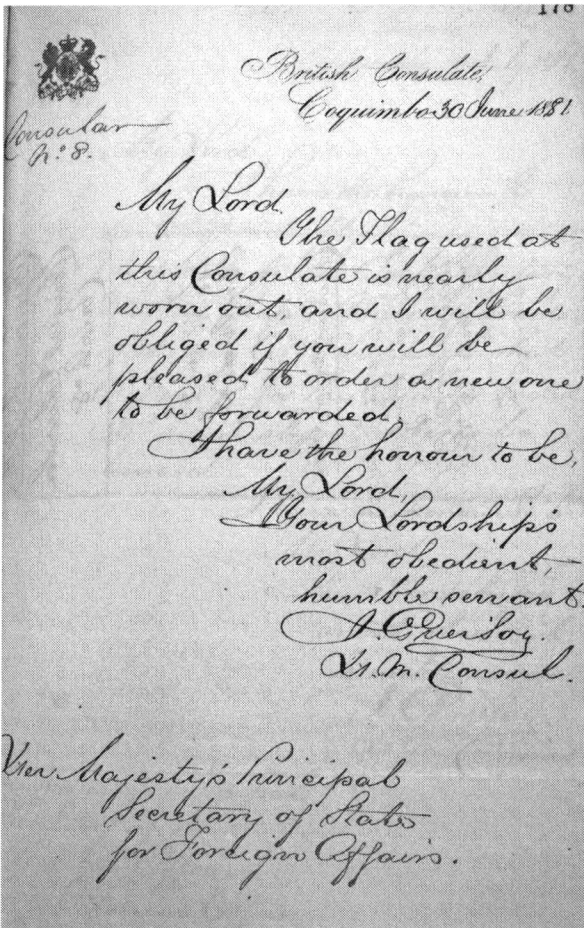

Letter from the British consul in Coquimbo to the Foreign Secretary in London, 1881, seeking a new Union flag for the consulate.

National Archive, London

– and Codelco remains a major public corporation financing much of the state's budget.

While it was not until the twentieth century that the exploitation of copper in Chile came to dominate the economy, the metal had been mined, refined and made into ornaments, tools and much else since the earliest civilisations in the region. During the colonial period copper was produced, but the focus of interest for the Spaniards was gold. The El Teniente mine near Rancagua, south of Santiago, was exploited by the Jesuits before being sold on to a succession of Spanish aristocrats. The new owners lacked interest in investing further, so the mine stagnated. After independence, and through the rest of the nineteenth century, copper output marked time: foreign investors were entranced by the nitrate boom. However, Joshua Waddington, the English capitalist, opened up deposits north of Copiapó in the 1840s and the Panucillo Copper Company of England exploited the mineral in Coquimbo. At much the same time, several British interests were engaged in copper projects around Caldera.

Charles Darwin visited the Jajuel copper mines near Quillota during his travels in Chile in 1834. Apart from noting the desperate working and living conditions of the local miners employed there, he recounted one particular improvement brought by the Cornish miners who managed the site. This was to extract, by reduction, silver from the copper pyrites which the local miners traditionally threw away as useless. The Cornishmen knew the value of that particular waste since back home its exploitation was common.

"The Chilean miners were so convinced that copper pyrites contained not a particle of copper that they laughed at the Englishmen for their ignorance, who laughed in turn, and bought their richest veins for a few dollars."

By the end of the First World War, British copper interests in Chile had declined to a total of little more than two million pesos. Investments by North American firms, on the other hand, had by then reached 115 million pesos. It was to be American capital that ignited serious, large-scale copper mining in Chile, from the beginning of the twentieth century onwards. Under what would become the Kennecott Copper Corporation, the El Teniente mine, once the source of artisanal copper tools and utensils for the Jesuit brothers, began serious production in 1904.

In 1910, the Guggenheim family established the Chile Exploration Company to produce copper from the vast Chuquicamata reserves, at an altitude of nearly 3000 metres in the Andes, close to the town of Calama, north-east of Antofagasta. This was one of the Guggenheim brothers' most profitable investments and used their own technology. When they sold out to the Anaconda

Copper Company in 1923, for US$ 70 million, the Guggenheims were con-
firmed as among the richest families in the world. It would be Anaconda and
Kennecott assets at the centre of the "chileanization" policies of the 1960s and
early 1970s. Today, as part of Codelco, the El Teniente mine employs some
5000 workers and produces nearly 450,000 tonnes of refined copper a year.
Chuquicamata's output is 340,000 tonnes with 6,500 employees.

Did the indefatigable John Miers, during his scouting of the country in the
1820s, at least have the vision to forecast the staggering success of the copper
industry in Chile? Well, in one respect he was correct in his assessment: it
would not be Englishmen who would bring this particular mineral wealth to
profitable exploitation. His confident, and negative, view was as follows:

"No expectation can be entertained by anyone acquainted with the country that the quantity of copper manufactured there can be much increased.
Any attempt to mine there [Coquimbo and Copiapó] by Englishmen, or under
English management, must fail; any show of intention to mine on an extensive scale, by foreigners, would immediately cause such an enormous advance
of wages, as would totally destroy all chance of profit, even could hands in
sufficient numbers be procured, which is impossible, to say nothing of the
expense of superintendence, tools, and buildings, and nothing of the monstrous
expense of digging coals at Concepcíon in the south and conveying them to
Coquimbo in the north of Chile. ... It seems extraordinary that many of the
persons whose names appear in these prospectuses [promoting copper mining
investment projects in London] should have permitted their insertion in such
delusive projects."

Miers' views were at least partly born of bitter personal experience. He had
only travelled to Chile, initially, as part of a speculative venture to invest in
and build copper processing plants. He was frustrated at every point, including
by what he saw as the Chilean government's failure to deliver on promises and
undertakings to facilitate the project. He had a negative view of the country,
which his comments on the likely profitability of all investment by foreigners
make no attempt to conceal. But he was perpetually wrong.

Coal for copper ore, a strange Welsh trade

Copper refining needed coal and, in the middle of the nineteenth century,
Chile had little available. True, some inefficient smelting was done on the spot,
but most of the ores were simply put on ships and sent back to Europe for smelting there. In the 1840s, coal veins near Concepción were being exploited by
Chilean mining companies, but it was Matías Cousiño – the family patriarch

who was launching vineyards using French grapes, constructing railways and mining copper in the Atacama region – who ultimately gathered the finance, expertise and manpower to exploit the great coal reserves of Lota. The town and nearby Coronel, some forty kilometres south of Concepción became synonymous with Chilean coal for more than a century. Visitors from Europe were faced with a landscape that could only have recalled the blackened pit towns of South Wales, Scotland, the Ruhr and northern France. The only London-quoted company to be formed specifically to exploit Chilean coal reserves was the Arauco Company. Thirty years after its establishment in 1885, with both railway and coalfield interests in the south, the company accounted for eleven per cent of total Chilean coal output.

So Chile continued to import coal from Britain, Australia and the United States, but mostly from Britain, which, in the early years of the twentieth century, supplied almost one million tons annually. Indeed, so great was Chile's hunger for the black gold – and so troubled its relations with neighbouring countries who might otherwise have been more natural suppliers – that the nation's diplomatic service was constantly directed to secure more coal from Britain and Australia. In the latter decades of the nineteenth century and the early years of the next, consuls in those two countries were often coal merchants or, at least, closely identified with the trade.

One end of the supply chain was South Wales, and notably the port of Swansea. By the end of the nineteenth century there was a large fleet of ships, "the copper-ore barques" as they became known, ferrying coal from South Wales to Valparaíso and returning with copper ore. In fact, the link was long-standing since Welshmen had, for decades, established and laboured in copper smelters set up in Guayacán outside the port of Coquimbo. The industrial revolution had brought lines of metal refining plants along the south coast of Wales – all dependent on the locally-mined coal. Copper mining in England itself was concentrated in the counties of Cornwall and Devon in the south-west. But each ton of copper ore needed four tons of coal to smelt it into metal. So, the location of smelters as near to coal mines as possible was an economic necessity. Thus, the copper plants of Swansea coupled with the coal pits of the South Wales valleys became the foundation for a fabulous export/import business.

It sounds enterprising, simple and profitable. It was not. The transport of coal in the holds of sailing ships and, later, steam vessels was hazardous. In essence the mariners were asked to sit on an incendiary device for three months and hope the cargo stayed quiet. It was not always the case. The near disaster of the voyage of the *British Isles* in 1905, when the crew spent four days battling a coal fire beneath the deck, was told in Chapter 1. Thirty years earlier, the loss of the wooden coal-barque *Patmos* provided another tragic seaman's tale.

Commanded by Captain Charles Nichols, the American-built ship set out from Cardiff laden with coal for Valparaíso. Eight weeks out, gales struck as it approached Cape Horn, forcing the barque on a southwards track. Despite the cold, intense smoke was suddenly noticed in the fo'c'sle[3]. The coal below had ignited spontaneously. It was smouldering and somewhere at the centre of the cargo was a glowing core of burning carbon. The crew battened down the deck hatches, the captain steered on to a northerly course but a heavy, icy westerly wind was driving the ship backwards, away from the Cape. Despite being

The new East Dock at Swansea was opened by the Prince of Wales in October 1881 to handle the "copper-ore barques" from Coquimbo which were sent back to Chile laden with Welsh coal.

The Illustrated London News

awash, the deck seams began to leak as the pitch sealing them melted from the heat below. The cabins had to be evacuated as the fire between the decks ravaged the vessel; the charred hatch covers eventually gave way to the pounding of the storm allowing water to flood in. As recounted[4] by a modern expert on

3   The forward part of the upper deck, the forecastle, in which the sailors' quarters were often located.

4   See www.headline.org.uk/maritime-history/

Welsh maritime history, Viv Head:

"The scene, as night came on with the wind roaring above the furnace, was terrible in the extreme. Never had such a more distressed ship struggled against the elements. Flashes of fire streamed to leeward in showers of sparks; spars cracked; the stay sails were afire. Only the long white slits of the lower topsails showed above the hell below. How long would it be before the masts burnt through?"

The following morning, the longboat was launched, the captain carried his wife who was wrapped in oilskins, and the exhausted, soot-covered crew began to row away from the *Patmos* whose survival was already nearly hopeless. Even as the waves appeared to be dousing the flames, columns of smoke spelt the end as the barque sank lower in the water with the crew looking on disconsolately from a distance. Now, their job was to keep the long-boat afloat as the storm raged around them. They fought till the following dawn, baling frantically and rowing as they could. Finally they spotted a shoreline of mountains – the coast of Tierra del Fuego.

Relief was only reinforced when the cry went up: "Sail ho! Sail ho!" A rusting, iron-hulled British merchant ship, *Pretricia*, also carrying Welsh coal to Chile, had been spotted. It took several hours of manoeuvring the longboat in the roiling surf before Mrs Nichols, the crew and, finally, Captain Nichols, were hauled on board. Yet, they were far from safe. The *Pretricia* itself had been fighting for hours to avoid being dragged by the storm on to rocks to the west of Cape Horn. The crew was close to collapse with the effort. However, with their numbers suddenly reinforced a new determination filled the vessel. Additional sails, though sodden from the wash, were laboriously raised to the masts. The iron sailing ship was turned into the wind, groaning under the strain, leaning frighteningly close to the waves, but finally making way under the dogged insistence of her men. They passed the Cape and sailed on. Against all the odds, they all made it to Valparaíso.

The extremity of such a trial of human stamina and endeavour was perhaps not the norm for the ships bringing coal to Valparaíso and returning to Wales with copper ore. Still, it was representative of the kind of risks taken by ordinary men and women to turn what appeared an attractive paper transaction into solid, but painful, reality.

Valparaiso Bound!

11.

Booms, bubbles, busts …
and a bombardment

At last we rounded that stormy cape,
Fair nights and pleasant days.
The next place that we anchor
Will be Valparaiso Bay.
For there the girls will welcome you,
I solemnly declare,
For they're not much like the Liverpool girls
with their curls and glossy hair.

Traditional sailor's song

In 1720, Valparaíso was nothing but a shabby harbour with a village attached, not at all the 'Jewel of the Pacific' as it would one day be known. For the few goods that arrived by ship legally – largely from Lima's port, Callao, since it was only the capital of the viceroyalty that had the right to trade – there was not even a customs house; all merchandise had to be taken by mule along the dusty meandering track to Santiago.

Commerce within the empire had been stifled, if not definitively asphyxiated, for two centuries; the Spanish monarchy practised the most extreme form of mercantilist protectionism. What was absolutely necessary for the upkeep, defence and survival of the conquistadors flowed one way, and gold – as the royal preference – flowed the other. The first era of globalization and free trade needed the end of the empire. In the meantime, the ructions among the royal houses of the Old Continent, and the succession of wars and treaties they provoked, had transatlantic and Pacific trade – the control of sea routes and raw materials globally – as a vital sub-plot. And as the British, the Dutch, the Habsburgs and the Bourbons fought it out, half the world away pirates, privateers and contraband merchants profited from the absence of enforceable rules and strong naval forces policing the seas and ports.

From the end of the fifteenth century, Spain had regarded commerce with the Indies as a colonial monopoly – sanctioned by the Pope in Rome through papal bulls in 1493. Its control over trade routes was absolute. All commercial traffic with the colonies was controlled from Seville as the sole designated port in the mother country. From that city the annual cargo convoy, the *'Flota de Indias',* departed for the ports of Veracruz in Mexico, Portobelo (Panama) and Cartagena (Colombia). Goods destined for the viceroyalty of Peru had to be hauled overland. When the Strait of Magellan and, later, the passage round Cape Horn became options for sea captains it was the British, but even more so the French, who took advantage. Few Spanish merchant ships were prepared to risk the new direct routes. William Bretagh, a British naval officer, wrote of the problem in his book on a circumnavigation starting in 1719. Belittling the skills and courage of Spanish sailors in taking on the southerly routes, he commented:

"The great advantage of the trade of Chili this way is so manifest, that his Catholic majesty is obliged by treaties to shut out all nations from it, as well as the English, though he makes nothing of it himself: and it's very rare that a Spanish ship has gone by Cape Horne. From hence arises the extraordinary price all European goods fetch at Chili and Peru: I have been told at Lima that they are often sold at 400 per cent profit; and I may say the goods that are carried from France by Cape Horne are in themselves 50 per cent better than those that go in the Flota from Cadiz[1] to Cartagena or Veracruz: because the former are delivered fresh and undamaged in six months, whereas the others are generally eighteen months before they can come to Chili: so that the French ... made their markets, furnished themselves with provisions, and got home again in twelve or fourteen months' time."

In the early eighteenth century, trade by enthusiastic French merchants was theoretically forbidden in the Spanish colonies: confiscation, large fines and even imprisonment were the fate of French smugglers, at least according to the regulations. In reality, French luxury goods were enjoyed in all the best homes and families. Despite the trade ban some forty French ships were peacefully plying the Chilean coast in 1715. According to G F Scott Elliot:

"Their trade in European and especially French goods kept on expanding, year by year, and the whole social and intellectual life of Chile began to be affected by that tincture of French culture which is still obvious."

French sea captains would be thrown in prison for smuggling, only to bribe their way out quickly. While dreadful penalties would be announced publicly,

---

1   By the time of the Bretagh voyage, Spain's designated port for trade with the colonies had been moved from Seville to Cadiz.

it was alleged that even the governor was making 30 or 40 per cent on the illicit sale of smuggled goods. Locally, there was little public or political pressure to do otherwise: understandably, French smugglers were far more popular than the English pirates.

It was not that the governments in Madrid did not realize what was happening, to the detriment of the monarchy and its empire. But reforming the system was a challenge and it took something close to military and political catastrophe to secure even the smallest steps. The trigger was the War of Spanish Succession of 1702-13 which ultimately settled the disputed throne of Spain. Initially, the dying king, Charles II, named Philip of Anjou, the grandson of the Bourbon Louis XIV of France as his successor. Fearing the potential power of a united Spain and France, the English, Dutch and Portuguese backed the rival claim of Archduke Charles of Austria, a Habsburg. Their allied forces seized Gibraltar in 1704, and Barcelona with Valencia and Zaragosa fell two years later. Archduke Charles installed his court in Barcelona. Madrid was taken the following year.

Lima's busy port, Callao, in the 17th century.

That was probably the high point for the Habsburg alliance. In 1707, a Spanish-French force routed the English, Portuguese and Dutch at the Battle of Almansa. While the French suffered defeats in Italy and the Netherlands, and Louis XIV temporarily was forced to withdraw troops from his engagement in Spain, Philip fought on. When the French returned to battle in 1710, following the failure of peace talks, the English and Austrians suffered heavy losses, finally convincing Charles – who took the Habsburg throne on the death of Emperor Joseph in 1711 – that he could not win militarily and that the unification of the Habsburg and Bourbon empires might be a good alternative. This was anathema to the English. Peace was restored through the Treaties of Utrecht in 1713. That left only the Catalans resisting Bourbon domination until Barcelona was retaken by Philip's army in 1715.

Valparaiso Bound!

Spanish strangle-hold on commerce is broken

The Treaties of Utrecht divided up Europe but left Philip with his Latin American empire intact. The British were satisfied by being granted a monopoly on the slave trade with Spanish colonies and the right to send one 500-ton ship each year to the trade fairs in Veracruz and Portobelo – thus beginning to break the grip of Spain on transatlantic commerce with Central and South America. Portugal's claim to the Colônia do Sacramento on the Río de Plata (now in Uruguay), was recognized, opening a crucial door for contraband that could find its way across the Andes. Moreover, the French were already entering ports on the Pacific side, having been granted that concession by Philip during the war in order that Spanish colonies would continue to be supplied. They continued to trade illegally after hostilities ended.

Even if the empire and the throne were secure, the Spanish economy had collapsed, the monarchy was riddled with debt, its trade was depleted and the navy was no longer capable of defending all the nation's interests across the world. Reform was inevitable. Initially, changes were steered by one of the King's court favourites, Cardinal Julio Alberoni, and subsequently his protégé, José Patiño who headed the Ministry of the Marine and the Indies. Alberoni sought to dismantle the concessions made in the Treaties of Utrecht and to stamp out contraband. However, it was little more than the pretence of reform, while continued clashes provoked by the ambition of the Bourbons to take back territory in Europe diluted the impact of even those minor steps. Another round of commercial reforms began in the 1740s, but they continued to be more focused on reinforcing Spain's grip on legal trade across the Atlantic and in the Pacific and the suppression of contraband than opening up to competitors. Revenues from royal monopolies on the sale and distribution of commodities like tobacco filled the King's coffers, at least for a while. Further limited reforms were introduced as the century went on, with several new ports being opened up for trade with Spain. Valdivia, Valparaíso Talcahuano and Coquimbo in Chile were finally permitted to welcome Spanish – but only Spanish – vessels. Additionally, the colonies were granted some rights to trade with each other.

A century after the first Bourbon reforms, with Spain's hold on the region broken, Captain Basil Hall of the Royal Navy could look back on the practical realities of trade in the colonial era in his 1826 account of a voyage during the years 1820-23. It was a scathing judgment:

"The old principle that the colonies existed only for the benefit of the mother country, was acted up to completely. The sole objects thought of were to gather wealth into the hands of Spaniards by abstracting the riches of South America;

198

and to take care that the Americans neither supplied themselves with any article which Spain could possibly produce, nor obtained these supplies from any but Spaniards."

Hall's more analytical assessment of the barriers placed on doing trade, or even simply residing, in the region showed the protectionist extremes to which the Spanish had gone, with or without the Bourbon reforms. According to the English naval officer no South American could own a ship, nor could a cargo be consigned to him; no foreigner was allowed to reside in the country, unless born in Spain; no financial capital, not Spanish, was permitted to be employed

Valparaiso Bay in 1859.   *The Illustrated London News*

in these colonies; and, normally, no foreign vessel, on any pretence, was able to touch at a South American port. Foreign ships in distress were to be seized as prizes and the crews imprisoned. Even ships in difficulties that anchored off Juan Fernández Island were to be treated that way. The viceroy was furious when one United States ship not only was given aid, but permitted to leave. He subsequently ordered the intendants of ports on the Peruvian coast to herd cattle and other farm animals inland if there was any danger of the crew of a foreign vessel, seeking supplies, taking advantage of them.

The self-defeating end-result of this system was piracy and contraband, conducted by ships of other nations, on an ever-growing scale. As Hall put it:

"This singular system of warlike commerce was conducted by the Dutch, Portuguese, French, English, and latterly by the North Americans. In this way, goods to an immense value were distributed over South America, and although the prices were necessarily high, and the supply precarious, that taste for the comforts and luxuries of European invention was first encouraged which afterwards operated so powerfully in giving a steady and intelligible motive to the efforts of the patriots."

Given that these restrictive commercial policies had amounted to little more than a self-inflicted wound over nearly three centuries of Spanish rule, it is hardly surprising that one of the earliest acts of an "independent" Chilean government (the junta administration), in 1811 (see Chapter 5), was to throw open its ports to trade with the world. This was the nation's first law to be enacted. Even if contraband trade continued and, for some years, frustrated the eventual benefits of free-trade, the economy was transformed; nothing would ever be the same. It was the clearest possible break with colonial practices.

Certainly, the national commitment to free trade experienced some turbulence, especially in the early years as near-bankruptcy from the independence struggle forced significant hikes in customs tariffs to pay debts. Later, duties and taxes were set to protect domestic industries like footwear, clothing, wheat and meat. Still, the political system and the economy stabilized in the 1830s and the administration of President Diego Portales cemented solid reforms. Among them was the consolidation of Valparaíso as the principal port on the Pacific coast. The town's great bay became the crowded gathering point for ships flying the flags of nearly every nation on earth.

A Welshman starts a banking dynasty

International commerce still needed two conditions to thrive: healthy banks and ready investors. In the immediate aftermath of independence there was no banking system and few investors. But as the potential for developing natural resources was recognized, so the financial system evolved even if, for decades, Chile had to rely largely on foreign, and especially British, capital. Trade was made possible initially by letters of credit drawn on European banks and issued through the trading houses that sprang up in Valparaíso and other ports. By 1827, Waddington, Templeman y Cia., was already active in the city as was Andrew Blest, a founder of the British commercial presence in Valparaíso. Both Joshua Waddington and Blest married into wealthy Chilean families.

Commercial banks were not long coming. Since the development of mining, railways and shipping services on the Pacific coast – as in most of rest of South

America – was supported mainly by capital raised in the City of London, it is not surprising that British banks arrived early. However, the pioneering days in Chile and Peru were dominated by a Chilean of British descent whose vast dynastic family wealth and influence has marked Chile until the present day. Combinations of names like Edwards, Ross, Eastman, MacClure and Ossandón are found everywhere at the summit of politics and business, the press and civic organizations, as well as being inscribed on the most lavish mausoleums to be seen in the grandest cemetery plots in Chile.

It was the family's patriarch, John Edwards, a young Welsh doctor serving as ship's surgeon aboard British privateers, who first landed in Coquimbo in 1804 and was drawn by love to stay. It seems to have been a genuinely romantic start to a near-monarchic dynasty. During the looting of the town, Edwards found himself in the house of Diego de Ossandón with whose daughter, Isabel, he was besotted instantly. He decided to desert his ship and, by one account, spent three days hiding in a wine vat in the house while the rest of his crewmates scoured the town in his pursuit. The arrival of Spanish reinforcements drove the English vessel back out to sea and Edwards was duly arrested. Released the following year, he married Isabel in 1807. The couple had a large family and John worked for years in La Serena as a doctor while building the beginnings of a fortune lending to local miners prospecting silver and copper in the Coquimbo area.

The wealth amassed allowed Edwards, who detested the Spanish, to fund the independence movement. In particular, he donated substantially to the funding of the naval fleet that would be commanded by Lord Thomas Cochrane. He was rewarded in 1818 by Supreme Director O'Higgins who presented him with citizenship papers. Later he became a deputy in the national assembly. His son, one of eight children from his marriage to Isabel, Agustín Edwards-Ossandón had been born in 1815 and was destined to become the richest man in Chile. Agustín started early, supposedly rearing chickens and selling eggs at the age of eleven; by the time he was seventeen he had enough capital to lend it out to silver prospectors crowding into the region after the first discoveries in Chañarcillo. At that stage, there were no banks in Chile. Edwards was regarded as a man of such integrity and prudence that he could carry on what amounted to banking operations solely on the basis of confidence in his word and his hand-shake. However, in 1851, already resident in Valparaíso, he founded what became Chile's longest surviving bank, Sociedad A. Edwards y Cía. – now part of Citibank. He added branches in several northern mining towns and continued to prosper, not only through banking but with investments in copper, silver and, as a partner of William Wheelwright, in the early railways.

Quickly other local banks sprang up in Valparaíso and Santiago, most based on mixed Chilean and British capital. But the need to finance the flourishing trade in raw materials between Latin America, Europe and the United States, as well as a series of speculative investment 'bubbles', attracted large European institutions. Early entrants were the London and River Plate Bank and the London and Brazilian Bank in 1862, followed a year later by the British Bank of South America, the English Bank of Rio de Janeiro and the London Bank of Mexico and South America. As the booms receded so banks went bust or merged to form some of the giant groups of today.

Lloyds Bank, for instance, brought together significant operations in South America originating with the London and River Plate Bank and the London and Brazilian Bank. Both firms managed to survive a devastating financial crisis that hit Argentina in 1890, and during the First World War they financed allied trade with South America. In 1923, with Lloyds Bank having acquired a controlling stake in both, the two banks merged to form the famous Bank of London and South America (BOLSA). In 1936, BOLSA took over the Anglo-South American Bank, which had once been the Bank of Tarapaca and London, established by John Thomas North, the 'Nitrate King', to support his investments in the saltpetre industry. That institution had developed additional interests in coffee and cocoa, and in 1923, before the Great Depression took its toll on business, had acquired a 60 per cent stake in Banco A. Edwards y Cie. BOLSA became a major financial player in Valparaíso and would remain so, finally being integrated fully into Lloyds Bank's international operations, having, along the way, merged with merchant traders Balfour, Williamson & Co.

Why would anyone put their money there?

As we have already noted, the Englishman John Miers had personal reasons for his scepticism about the scope for profitable investment in Chile:

"I should lament to hear that any British capitalist, however flattering the offers made to him, should invest his capital in any enterprise upon the soil of Chile: having myself failed in such an attempt, from impediments that exists in the country, together with the absurd obstacles opposed by the general and local authorities, as well as the obstinate jealousies of the natives, notwithstanding all the flattering inducements that were held out, and the outward show of protection afforded in an especial manner to me individually."

Thankfully, nobody took much notice of the sour and gloomy Miers. In the decades after his departure, investment poured into the region from Europe and as the century drew towards its close, North Americans also were also ploughing money into mining projects and railways.

Just how great was the British financial commitment? By the end of December 1909, over £766 million of British capital was invested in Hispanic America as a whole. This included almost £290 million in municipal and government bonds and over £18 million in banks and shipping companies. With interest in mining on the decline, nearly half of this capital was placed in railways. As a comparison, in 1914, British investment in continental Europe was just 28% of that in South America. Investments in Chile, specifically, occupied either fourth or fifth place in the regional league table of popular targets for British-sourced financing. Much of the riskier speculative capital headed for Chile was raised through offerings in the City of London. At the end of January 1909, the total quoted on the London Stock Exchange was £44 million[2] of which nearly £15 million was in railroads, over £8 million in nitrates and associated investments, and over £20 million in government bonds. By 1911 British publicly subscribed investments in Chile were put at £46 million (half those in Brazil and around a quarter higher than those in Peru and Uruguay). By 1913 the total was something over £61 million. Chile continued to fight above its weight as an investment target thereafter, a reflection of its atypical political stability.

Travellers were often struck by the proliferation of familiar British company names. Arriving with John Thomas North at Coquimbo in 1889, the English journalist William Howard Russell was astounded by the number of British insurance companies he counted in the town: South British, London Imperial, London Corporation, Lancashire, Queen, Commercial, Union, Northern and the Chilian Valparaíso Company.

Still, it was the great trading houses that finally made sense of all the investments. Without them – and they were as much French, German, Italian and Spanish as British – the newly-discovered minerals, wheat and other bulk products would have had no markets and no organized shipping services to reach them. In the following pages, we will look at two such firms.

"The Turds of Foreign Birds": Guano and the story of Gibbs

The London firm of Antony Gibbs & Sons was one of the early commercial houses active on the Pacific coast. The company's story is well told in W M Mathew's "The House of Gibbs and the Peruvian Guano Monopoly". It was a business founded on sea-bird droppings. That Gibbs ended up making a

---

2   As much as £40 billion in investment value today.

fortune from the substance provoked a popular rhyme in the City of London:

"The house of Gibbs that made their dibs
By selling turds of foreign birds"

Guano is a very rich nitrogenous fertilizer. In the decades before saltpetre-based nitrates from the Atacama Desert became dominant, fortunes were made based on centuries of excrement deposited on the shores and islands of the neighbouring Pacific coast. These fertilizers were almost as sought-after as gold and provoked no less trouble: men fought over them or died in the struggle to exploit them; governments tumbled and speculators filled their pockets.

It was not until 1840 that the cash-strapped Peruvian government finally took serious advantage of this valuable natural resource and signed a contract for its exploitation with a Peruvian entrepreneur named Don Francisco Quiros.

Guano ships at anchor around the Chincha Islands, Peru, 1863.

The Illustrated London News

He was backed in the venture by several French firms and the Liverpool trader William Myers & Co, a company that would become one of Valparaíso's leading commercial houses. Myers had been instrumental in the decision to set up a venture for guano exports to Great Britain. At the request of the entrepreneurs in Lima, Horace Bland, an English merchant in Valparaíso, had handed on samples of Peruvian guano for testing by farmers in Britain. Myers, with extensive farming interests and contacts, quickly concluded that the product could make money and offered financial backing.

The first contract provided an export monopoly to the consortium in the export of guano to foreign markets for an initial period of six years. The terms proved a give-away by the Peruvian state. On the other hand, getting the new product accepted by farmers in Britain was slow: it may have been a uniquely high-quality fertilizer, but it was also expensive (at around £25 a ton) in comparison to the crushed animal bones which were in common use at the time.

Inevitably, news of the very high prices being paid by British farmers for the few shipments so far landed, compared to the low contract price accepted by the government, soon became a source of grievance in Lima. A second contract, much less favourable to the companies, had to be drawn up within a year – the Peruvian state, having declared war on Bolivia, was in need of funds. At that point Gibbs – established in both Peru and Chile since the early 1820s – began to show a discreet interest. The local representative was courted to participate but, under pressure from the London base, he declined. On seeing the terms a few weeks after signature, the head of the firm, William Gibbs, wrote to his man in Lima to: "*Congratulate* you on your *failure*, your non-success a great relief to us..."

Yet, the firm's diffidence would not last another twelve months. Not only did the Peruvian government need to raise yet more funds from its guano resources, but the original consortium could go no further in advancing loans against guano exports. A firm with greater financial standing, preferably one deeply embedded in the City of London had to be part of the deal. Gibbs would share the sales monopoly with Myers who, in turn, were starting to go cold on the trade. The new terms were tougher than ever, the balance of advantage probably swinging towards the Peruvians. Another 200,000 pesos were duly provided up front. In London, William Gibbs, unable this time to contain the enthusiasm of the Lima branch, described the transaction as "an act of insanity".

In the words of a British diplomat of the time, the Peruvian government had simply taken advantage "of the avidity of the Monopolists and Speculators." It had played off the firms against each other, by quietly injecting a degree of competition amongst those wanting a slice of the action. With profitability now in question, the consortium was hit further by the fall in British wheat prices in the early 1840s. Farmers shied away from expensive fertilizers. The slowly evolving British market for guano was quickly swamped. Myers favoured hanging on with high prices for their product, gambling that farmers would eventually buy up stocks; Gibbs wanted to cut prices and stimulate the market. Whichever direction they went, they had no chance of selling enough guano to get a return on the advances already paid to the Peruvians. They needed a contract extension. After a lot of haggling in Lima, they got one for three years on top of their existing five.

Yet neither firm was in control of its future. What was becoming a guano glut was worsened with the discovery of new supplies much nearer the market, on a tiny island called Ichaboe off the south-west coast of Africa. Within a few months hundreds of ships were plying the new guano – albeit of a slightly inferior quality to the Peruvian product. In the year 1845, African imports of guano, mostly from Ichaboe, reached prodigious levels. As shipments from Peru and Bolivia fell drastically, the monopoly seemed worthless and prices collapsed.

Happily for Gibbs, the African challenge did not last. Supplies from Ichaboe declined almost as soon as they had reached their 1845 peak; it was a bubble and the bubble burst with over-exploitation – there was no commercially worthwhile guano left. There were, however, huge stocks in the UK and no likelihood of their being quickly cleared. There was no choice but for Myers and Gibbs to allow the price of their Peruvian guano to fall. It dropped below the £10 a ton level and with that Myers decided that enough was enough; the company wanted out of the business and told Gibbs so in late 1847. In parallel, the Peruvians continued to outplay the various French and British interests in concocting terms for new contracts. Their economy was fragile, badly managed and heavily indebted, yet Lima tied down more large loans in London, secured on export rights for guano.

One by one the original players, including Myers, abandoned the guano game. As the 1840s ended, Gibbs was on its own controlling the British market. In principle it was a highly advantageous position; large farmers in England and Scotland were increasingly convinced of the value of the fertilizer, and scientific evidence backed up their experience. In the decade from 1850, there would be a boom and then a slump. The 1849 Peruvian contract gave Gibbs a monopoly not just in Britain but almost the entire European market, excluding France and Spain. That arrangement would eventually be extended until the end of 1861. A new advance, of $400,000 was required by the Peruvian government to be followed by others estimated at up to $2million. But, unlike previous arrangements, there was no limit on how much guano could be shipped. Henry Gibbs, now head of the company in London, commented: "if we can carry away the islands[3] bodily before 18 December 1861, we have strictly the right to do so."

But the deal caused heavy political fallout. In Lima, it was largely hidden from the Congress. President José Echenique was overthrown in January 1855 and the new Congress demanded the contract be terminated. However, given the relative benefits of the relationship with Gibbs, not only did the new head

---

3 Principally the Chincha Islands off south-west Peru.

of state, Ramón Castilla, do almost nothing to amend the terms, let alone end the contract, he extended the monopoly such that Gibbs now commanded the French and French colonial markets. Shortly after, the British trading house got Spain too. For better or worse, Gibbs and the Peruvian government were bound together in a marriage of convenience and profit that would prove painful to break.

Between 1850 and 1860, Gibbs dispatched a total of 3051 ships from the Chincha Islands containing nearly two million tons of guano. There was no doubt that it commanded a premium position in the agricultural markets of Europe, and especially Britain. The *Farmer's Magazine* bestowed near mystical powers on the fertilizer in one issue of 1854:

"If ever the philosopher's stone, the elixir of life, the infallible Catholicism, the universal solvent or the perpetual motion were discovered, it is the application of guano in agriculture."

Yet the elixir was expensive and the Gibbs monopoly was a politically explosive issue at both ends of the chain. The Peruvian government pressed the firm to push up the price still further even though farmers in Europe were already having to pay more as demand increased and stocks wound down. Naturally, the farmers – and especially those large land-owners who sat in the British Parliament – wanted to lower costs, particularly as wheat and other commodity prices were falling in tandem in the early 1850s. Sir Robert Peel, the great reforming Prime-Minister of Britain, who had by then retired to the life of a farming landlord, wrote to the Foreign Secretary, Lord Palmerston, in 1849, complaining that high guano prices were harmful. He believed that ending the Gibbs monopoly would force prices down from around £10 a ton to nearer £6 a ton. Peel could not be ignored; instructions were sent to the British *chargé d'affaires* in Lima to act on the complaint. Inevitably, the President Castilla refused to budge – his exchequer and debt repayment were the priorities.

The diplomat's report back to London concluded that the only answer was to find new sources of guano or alternative fertilizer products. But there was also the question of the Lobos Islands. One activist member of the Royal Agricultural Society who also happened to be a naval officer, Thomas Wentworth Buller, had rediscovered references to these small islands off the North coast of Peru which had been shown to have large guano deposits. He wrote to Palmerston claiming that the islands were not controlled by Peru and that a British warship should be dispatched to protect any merchant vessel loading guano there. Neither Palmerston nor his successor as Foreign Secretary, Lord Malmesbury, wished to provoke a diplomatic incident, if not a war, on such a flimsy claim.

Valparaiso Bound!

But Buller persisted into 1852, dragging in opposition politicians behind his position. He wrote to *The Times*, insisting that Peru had no legal claim to the islands and was operating a guano monopoly "injurious to the whole civilized world"[4]. The Peruvian embassy in London insisted not only that the islands were within Peru's jurisdiction but that its navy patrolled the waters around. Unmoved, shippers and traders in Liverpool and Aberdeen prepared to send merchant vessels to take the Lobos guano and demanded the protection of the Royal Navy. Farmers excitedly backed the proposal.

Finally, a powerful delegation including Buller, for the Royal Agricultural Society, and some of the biggest and most influential landowners in the country met the Prime Minister, Lord Derby, on 11 June, 1852. The Prime Minister listened patiently but then told the group firmly that, like it or not, Britain had no claim on the Lobos Islands which were entirely in the hands of Peru. The delegation left Downing Street defeated, dejected and with nothing other than an assurance that naval captains would be advised to include the identification of guano deposits in their various surveying activities around the world.

At the end of 1856, Gibbs and the Peruvians raised the price of guano again, to £13 a ton. The market reacted badly. Sales in Britain halved the following year and, although there was some recovery, the peak was passed and the end of the guano era was in sight. Alternative products, like superphosphates, were cheaper for farmers. Nitrate from saltpetre would soon be the predominant fertilizer product exported from South

By the 1920s, Gibbs & Co. were importing everything from Paraffin wax to expensive French Champagne. *South Pacific Mail*

America.

The Gibbs contract terminated at the end of 1861 and the firm had little interest in seeking another. It was clear that trading rights for guano would now pass, in large part, towards Peruvian companies. The prevailing political sentiment in Lima would not permit a continuation of monopolies based on European interests. Gibbs management shed few tears. The company had risen to be one of the foremost houses of the City of London, largely on the back of the guano trade. Now it would concentrate on financial transactions, and prosper. One branch of Gibbs thrived as a merchant house in Valparaíso and the firm engaged in the saltpetre industry that would shortly boom.

The guano trade continued to be crucial for Peru at least into the 1870s. Between 1851 and 1872, a total of more than ten million tons of first-class guano was extracted from the Chincha Islands, mostly for export and worth, according to a 1913 estimate, about three-quarters of a billion dollars. It was a dirty trade in more ways than one. As well as the smell, the deposit had to be chipped or often blasted off the rocks. The heat was almost unbearable and the overseers charged with keeping the labourers at their toil as brutal as could be found anywhere. So bad were the conditions that poor, local natives would often not take on the work. The business depended on slavery. Not black slaves from Africa – although emancipation was not fully enacted in Peru for three decades after independence – but Chinese coolies. Estimates suggest that some 100,000 slave workers were sent from China to Peru between 1849 and 1873, with as many as ten per cent being lost during sea passages every bit as horrific as those suffered by African slaves in the centuries before. It was a scandal taken up by the British government, but not so forcefully as to disturb Gibbs's business overmuch.

Three Scottish adventurers build a business empire

If the early days of Gibbs' South American adventure were firmly entrenched in Peru, those of another solid British trading firm, Balfour, Williamson and Co., were associated with Valparaíso in the second half of the nineteenth century. Whereas Gibbs made a fortune from trade in guano, Balfour, Williamson would do so largely from the exploitation of saltpetre nitrate in Chile, Bolivia and Peru.

According to the company's official history, *"Heirs of Great Adventure"* by Wallis Hunt, the partnership was first established in Liverpool in 1851. Three young Scotsmen, Alexander Balfour, Stephen Williamson and David Duncan, thought they could make money shipping goods to the West coast of South

America. They were bright but poor; it would be for Stephen Williamson's uncle, William Lawson, to put up the £10,000 necessary to start business in Liverpool and Valparaíso.

Initially, Balfour stayed in Liverpool while Williamson and Duncan voyaged to Valparaíso to establish offices there – Duncan surviving a near-shipwreck, an engine-room fire and yellow fever on the way. At the start, they concentrated on shipping textiles and clothing. Although their very first shipment ended up in San Francisco by error, causing the new house heavy losses, they soon gained the confidence of manufacturers in the north of England, of whom their financial sponsor, William Lawson, was one. To be profitable they needed a two-way trade; soon they began to send cargoes of nitrate, guano and wool back to Liverpool.

It was not easy. The two sides of the firm quarrelled incessantly. Costs at the Liverpool end ran out of control in a bad economic environment with Britain suffering the impact of the Crimean War and the 'Indian Mutiny'. Profitable trading in Valparaíso, on the other hand, grew quickly, almost as quickly as the ambitions of the two local partners. Unfortunately they over-reached themselves and a financial crisis ensued. The firm's ruin was barely averted.

There was upheaval among the partners so Stephen Williamson returned to England to rebuild the business. While doing so, he married Annie Guthrie, the daughter of a well-known preacher from Edinburgh. He returned to Chile soon after and, at the same time, the other two partners swapped places. Alexander Balfour took a passage to Chile while David Duncan returned to England, preceded by his invalid wife and two children, to run the Liverpool office. Nevertheless, the bad feeling between Balfour and Duncan continued. Duncan believed his partner had been incompetent in handling the financial crisis, and ultimately declared that he could no longer work with Balfour. Williamson felt he had no option but to dissolve the partnership. He also could not avoid making a painful choice between his two old friends and business companions. After much heart-searching, he opted for the older, more conservative Balfour rather than the adventurous Duncan. Still, Duncan soon made good: he joined H F Fox, a partner in Ravenscroft Brothers which had been active in Valparaíso since 1843, to form Duncan, Fox and Company.

Balfour, Williamson y Cie. became the standard-bearer for the company in Chile. By 1865, Williamson convinced himself that the company needed a presence in North America and that it was for him to steer the process. He left Valparaíso for ever, in October of that year, on the last merchant vessel to leave the port before the Spanish blockade that lasted until April the following year (see below). Back in Liverpool, he oversaw the assessment of the proposal to set up an office in San Francisco given the impending arrival of the new railroad from the US East coast and the huge potential for trading wheat and other commodities. In 1869, two young managers from the Liverpool office established Balfour, Guthrie and Co, in the Californian boom-town. The company would become a significant player in the opening up and development of the American West.

Alexander Balfour himself occupied the Williamsons' 'home on the hill' on Cerro Alegre in Valparaíso until 1868 when he returned to Liverpool, at a point when both ends of the business were thriving. Later, the firm expanded into new activities in Chile: it owned and operated a flour mill and then vegetable oil mills; it became an agent for British insurance companies and stepped up its engagements in shipping nitrate, copper and other ores. The company became especially active in the nitrate industry, exploiting its own concessions and establishing an office in Iquique. However, as high prices plummeted in the 1880s, the firm quickly reversed its commitment and pulled out. Balfour, Williamson also gathered shares in merchant ships. By 1876, it had some twenty vessels plying routes across the globe.

Back home in Scotland, Stephen Williamson was elected to Parliament as a Liberal in April 1880 – for the constituency where he had been born, St Andrews in Fife. He pursued causes dear to his heart, including the welfare and conditions of merchant seamen. By this time it was Williamson's sons who had taken the reins of the firm in Valparaíso and San Francisco, and they would eventually become partners. While the mid-1880s were difficult for business, the firm went on seeking new opportunities in Chile. In 1888, Stephen Williamson agreed with the Valparaíso partners that the company needed a presence in the newly developing territories of southern Chile. They opened the 'Bodegas de Trigo' in Traiguén for wheat trading and an office in Concepción for general trading through the port of Talcahuano. They also built a flour mill at Concepción.

Alexander Balfour died in 1886 after a battle with cancer and was honoured locally in Liverpool. Stephen Williamson finally lost his parliamentary seat in 1895. He fell ill in 1900 and retired from business a year later. He died in June 1903, just before his seventy-sixth birthday. Writing to William Henderson, one of the early employees and later partners in Valparaíso, he concluded:

"I arrived in Chile in May 1852 – a long, long time ago. If I had to begin my career again, I could not choose one which would be more in harmony with my tastes and feelings and, perhaps I might add, aptitudes. I have always liked my work."

He had started with a loan of £5000 and, when he retired, the various trading houses that then comprised the firm, especially those in Chile, probably commanded a collective capital of around £1 million.

Stephen Williamson departed Valparaíso just as a Spanish fleet was imposing a blockade on the old port. The story of the blockade, and the bombardment that followed six months later, on 31 March 1866, is one of the stranger episodes in the history of European involvement in Peru and Chile, in the nineteenth century. It has been explored in detail by this author in a previous book[5]. But it is worth retelling briefly here before moving on to more serious and tragic events that reflected European – especially British – business influence in the political and economic affairs of the two countries.

An insulted Spanish queen burns down Valparaíso

In 1864 a small Spanish fleet seized Peru's Chincha Islands and took control of the guano industry. By that time, Gibbs had already given up the trade which had passed largely into the hands of the Peruvians themselves. The export revenues being generated continued to be vital for the country's economy and for the repayment of its large debts abroad. At the time, Spain's economy was also in shreds with the monarchy desperate to restore its standing in Europe; the loss of an empire and political instability at home had reduced the nation to a secondary power of little interest to the rest of the continent. Its new adventure in the Pacific, which would last until the middle of 1866, was a last-gasp attempt at playing in the senior league of nations.

The Spanish vessels – comprising what was initially vaunted as a 'scientific expedition' – had received a friendly welcome in Valparaíso in 1863, before continuing north to Callao in Peru, Panama and San Francisco. On its return voyage, with several of its scientists having been lost through illness or chosen to go their own ways, the fleet was joined by a murky figure, named Don Eusebio de Salazar y Mazarredo. Determined to punish Peru – at a time when Spain considered that its old colony should have been paying reparations for the impertinence of being independent – Salazar set about concocting a crisis. Claiming that Spanish – in reality, Basque – settlers were being ill-treated, he incited the admiral commanding the expedition to retaliate. Salazar returned to Spain to get royal approval. Arriving back in Peru he claimed (falsely) to have secured that support and, in addition, an appointment as personal representative of Queen Isabella.

---

5   "The Bombardment of Paradise", David Woods, 2011.

That made Salazar responsible for negotiating a settlement in Lima, which, predictably, he failed to do. In April 1864, he initiated the Spanish retaliation: the Chincha Islands were taken, the governor arrested and a ransom demand of three million pesos presented to the government. Foreign powers sought, unsuccessfully, to intervene and the government in Madrid was severely embarrassed – notably since it had rescinded Salazar's mandate within days of his setting sail for Peru. Still, the Peruvians needed the guano revenues badly, so its autocratic president was forced to pay up against the wishes of the congress. As a result, several months later, Peru's President Juan Pezet was overthrown by a popular revolution and military coup.

Hours before the bombardment was due to start, the population of Valparaiso crowded towards the hills surrounding the town for safety. From a report by El Correo de Ultramar. *Biblioteca nacional, Santiago*

Even though the Spanish fleet, under its new commander Admiral José Manuel Pareja, duly left the Chinchas, the affair was far from over. Pareja harboured a pent up hatred of the Chileans; his father having died in the country decades before, during the independence war (see Chapter 5). So the Admiral looked south for a new opportunity for Spain to show its teeth. Pushed also by

Madrid, Spain's senior diplomat in Santiago concocted a list of alleged Chilean misdeeds during the confrontation with Peru over the Chinchas. In principle, Chile had stayed neutral during the conflict. In practice, its theoretical equal treatment of the two sides had caused particular difficulties for the Spanish – for instance, its restrictions on coaling and provisioning in its ports. Moreover, public opinion in Chile was naturally and sometimes vociferously anti-monarchy, stirred by scurrilous newspapers like *San Martín* which took huge delight in insulting the Spanish royal family.

Eleven grievances were drawn up for which explanations and apologies were formally demanded. While explanations were provided, the idea of apologizing in any manner to the old colonial rulers was out of the question for the Chileans. The breaking point was a requirement that Chile deliver a naval salute to the Spanish flag in the bay of Valparaíso. On 24 September 1865, Admiral Pareja announced, under his plenipotentiary powers, that he was breaking off all diplomatic relations and imposing a blockade of Chilean ports, notably Valparaíso. Of course, the small Spanish fleet lacked the capacity to blockade effectively, but it certainly had the potential to disrupt commerce.

The trading houses of Valparaíso were outraged. Diplomats of European nations were dragged into the confrontation and foreign ministries in capitals the world over began to take an active interest, especially in London and Paris. Their interest became all the more acute when Pareja added a threat to bombard Valparaíso in the event that a settlement was not found. This was a dire prospect, not only because lives and properties might be lost, but because the port was crammed full of merchandise and, particularly, millions of dollars' worth of European goods stored, duty-free, in the customs warehouses. And Valparaíso was without defences. Still, there was much confidence in the port that the Spanish admiral was bluffing.

The business community was also convinced that the naval vessels of Britain and the United States, present in the blockaded port, would not stand by and allow their property to go up in flames. Indeed, the English rear-admiral, Joseph Denman, seemed in agreement with his American counterpart, Commodore John Rodgers who commanded the most modern and deadly warship in the bay, that they would act together to defend the town. Only in the final days before the bombardment did they have second thoughts, pressured it seems by diplomatic concerns about the need to maintain neutrality.

Certainly, the two captains – both of whom had splendid records and were much admired and decorated – believed that the Spanish would ultimately back-track given their lack of firepower in the face of the two other squadrons that would face them. It was not to be. For Rear Admiral Casto Méndez Núñez, one of the most courageous commanders in the Spanish navy, it was a matter of principle. The honour of Spain was at stake, his predecessor having committed suicide after the tiny Chilean navy had taken one of his vessels in battle just a few months earlier. He told Denman and Rodgers that he would willingly go down with his ships to the bottom of the Pacific rather than fail in his duty to carry out the Queen's orders.

On 31 March, 1866, the Spanish fleet duly carried out its orders, pummelling Valparaíso for three hours. The crews of the British and American naval vessels, which had withdrawn some distance, looked on and did not intervene. Happily there were only limited injuries and no immediate fatalities. But homes, stores, shops, banks, offices and much else were destroyed or badly damaged. In today's money, some US$220 million went up in smoke, much of it in the customs warehouses. The volunteer firemen supported by some sailors fought the fires for over twenty-four hours.

The traders and other foreign businessmen were furious. They were influential men in Chile and no less influential through their parent companies back in Liverpool and London. They ensured that the failure to protect them came to the public notice. There were rows in the British parliament as ministers sought to justify the "cowardly" neglect of their countrymen's life and property. This was not the behaviour of "Lord Nelson's navy" protested one outraged parliamentarian. Outcries over the Spanish action were heard in Paris, Berlin and other European capitals while in Washington congressmen spoke out for and against the policy of neutrality. The world's press fulminated; even Spanish public opinion was divided over the justification for the action. When the same Spanish fleet sought to repeat the punishment on the Peruvian port of Callao, a few weeks later, it was almost destroyed by onshore defences and Rear Admiral Méndez Núñez was severely wounded. It was to be the last Spanish military adventure in South America.

After the bombardment, the port of Valparaíso was refurbished. Yet the forests of European flags and masts that the citizens of Valparaíso had become accustomed to observing in the Bay, would thin out. A peak of 1006 vessels – including 245 from Britain, 44 from Germany and 51 from France – docked in the year 1861. By the turn of the century, in 1901, that total had almost halved, although some 321 ships flew British ensigns and 132 the German flag. However, the vessels were no longer the small, fragile, wooden sailing ships that had been typical of the first half of the nineteenth century. Now, they were large and fast, mostly steel-hulled and propelled by steam. So, looked at in terms of weight, the picture was far from decline. Overall, the tonnage of merchant vessels using Valparaíso doubled from 1896 (860,000 tons) to 1913 (1,650,000tons), the year before the Panama Canal opened for business. By 1930, Valparaíso port activity had fallen back to levels of the beginning of the century. However, by that time San Antonio, the new port to the south, had built its custom to almost the same level at 757,000 tons.

Almost as numerous as ships in the Bay in the middle of the nineteenth century were the trading houses to be found scattered throughout the streets of the port. British certainly, German increasingly and French persistently. But

One of the French Bordes fleet, "Cerro Alegre", which carried nitrate from Chile to Europe between 1894 and 1915. Unlike many such vessels, it survived submarine and other attacks during the First World War.   *State Library of Victoria, Australia*

Italians, Danes, Norwegians, Spaniards, Russians and many other nationalities worked ceaselessly to meet the ever-rising demand for raw materials in Europe, and the no-less buoyant demand for luxuries, clothing, shoes, household decorations, engineered supplies, electrical goods as well as coal and other basic commodities up and down the West coast of Latin America. Italian traders included the Cancianis from Lombardy, Delpiano from Genoa and the Falconis from Venice; among the Germans were Schutte, the powerful Huth clan and Stuven from Hamburg; while France was represented, among others, by A D Bordes from Bordeaux and Le Havre.

One French observer, in 1888, declared himself satisfied with the prevalence of French fashions and luxuries but remained irritated by France's failure to trade as successfully as other European states. He noted that, in 1886, imports from England had amounted to 17 million piasters[6], those from Germany, 8.3 million, while France's performance lingered with just 5 million. It was "especially annoying" since the German performance was on the rise while the French figures were falling. As for exports, those to England were valued at 38.2 million piastres and those to France only 2.8 million.

The French may have fallen behind the pack, but at least they did it in style. Apart from dominating fashions in the capital, this was the era of the great French 'bounty ships' whose fine, majestic lines graced the Bay of Valparaíso as they did ports from Sydney to Manila to Rio de Janeiro. At a time when even the British merchant fleet was looking tatty, the French subsidized the construction, in French shipyards, of several hundred magnificent three- and four-masted vessels. From the 1870s – following France's commitment to free trade – until around 1910, these elegant ships were launched to ply the trade routes of the world.

---

6 It was common for French speakers of the time to refer to US dollars as 'piastres'.

Valparaiso Bound!

12.

The nitrate men ... and a war

We're bound out to Iquique Bay,
Hang down ye bunch o' roses, hang down,
We're bound away at the break of day,
Hang down ye bunch o' roses, hang down.

We're bound away around Cape Horn,
We wish 'ter hell we'd niver bin born.

Around Cape Stiff we all must go,
Around Cape Stiff through the ice an' snow.

Me boots an' clothes are all in pawn,
An it's bleedin' draughty around Cape Horn.

"Bunch o' Roses". A traditional sea song adapted for the saltpetre trade

Nations go to war for many reasons, most of them bad. But for fertilizer? Chile, Peru and Bolivia did exactly that in 1879 and Chile, through a civil war, arguably did so again in 1891. Natural nitrates were in huge demand in Europe for agricultural use but also as an essential ingredient of explosives for armaments. Trade in nitrate-based fertilizers underpinned the economies of all three countries in the middle of the nineteenth century. It also provoked the shedding of much blood in brutal conflicts.

Not much romance there! Yet writers and travellers were capable of being poetic about both the arid wastes in which saltpetre nitrates were found and even the life in the *oficinas* where the mines and processing plants ground out, day by day, night after night, the precious commodity. One was Lilian Elwyn Elliott, who visited the region in the 1920s. Her descriptions may be blind to the hardships suffered by so many in the great nitrate epoch, but they are worth quoting at length since so much of this story concerns money, not beauty:

"Before the realization of the properties of nitrate and its commercial exploitation upon a great scale, the burning pampas of Tarapacá and Antofagasta were solitudes, shunned by all animal life. This region, whose products were destined to give new life to a million cultivated fields, to bring orchards and groves all over the world into magnificent flower and fruit, lacked the ability to produce so much as a blade of grass.

"Yet today this region presents the liveliest scenes of the West Coast. Where a solitary waste lay under the sun, railways cross the desert with loads of heavy bags of chemicals; tall chimneys rise into the quivering air, the grey tin roofs of the nitrate works dot the pampas thickly. Each nitrate plant is the centre of an artificial town, to which every drop of water must be piped, every article of clothing, food, every scrap of wood and metal needed for dwellings and *oficina* must be carried. ... The scene appears to have no elements of beauty, for there is no hue but that of the sandy desert, the grey and black of the *oficinas* and the gleam of railway tracks; the outlines of the scored and pitted ground, the railway cars, the smoking chimneys, are harsh. Yet there is a sense of energy and prosperity, of intelligent activity, and in the pure dry air of the pampa almost everyone experiences a feeling of splendid health and well-being.

"Above the flat desert is an enormous bowl of clear, transparent sky and one looks far away to distances that seem endless. At sunrise and sunset the effects of light upon the sky and pampa are of a beauty never seen but in expanses such as these. I have watched the sky in an Antofagasta nitrate pampa when, as the sun fell swiftly, all the arch flushed with rose, and quickly flooded with sheets of purest violet while the orange and umber pampa took on deep amethyst shadows; before pastel or paint could record the sight, all the sky was transformed in a clear luminous lemon-yellow, upon whose bright surface streams of translucent green presently ran. The high peaks of far-distant Andes appeared as if floating, the snow-crowned heads of San Pedro and San Pablo alone visible against the changing sky, fading at last into the mantle of sapphire that gradually shrouded pampa and heights, with nothing moving but a host of brilliant stars, sparkling like diamonds on a live hand. In a few moments after sundown the scorching heat has given place to sharp cold, and he who rides by night across these deserts must carry a heavy woollen poncho; one sleeps indoors under blankets. Dawn is a miracle of pink and pearl, and in at the window comes the scent of the cherished flowers in the little garden, glistening with dew. The new day is of indescribable freshness and serenity. Long before noon the sun is pouring vertical floods of sunshine upon the desert, the very sand seems to quiver with heat, and a relentless scorching breath seems to fill the world.

"But to this all-the-year round heat the foreigner soon becomes accustomed

— everyone, as a matter of fact, workers and officials alike, is a "foreigner" to this pampa; human life is imported like every other commodity here. But the children born of white parents in the nitrate fields are strong and sturdy, and it is not surprising that they who have lived for a year or two on the pampas find themselves restless in other places, suffer a feeling of constraint, a longing for these wide skies and far horizons."

The nitrate industry was a global one, it was the epitome of nineteenth century capitalism, mostly founded in the City of London. It stimulated the rise and fall of business dynasties across Europe and in South America. We have already seen the rise of Gibbs and Co, but this firm was only the first; other capitalists, with names like North, Bordes, Sloman and Baburizza, would take their turns at reaping the riches that these dull but valuable substances generated.

What is a nitrate? While fertilizers traditionally use nitrate compounds of both sodium and potassium, what was initially known as "Peru saltpetre" and more recently as "Chile saltpetre" is essentially sodium nitrate, or nitrate of soda. The Incas knew about saltpetre, although they made most use of the richer guano fertilizer. The Spanish used saltpetre for explosives and fireworks. The manufacture of contraband gunpowder became common in Peru during the eighteenth century and the authorities in Lima did their inadequate best to stamp out the practice. But fireworks were popular with the colonial rulers while the Catholic fathers made sure they had plenty of the material for incendiary displays during religious festivals.

Moving caliche at the Oficina Solferino near Tacna, Peru, in 1889. *Biblioteca Nacional de Chile*

Saltpetre was not taken from the ground as ready-made gunpowder or fertilizer. It was mined and transported – normally on the backs of native or Chinese labourers – as rocks known as *caliche*. After being broken up the pieces of caliche were boiled in copper cauldrons until the nitrate content dissolved. The liquid was then transferred using ladles into vats where it crystallised. It was a simple process, but inefficient. It was an English chemical engineer, James "Santiago" Humberstone – whose tragic family history in the Atacama we have already noted – who introduced a far more productive method that revolutionized the industry. His version of the "Shanks" system transferred the *caliche* into a series of tanks through which pipes circulated steam. The liquor was progressively refined and drawn off until it could be dried and crystallised. The steam was produced using coal or fuel oil rather than wood. Humberstone's system remained predominant until well into the twentieth century.

Charles Darwin visits a nitrate plant

The principal deposits of nitrates were found in today's First Region of Chile – Tarapacá, with its capital, the port of Iquique – and the Second Region – centred on Antofagasta. The former was Peruvian territory before the Pacific War of 1879-83 and the latter Bolivian. Early efforts to trade the un-refined nitrate failed: a first shipment to Liverpool, in 1820, was simply thrown overboard for lack of buyers and the chemicals with which to treat the *caliche*. Another ten years would pass before further modest shipments found markets, notably in France where the use of nitrates was finally understood. Their importance gradually dawned on scientists and then farmers in Europe as reports by travellers reached them. Chief among them was probably Charles Darwin, who arrived at Iquique, in *HMS Beagle*, on 12 July 1835. The following day, he hired two mules and a guide and set off up the steep mountain track that leads from the port to see something of the infant saltpetre industry. Darwin's diary entry describes the sight of an endless array of skeletons of beasts of burden that had expired from exhaustion along the route.

The house in which Darwin passed the night and learned about the mining of nitrate belonged to one of the British pioneers of the industry, George Smith. Smith owned the *oficina* known as 'La Noria' which he and his uncle, Archibald Robson, had bought from Hector Bacque, a Frenchman. Smith, from Norwich, England, was born in 1802 and arrived in Peru in 1821. He established himself in Tarapacá and began to survey the potential for nitrate production in the region from 1827. He had been contracted for the study by the Governor of Tarapacá and worked with a young scientist, William Bollaert, who had previously assisted both Michael Faraday and Sir Humphry Davy at the Royal Institution in London. Bollaert, who later devoted himself to ethnological studies in Peru and Chile, was a long-time friend of Smith whom he regarded as the scientific father of the modern nitrate industry. The two were clearly devoted; Bollaert fondly describing later their "calm and stoic" travels across the wilderness of the desert.

For the thirty years between 1830 and 1860, nitrate production and exports from the Peruvian and Bolivian *salitreras* (saltpetre mines) crept slowly upwards backed by a mixture of European and local capital. However, with the guano trade under the Gibbs monopoly appearing to falter, that company moved into the Tarapacá nitrate business buying the firm originally formed by Smith and Robson. The Compañía Salitrera de Tarapacá would be one of the most powerful businesses in the region. Smith finally set sail back to England in 1866, after over forty years toiling in the arid mountains and deserts of Peru, to improve the technology and infrastructure of an industry that would, in the coming decades, make many fortunes. He died in London four years later.

As the century wore on, around 250 *oficinas* would extract and refine nitrates in the deserts of Peru and Chile – more or less evenly divided between the regions of Tarapacá and Antofagasta. This hard-won, salty compound would become so sought-after and expensive in Europe that it was regarded as the equivalent of a white gold. In 1835, some 39 ships were charged with a total of a little over 140,000 quintals (6,458 metric tonnes) of nitrate. Although most production was then within Peru, Valparaíso quickly established itself as

Oficina La Palma (later Humberstone), near Iquique, in 1881.
Biblioteca Nacional de Chile

the commercial heart of the nitrate trade, through which most shipments had to transit. By 1842, 65 vessels carried over 16,000 tonnes to European ports. In 1850 the total was 23,500 tonnes, and ten years later, 63,000 tonnes. The one million tonnes mark was reached in 1890 and a peak of just under three million during the First World War which was broadly maintained up to the onset of the Great Depression in 1929.

Nitrate exploitation in the region of Antofagasta, then controlled by Bolivia, began much later than that in Tarapacá, to the north. The great Chilean explorer and entrepreneur, José Santos Ossa Vega, had set out in 1866 with an expedition to search for silver in the Atacama Desert. What they found after an arduous trek was some of the largest nitrate deposits then known: the Salar del Carmen. Returning to Valparaíso, Ossa met with Augustín Edwards, the banker, to seek the capital necessary to establish the new industry in a region that was then barely populated. The third key part of the business triumvirate would be, once more, Gibbs and Company. George Smith took a stake and, with a number of other Chilean and European shareholders, the company Melbourne Clark y Cie was formed in 1868. A few years later, the firm was transformed into the influential Compañía de Salitres y Ferrocarril de Antofagasta which would be the driving force behind the subsequent development of the city whose name it bore.

It was the fortunes of the Compañía de Salitres y Ferrocarril de Antofagasta that would eventually lead to a war. There had been trouble between governments in Santiago and La Paz over the coastal claims of Bolivia for years. As far back as 1843, Bolivia's military dictatorships had claimed the littoral down to the 25th or 26th parallels, thus taking 150 to 300 kilometres of coastline south of Antofagasta and the guano deposits that went with it. Chile had claimed rights to the guano from the Bay of Mejillones southwards – that small port being 50 kilometres north of Antofagasta. By 1843, Bolivia was laying claim to the entire Atacama region.

It all spelled trouble, and the trouble came in a series of skirmishes at sea. National pride was dented on both sides and, since commercial interests were at stake, a solution had to be found. That was achieved in 1866. First, an agreement was signed in Santiago between the two governments in which Chile handed Bolivia territorial rights down to the 24th parallel, about 40 kilometres south of Antofagasta along with shared rights to guano and an accord on customs tariffs for exports of that product. Almost simultaneously, La Paz gave José Santos Ossa and his partner Francisco Puelma the first concession for the exploitation of the saltpetre nitrate deposits they had discovered in the Atacama Desert.

John Thomas North appears on the scene

It was inevitable that Ossa would one day meet another larger-than-life character in the nitrate story: John Thomas North, later known as the 'Nitrate King'. The manner of their meeting, if the anecdote recounted in the official history of the nitrate producers is to be believed, hardly reflects the grandeur and influence that North later attained. Supposedly, sometime in 1870, Ossa was travelling on the Carrizal railway to reach his home village of Freirina (between La Serena and Copiapó) when there was an accident. Ossa did his best to assist in the emergency while the engine-driver, an Englishman, had difficulty making himself understood among the passengers. This was North. He had arrived in Valparaíso, the previous year, starting work as an engineer in the railway construction yard of Caldera and then on the Carrizal railway. In 1871 he would travel further north, to Iquique, where he secured his first position in the nitrate industry, as a boilermaker in the Officina Santa Rita.

John Thomas North, the "Nitrate King," around 1880.
The National Archive, London

North would later generate his own mythology, including that of his very humble origins. In reality, he was the son of a prosperous coal merchant near Leeds, in Yorkshire, and became an apprentice at the age of fifteen in an engineering company one of whose partners was a cousin of his father. In the late 1860s and 1870s the nitrate industry in Peru was growing fast. Many Englishmen appeared in the region as engineers, constructors, miners and traders. Iquique's boom almost quadrupled its population between 1862 and 1876 when it reached just under 10,000. In 1879, the British government appointed its first vice-consul in the town, Maurice Jewell, who also became North's first partner. They imported machinery, tools and other merchandise for the *salitreras* and local businesses. North understood the prime importance of infrastructure and supplies in these remote regions. His early ventures gave him a foundation on which he could start building a stake in the industry, eventually acquiring *oficinas* of his own. For instance, water was scarce but an absolute necessity for the development of the nitrate business. In 1878 North began to manage the services of the Compañía de Aguas de Tarapacá, shipping in water from Arica, further north. A few years later, the English founder of that company left Iquique and North was recognised as the sole owner. By the end of the Pacific War, North had established a monopoly on the supply of water.

Railways would also play a big part in the success of the nitrate industry. Correspondence in the records of the Royal Gunpowder Factory at Waltham Abbey in England, includes a letter from a civil engineer called William Lloyd to the Managing Director of Heaton's Steel and Iron Co, dated February 1869. Lloyd claimed to be able drastically to reduce the costs of imported nitrate of soda from Peru. Basing himself on a paper read at The Royal Geographical Society by George Smith's partner William Bollaert, he noted that for the one hundred nitrate works already operating in the area of Iquique most of the 20,000 men and 15,000 animals employed were simply transporting fuel and provisions to the works and bringing the nitrate down to the ports for shipment. Building a railway from Iquique to the mines – then barely 23 miles apart – would cost no more than £250,000, he stated, and would be paid for within one year given annual shipments of 100,000 tons of nitrate. More savings could be generated by constructing a *"mole"* (jetty) to facilitate loading in the port. With these innovations, insisted Lloyd, the cost of delivery to European ports of £8.13s.10d would be reduced by £2.11s.6d, a saving of over 25 per cent.

All this was vital for farming costs. As Lloyd pointed out, the potential for the South American saltpetre nitrates was becoming accepted. A paper by a Mr Pusey in the Journal of the Royal Agricultural Society in 1853 had been ebullient in its assessment of increases in wheat yields in Britain and the possibility of a dramatic reduction or eradication of wheat imports. Mr Pusey had been effusive:

"It is wonderful, certainly, to have found a mineral which at the present high price yields us wheat at a cost of 24s [British shillings] a quarter, and if cheapened, as apparently it might be, by one-half, would of course yield it at 12s a quarter[1]. Thus, instead of 3,000,000 quarters of wheat, costing $6,000,000 sterling, we might import yearly 200,000 tons of nitrate, costing little more (at £8 a ton) than £1,600,000 only, and so our farmers might obtain from their own farms the whole foreign supply of wheat without labour and with but a few months' outlay of capital."

The importance of Peruvian and Chilean saltpetre was also not lost on arms manufacturers in Europe. By the end of the 1870s, the Royal Gunpowder Factory in Britain was fretting about the cost of Indian Bengal saltpetre and looking for other supplies at a reasonable price.

Clearly, the economic and military interests tied to supplies of competitive nitrates were very high in Europe and no less so in the three countries most closely engaged in their extraction, refining and export. As we have seen, the Peruvian government had persistently overstretched itself with foreign loans for large public works and wars. It needed export revenues desperately to meet repayment schedules. In January 1873 the government in La Paz – for the first time under a civilian president, following regular *coups-d'état* – sought to create a sales monopoly for nitrates and become the sole exporter. A law was passed to that effect but, in the face of fierce opposition, never enacted. In 1875, however, the government decided on a different approach. It obtained from Congress the authority to raise a new loan of £7 million sterling, in part to be used for the expropriation of privately owned Tarapacá nitrate *oficinas*. The owners were initially paid in certificates that the government undertook to redeem in two years at eight per cent annual interest. In the event, Peru failed to raise the loan to redeem the certificates, a catastrophe for the original owners but later the basis on which fortunes would be made, especially that of John Thomas North.

However, the immediate impact was a collapse in nitrate production, exacerbated by a violent earthquake in 1877. Tarapacá nitrate exports fell from 7,300,000 quintals[2] in 1876 to 5,000,000 the following year. Heavily invested trading houses in Valparaíso observed events in Bolivia, appalled. The Chilean government began to consider its options; war would only take one further spark. This came in 1879. A diplomatic dispatch from Santiago on 28 January

1   A quarter was the equivalent of 8 bushels or 480 pounds of wheat.
2   A quintal was the equivalent of about 100 pounds or 45 kilos.

noted reports that Bolivia was placing extra taxes on nitrates taken from the Salar del Carmen and other deposits near Antofagasta. The regime was also demanding arrears from August 1874 when the treaty was signed under which the Compañía de Salitres y Ferrocarril de Antofagasta had received the rights to extract and export without additional duties. The sum involved was US$90,000. Failure to pay would lead to an embargo of the company. It would also have entailed the arrest of its English manager, George Hicks, had he not managed first to get aboard a Chilean naval vessel in Antofagasta bay.

Shipping nitrate from Pisagua in 1891.   *The Illustrated London News*

This was poison for the political establishment in Santiago. There was a lingering resentment over the ceding of territory around Antofagasta in a 1866 treaty – signed after Bolivia and Chile had joined forces with Peru to confront Spain during the Chincha Islands crisis and the subsequent blockade and bombardment by the Spanish fleet. Further, even in 1878, census figures show that nearly 80 per cent of the population in the province of Antofagasta – the city, coast and inland – was Chilean. The rest of the inhabitants were Bolivians, Peruvians and Europeans.

War becomes inevitable

There had already been skirmishes between Chile and Bolivia – one country presided over by a soldier, Hilarión Daza Groselle, with a shaky economy and an iron fist, the other by an instinctively pacifist, professional politician and administrator, Aníbal Pinto, whose army had been depleted through budget cuts. War appeared inevitable, however, as the Chileans in Antofagasta panicked at news that the Peruvian fleet might move southwards to support reinforced Bolivian defences. The Chilean press, egged on by the larger nitrate investors, demanded action.

The government in Chile first sought an urgent diplomatic resolution of the problem but claimed Bolivia showed no interest. Thus, on 10 February 1879, Sir John Drummond Hay, Britain's senior diplomat in Santiago, reported to London:

"The general impression here as to the operations about to be undertaken is that Chile will now endeavour to retake the strip of coast which of her own accord she gave over to Bolivia in 1866 for the sake of peace and quietness and to put an end to the bickering on the subject of boundaries. This portion of land has now acquired a certain value from the discovery and successful working of the large nitrate deposits existing there and the proceeds of which would go far to defray the expense of the war."

In the morning of 14 February 1879, Chile successfully landed troops at Antofagasta without opposition, thus taking back the land and coastline previously ceded. Bolivia declared war two weeks later with Daza assuming that naval support from Peru would soon settle things in Bolivia's favour. For a short while it did so, the early sea war went badly for Chile. At the time, the Navy's commander was Admiral Juan Williams Rebolledo, a hero of the 1865-66 war with Spain. However, by the 1880s, the Admiral had personal political ambitions. Ordered by President Pinto to move the fleet north and engage the Peruvian enemy at Lima's port of Callao, Williams Rebolledo chose instead to go only as far as the nitrate port of Iquique which he blockaded, assuming the Peruvians would come south to engage him.

When frustration set in in Santiago, the Chilean commander reluctantly sailed his strongest iron-clad vessels to Callao, leaving two old wooden ships, *Esmeralda* and *Covadonga*, to maintain the Iquique blockade. It was a catastrophic misjudgement; the Peruvians had already left port en route for Iquique where they were able to engage the hopelessly out-gunned Chilean ships, sinking the *Esmeralda*. Nevertheless, the Battle of Iquique was far from a total loss for Chile. First, the old *Covadonga* led the Peruvian iron-clad *Independencia* to run aground during a chase, effectively halving Peru's naval strength. Second, Chile gained a national hero in the form of Captain Arturo Prat. With his ship sinking beneath him, and armed only with his sword, Prat leaped aboard the Peruvian warship *Huáscar* and tried to take the bridge. He was shot and killed, but the huge outpouring of patriotic grief and admiration for Prat brought new support for an aggressive conduct of the war against Peru and Bolivia.

Ironically, perhaps, while suffering blows to its naval prowess in battle, Chile was also provoking some angry reactions to its conduct, including an "utter disregard for the rights and interests of neutrals", according to the British minister, Spenser St. John, in Lima. Indeed, the envoys of the United States, Great Britain, Italy, Germany and France addressed a joint complaint to Admiral Williams Rebolledo. Among their grievances: the Chilean iron-clad *Almirante Cochrane*, under the command of Captain Enrique Simpson, son of a distinguished English naval officer in the War of Independence, had seized merchant vessels and destroyed port facilities, including British property, at Mollendo. Williams Rebolledo himself came in for criticism, for allegedly seeking to destroy the port of Pisagua. In the face of only mild resistance and defensive fire, he had shelled the town "and did not cease until nine-tenths of it were destroyed", including the English consulate. As for the doomed Esmeralda, the diplomats charged that, prior to the blockade of Iquique, the vessel had fired on a train taking women and children out of harm's way while the town was bombarded. Happily, there were no casualties.

In August 1879 Williams Rebolledo was replaced by Admiral Galvarino Riveros who refitted his ships and went in pursuit of the Peruvians. In October several Chilean vessels trapped the key enemy iron-clad warship *Huáscar*, under the command of the skilled and much admired Admiral Miguel Grau Seminario, off Angamos Point, near Mejillones. After a fierce engagement, the *Huáscar* was captured, with Grau and more than thirty Peruvian mariners dead. The battle completely reversed the direction of the sea war, giving Chile firm control of the coast up to Callao and, therefore, Lima.

The land campaign would last from November 1879 to January 1881 and, as the Chileans battled northwards, would amount to a bloody and vicious war in which the price paid, in men and fortune, on both sides, was almost beyond public and political acceptance. It was marked by incompetence on all sides, failure of the supposed military alliance between Peru and Bolivia and political duplicity in Santiago.

In November of 1879, more than 500 Chilean troops were killed during a counter-attack by Peruvian forces on the village of Tarapacá shortly after the first successful landing by Pinto's army in Pisagua. Nevertheless the Peruvians withdrew northwards, making the province of Tacna the next military objective for Chile. In May 1880, under a new commander, General Manuel Baquedano, the town of Tacna was taken with three out of every ten Chilean soldiers – over 2000 in all – killed or wounded. The port of Arica was taken in July that year in a lightning and heroic assault, lasting just fifty-five minutes but leaving 120 Chileans dead. Public outrage in Santiago at the heavy losses being sustained by its army incited calls for the taking of Lima itself.

That objective was close to being achieved in January 1881 after two devastating battles, at Chorrillos and Miraflores on the outskirts of the capital. Chilean losses were at least 1300 dead with over 4000 wounded. Peruvian casualties were even higher. It was a tense period, fraught with danger. Diplomatic reports were again complaining of the behaviour of the Chilean forces, notably in Tacna and Chorillos. There were claims of pillaging, the unnecessary burning of towns and the murder of prisoners. Diplomats feared similar brutality in Lima. Indeed, neutral powers began to envisage the use of foreign fleets to act against any indiscriminate attack on the centre of Lima and the port of Callao. However, Baquedano gave his word to hold back from fully taking Lima, at least until the city had had an opportunity to surrender. With diplomatic encouragement ceasefire terms were agreed.

At that point Peruvian army survivors went on the rampage against foreigners in Lima. According to the British minister in Lima, "at least 700 ladies and children" took refuge in the English legation for the night. Thus, when the Chilean troops and a contingent of Santiago policemen marched in the following afternoon, 13 January, they were welcomed by many in the city as bringing a new sense of order and security. A similarly strained situation in Callao was also restored to relative tranquillity.

A Committee of Chinese Merchants later wrote to the British diplomat Spenser St. John seeking the aid of the British crown in their claim for compensation from the Peruvian government. The merchants noted that several of their countrymen had lost their lives and over £364,000 in losses had been sustained. All this despite the fact, they complained, that the shopkeepers had painted the words *'Bomba Inglesa'* on their shop doors. In other words, in a devious attempt to secure the protection of the British flag they had all joined the Chinese Company of the English Fire Brigade!

The frontiers are redrawn

Yet the war was not over. Chile initially wanted to keep the provinces of Tarapacá, Arica and even Tacna, as well as Antofagasta. The Peruvian government would not concede and there were military leaders at large prepared to offer guerrilla-style resistance to the occupying forces. According to British Foreign Office reports of the time, the United States offered some one-sided mediation to deter what the State Department saw as British imperialism exerted through commercial interests. Foreign bond and nitrate certificate holders, on the other hand, feared that the United States was mediating in order to hand control of the nitrate fields to an American company. The Chilean preference to leave Lima quickly was complicated, in July 1882, when a guerrilla force massacred an entire Chilean detachment of seventy-seven soldiers at La Concepción, east of the capital.

The settlement that emerged towards the end of 1883 handed the province of Tarapacá to Chile. The provinces of Tacna and Arica were to remain occupied for ten years after which popular referenda would decide whether they should revert to Peru or not. As for Antofagasta, the Bolivians signed an armistice in April 1884 granting Chile a right to govern and administer the province, at least while the truce was in force. A treaty signed in 1904 by the two countries settled the line of the frontier but left Bolivia without a corridor to any port on the Pacific coast. The referenda on Tacna and Arica never took place. Instead a treaty signed in 1929 returned Tacna to Peru while Chile kept Arica. To this day, there remains a dispute over the maritime limits between the two countries, a dispute that was taken to the International Court of Justice in 2008.

Historians have long debated the extent to which foreign interests intervened directly to provoke this brutal conflict. The evidence is shaky according to the British historian Harold Blakemore who delved deeply into these events, with the aid of much intra-company correspondence of key players like Gibbs and Co. But that is not to say that European companies were disinterested. The manner in which the nitrate riches of the Atacama were administered before, during and after the War of the Pacific had global significance that mere territorial changes hardly reflect.

By April 1880, with the provinces of Tarapacá and Antofagasta now occupied by the Chilean army, diplomats and government officials on all sides were already seeking to ensure continued trade in guano and saltpetre nitrates. Given the huge debts of Peru and Bolivia in London, and the demands of bondholders, this was vital. La Paz and Lima were desperate to maintain some hold on the reserves and the revenues they generated, not least to finance the continuing hostilities with Chile. The Bolivians initially proposed that their debts be paid off through an extra levy on guano exports. That was impracticable since the reserves were in Chilean hands. An alternative was to sell guano already held in stock in Europe; a reasonable enough idea were it not that Bolivia had no capacity to orchestrate such sales. Meanwhile, the Chilean government had already decreed that foreign holders of Peruvian bonds would be free to load guano deposits. These would pass through Valparaíso where a levy of 30 shillings for every ton would be paid before onward shipping.

Chorrillos, on the outskirts of Lima, more than a decade before the Chilean army bloodily over-ran the town in 1882.   *Library of Congress, Washington*

Of course, altogether bigger stakes were in play when it came to handling saltpetre nitrates from Tarapacá. This was not Peruvian property to dispose of even had the government had the means to access it in occupied territory. Furthermore, Lima was faced with a decree issued in Santiago which rescinded all saltpetre contracts signed with Peruvian authorities. Delivery from 20 February 1880 onwards would be to Chilean authorities with the product set for eventual public auction and the proceeds for the Chilean exchequer.

"Colonel" North – as he sometimes grandly, but inaccurately, referred to himself – and his associates had taken a calculated bet on the outcome of the war. They had judged that Chile would not only win militarily but also return

233

the mines to private ownership. Indeed, while hostilities were still raging, the Chilean government appears to have decided to do just that, using the pre-war nitrate certificates issued by the Peruvian government as the vehicle for a change of ownership. North and two English friends, Robert Harvey and John Dawson, speculated on the future value of these certificates. Harvey was a fellow engineer by trade but, before the war, and usefully for North, he became an employee of the general inspectorate for the *salitreras* (the saltpetre mines) set up by the Peruvian government. So respected was he in Lima that he was also appointed an honorary colonel in the army. His luck held: with the rout of the Peruvian military by the Chileans, Harvey found himself briefly taken prisoner but, soon after, named by Santiago as Inspector-General of Nitrates. John Dawson was a banker managing the Iquique branch of the Bank of Valparaíso. He helped supply the funds with which North and Harvey bought the nitrate certificates that would make their fortunes.

Given the uncertainty during the war, the certificates had been traded as their intrinsic value fell. Shortly after the military disasters of Chorrillos and Miraflores, in early 1881, they were changing hands at ten per cent of their nominal value. The result was to put these assets in foreign hands. Mainly British speculators bought up the certificates and subsequently exchanged them for the appropriate *salitreras* whose values after the war, when production and trade picked up quickly, were then much greater. Huge paper profits were earned. In 1878, British capital had controlled 13% of the nitrate industry in Tarapacá; by 1884 the proportion was 34%.

Nobody did better than John Thomas North. Certainly he was a natural gambler in business with an informed, experienced but uncannily prescient instinct for profitable opportunities. That he had some prior knowledge, through Harvey, of the Chilean intention to return the nitrate industry to private hands seems evident. In any event, North and Harvey bought, for a pittance, certificates covering some of the most attractive nitrate *oficinas*.

None of this passed without reaction by those left high-and-dry with almost worthless nitrate certificates. In June 1883 a group of the English Nitrate Certificate Holders wrote to the Foreign Secretary in London. They insisted that their certificates remained a valid title and that Chile had no rights to the assets covered. The group demanded that British diplomatic representation in Chile join with that of other European governments, representing their own certificate holders, in demanding that Chile recognize their rights.

With most of the valuable *oficinas* now in different, but nevertheless British hands, the Foreign Office sat on its hands. Meanwhile, the government in

Santiago had set up a Consultative Commission on Guano and Nitrates which reported in rather different terms, among other things emphasising the well-established tradition of non-acceptance of national debt by occupying nations:

"Effectively, in the Franco-Prussian war, Germany annexed Alsace and Lorraine without taking upon herself a single centime of French debt. Italy recovered the Lombardo-Venetian Kingdom from Austria without recognizing any Austrian debt. Russia dismembered Turkey, and neither the whole nor a portion of the latter's debt was recognized by the former."

This was disputed by the certificate holders, but to no avail. Peru and Bolivia could do nothing. The Commission's findings became the foundation of North's fortune. He and his associates would go on to reap ever greater success and profits.

One family's story of escape from the conflict

This chapter started with a rose-tinted account of a visit to one of the *salitreras*. As we shall see, there were uglier sides to the industry. The War of the Pacific created hardship and anxiety in the *officinas* scattered, undefended, across the desert where the conflict raged. The processing plants ground to a halt, leaving skeleton caretaker teams and usually European management in place. Workers and their families were moved to the principal towns around the nitrate fields. News was sparse, but all were conscious that the fighting was moving relentlessly towards them.

There are many stories of near escapes. One is that of James Humberstone, the Kentish engineer responsible for many of the technical and managerial innovations that transformed the industry. In 1929, then retired, he wrote out his memories of three dramatic weeks at the start of the war in a pamphlet titled: *"Flight from Agua Santa in 1879"*.

Humberstone was then the manager of the Oficina Agua Santa – part of the nitrate empire of the British firm Campbell, Outram and Co – situated in the desert, east of the port of Mejillones, and connected to the export port of Pisagua by railway. When the Chilean army landed in Pisagua on 2 November, 1879, the *oficina's* output had already been halted for months as the port's facilities had been under constant naval bombardment. Just fifteen or twenty of the older workers and their relatives remained, along with eight foreign employees and their families. Among them were Humberstone's own wife Irene, his mother-in-law Mary Jones, their two-year old daughter Luisa, and the new-born Amy, just six weeks old. The staff also included an English accountant and his Chilean wife, a French engineer and family, two unmarried Englishmen, two Italian storemen and two Argentinian gauchos, one of whom would be the group's guide across the desert.

Humberstone had already decided that for the safety of the women and children, the group would need to move. It was clear, there would be military actions in the area as the Chilean army moved through Tarapacá and north towards Tacna. The *oficina's* horses, mules and wagons had been requisitioned by the allied Bolivian-Peruvian army and they had experienced some hostility as foreigners. With the these allies falling back quickly, word came on 5 November that the military authorities could no longer guarantee the safety of the Europeans.

Two horses were procured – for Humberstone and Irene – several mules and a wagon for most of the women and children. They decided not to take the main route north, which would be crowded with refugees, troops and deserters, but to use a remote track that crossed a series of steep ravines, running east-west, between the cordillera and the coastal range. This would take them to the village of Tarapacá and, if necessary, eventually to Arica on the coast. But it would also be long, dangerous and tiring.

Although starting early, they were soon struggling under an intense heat made worse by clouds of dust that regularly turned into gusts bombarding them with small stones. For a while they lost sight of the track and feared complete disorientation. Nevertheless, in five days they arrived in Tarapacá where Humberstone met the governor. The original plan to leave the women and children in the town while the men moved on to Arica and Tacna was ruled out by the official who saw the arrival of the Chileans, and therefore a battle, as imminent.

After a peaceful night in a small villa, the group prepared to set out once more northward. However, they now faced the most violently steep climbs and descents that the desert could offer. Such were the precipitous conditions that a distance of around 200 kilometres ruled on the map would be translated into a journey of around 380 kilometres. There was no possibility of using the cart. They would have to travel on three horses and five mules: eight mounts for eight men, five women and three children. The only answer was for the men to take in turns to ride and walk. Two mules would carry the luggage. It was far from ideal, but there was no choice.

In the middle of the following night, the governor arrived to warn that they should leave rapidly; a unit of Chilean cavalry was approaching following news from survivors of a bloody battle near Agua Santa. The *oficina* had been set alight: there was now no reason for Humberstone to return quickly. His real concern was to get his wife and young daughters through the tests that would await them on the way to Arica. They were ready at dawn, the adults swallowing drafts of pisco before moving off towards the first steep climb.

Soon after, the mule carrying Mary and the little Luisa, bolted, throwing Humberstone's mother-in-law and daughter into a stony ravine. Mary "valiantly" protected Luisa from any injury, but suffered multiple cuts and bruises in the process. Nevertheless she was soon back in the saddle, with the youngster now consigned to ride with one of the men. Then followed hours of increasing heat in exposed, desolate country. Their water supplies ran out, and the group found themselves no longer able to speak and barely to breathe. Humberstone noted: "I could see that Irene had reached the limit of her resistance; after all it was only six weeks since she had given birth to her little daughter."

When they reached a small valley, they stopped, Humberstone put his fam-

The unforgiving terrain of Tarapacá - the kind of country through which the Humberstone family struggled.

ily in the shade of a boulder, and gave the horses to two of the men with instructions to ride ahead, get water and return. An hour and a half later, the water arrived and the group set off once more for a valley with a few trees.

"After a long rest we saddled up again and set off half-asleep, but in amazingly good spirits despite our swollen tongues, split lips and peeling noses. In this state we arrived at a house outside Ariquilda. I think this has been the worst day of my life in terms of physical suffering. It was not so much the heat and the thirst but the muscular fatigue caused by long periods walking, each step being an ordeal that was not relieved by sitting or lying."

Yet no-one complained. Humberstone noted with admiration that the women had been obliged to walk down the rough slopes wearing their smooth-soled, high-heeled boots, buttoned to the ankles. After a day of rest they continued on, along the way claiming back from a group of armed Bolivian men four mules marked with the Campbell, Outram brand. This allowed more of the party to ride rather than walk.

Several days more of crossing valley after valley, left them again without food or feed for the animals. With their situation once more critical they again sent ahead the Argentinian gaucho, Reinoso, who knew the area, to reach the next village and send back guides with water and food. In the meantime, moving slowly in the gathering darkness, the party came close to taking wrong turning and losing themselves. They were saved only by the insistence of one of their horses and a mule who knew the route sufficiently to take their own decisions. As night fell, they reached the village to which they had been headed and had their first square meal in days.

Sixteen days after leaving Agua Santa, the group reached Arica safely. The final stages had been easier. Humberstone had several encounters along the way, none more unexpected than that with the President of Bolivia, General Hilarión Daza. Meeting in the dictator's tent, in a valley south of Arica, Humberstone had received nothing but sympathetic concern for his family. Outside, the dictator was already being scorned for disastrous leadership in the campaign, leaving his Peruvian allies to face alone the bloody advance of the Chilean army.

After leaving his family in safe hands, James Humberstone returned quickly to Agua Santa where he found the *oficina* in ruin. His house had been burned to the ground as had other major buildings and part of the plant itself. Humberstone was distraught at the sight. But little by little, the workers and managers returned and started to rebuild. On 8 February 1880, he joyfully went down to the port of Pisagua to greet his family, finally arrived back, by ship, from Arica.

13.

Railways, the nitrate men ... and a revolution

Heave away, bullies, ye parish-rigged bums
Way, ay, roll an' go
Take yer hands from yer pockets and don't suck yer thumbs
Heave a pawl, O heave away!
Way ay, roll an' go!
The anchor's on board an' the cable's all stored,
Timme rollockin' randy dandy O!

Roust 'er up, bullies, the wind's drawin' free,
Let's get the glad-rags on an' drive 'er to sea.

We're outward bound for Vallipo Bay,
Get crackin', m' lads, 'tis a hell o' a way!

"Roll and Go" Traditional sea song of the "Cape-Horners"

Road, sea and air transport now dominate travel on the Pacific coast, but, just as railways were a foundation of the industrial revolution in Europe, and joined the east and west coast of North America to spread farming, industry and commerce across that continent, so they were once also omnipresent in Chile, Peru and Bolivia. The saltpetre nitrate industry, in particular, required thousands of kilometres of railway track and copious rolling stock. Railways would eventually help provoke the 1891 revolution in Chile.

It was American engineers who were most associated with railway development, and especially the more ambitious lines into the Andes. William Wheelwright and Henry Meiggs are the most celebrated. Wheelwright, born in Newburyport, Massachusetts, in 1798, built Chile's very first rail link, between the mining town of Copiapó and the port of Caldera. The line went into service in December 1851. But while Wheelwright was famed throughout South America for his railroad construction, he had also founded, much earlier, the Pacific Steam Navigation Company (PSNC) which ran steamer services up and down the Pacific coast and eventually to Europe and the United States.

The PSNC was British-financed after extensive, but vain, efforts by Wheelwright to interest the Astors and Vanderbilts among other wealthy American investors. Similarly, while early railway projects were funded by important Chilean families, the City of London soon predominated, its investors continuing to place their wealth in the railways well into the twentieth century. At the end of December 1909, over £343 million of British capital was invested in railroads in Latin America – far more than in nitrates and other mining activities.

By 1916, there were about 6400 kilometres of railway in Chile, of which 3,300 were state owned. At that time, rapid railway expansion was still underway, with the government spending nearly $20 million in 1912. The 'longitudinal system' launched by President Pedro Montt in 1908 was intended to run some 3,400 kilometres from Arica on the Peruvian border to Puerto Montt in the south. The key transversal line ran from Valparaíso to Los Andes, north of Santiago, where it linked to the Chilean Trans-Andine Railway for the crossing to Mendoza, and finally to the Argentine Trans-Andine Railway which completed the 1425-kilometre connection between Valparaíso and Buenos Aires.

Wheelwright had surveyed the key Valparaíso-Santiago line a few years after finishing the Copiapó-Caldera line. The complicated and testing construction was initiated by another American, Samuel Ward Greene of Rhode Island, continued by the British engineer, William Lloyd, but completed, in 1863, by Henry Meiggs. A native of Catskill, New York, Meiggs pursued largely unsuccessful business ventures in Boston, New York and, most disastrously, real estate speculation in California during and after the 1849 gold rush. Pursued by his creditors, he fled to Chile in 1857 where he launched a much admired career building railways and other large projects. He impressed everyone with his dynamism, including the government in Santiago with which he made a deal to complete the Valparaíso-Santiago line. Meiggs was given three years to do the job. Any delay in completion, Meiggs would have to compensate to the tune of $10,000 a month. On the other hand, he would earn as a bonus the same amount for each month gained. With sixty American engineers and some 10,000 workmen, the line was completed in less than 2 years.

With his substantial bonus, Meiggs continued accumulating a fortune and supposedly repaid his debts. His other remarkable construction projects included the Oroya (Central) Railway in Peru. This line, the highest railway line in the world at the time, starts at the port of Callao and in just 170 kilometres climbs to nearly 4,900 metres – marginally higher than Mont Blanc. The project required unprecedented feats of design and engineering. The energy required of Meiggs, as well as the stress, probably precipitated his death in 1877, with the project still unfinished.

Other foreign engineers and architects, as well as financiers, were responsible for numerous construction projects in Peru, Chile and Bolivia during the nineteenth and early twentieth century. They built many of the urban tram networks, the famous elevators of Valparaíso; and Gustav Eiffel, the Frenchman responsible for the celebrated tower in Paris and the Statue of Liberty, applied

Inauguration of work on the Valparaiso-Santiago railway line in 1852.

The Illustrated London News

his iron-frame construction techniques in Arica and other cities in Chile, Bolivia and Peru.

However, it is the nitrate railways that will concern us here, since, at least in part, they were responsible for one of the most dramatic and painful events in Chile's history. Once more, "Colonel" John Thomas North was heavily implicated. The essential Englishness of the railway system across the Atacama Desert and down to the Pacific nitrate ports, was observed by the journalist William Howard Russell during his visit to Iquique with North:

"At the station of the Nitrate Railway you see a bustling staff of English clerks, engineers and drivers; piles of jute bags from Bremen or Dundee; Heath's patent fuel, Cardiff; machinery from Leeds and Glasgow; Fowler's and Fairlie's engines; American carriages – a little Crewe[1] full of life and energy.

When North returned to England, after the Pacific War, he had in his hands

---

1   A centre for railway stock construction in northern England

the title deeds – emanating from his astutely, or perhaps dubiously, procured nitrate certificates – for a business empire that would bring his eventual coronation as the "Nitrate King". In February 1883, he and his prominent associates registered the Liverpool Nitrate Company in the City of London with a paid-up capital of £150,000. This was followed by the Colorado Nitrate Company in 1885 and the Primitiva Nitrate Company in 1886.

Nitrate production had increased sharply after the cessation of Pacific War hostilities in 1883, in part boosted by Humberstone's new refining process. But output quickly outstripped global demand. The response by the major producers, in 1884, was to form the first of several price-fixing 'combinations' (cartels). Production quotas, or ceilings, were agreed for each nitrate oficina, while the industry awaited an upswing in world demand. Nevertheless, despite the revenue-stifling impact of the combination, North's new companies did well for their shareholders. The Liverpool Nitrate Company paid dividends of 26 per cent in 1885 and 20 per cent in 1886.

The City of London makes a killing

However, the real boom in share prices came when the combination collapsed at the end of 1886. The European markets for fertilizer were expanding again and modern plant was permitting some *oficinas* to produce ever more cheaply. New companies were floated on the London Stock Exchange in 1888 and 1889 to huge enthusiasm among investors. Some were companies promoted by North and his long-standing associate Robert Harvey. Other entrepreneurs got in on the act, but the undisputed leader of this new nitrate business mafia was always North. As *The Financial News* of London commented:

"Put Colonel North's name on a costermonger's[2] cart, turn it into a limited company, and the shares will be selling at 300% premium before they are an hour old... Whatever he touches turns, if not to gold, at least to premiums."

Some commentators called him a "regular charlatan", among other things, while competitors, like Gibbs and Son, resented his ascendancy in the very business they had spearheaded. *The Economist*, questioned the real value of the businesses being so effectively hyped on the stock exchange. But North basked in public popularity and fame. He became a social figure, having bought and renovated a mansion in Kent. He threw huge and extravagant parties, ran a stable of racehorses, hunted with the aristocracy, and maintained friends and acquaintances in very high places, including the Churchills, Rothschilds and even the Prince of Wales.

---

2   The term for a London street fruit vendor of the time

From the mid-1880s, whatever the doubts in London and among local bankers and traders in Chile, there evolved a profound identity of interest between North and the Chilean government. As nitrate exports multiplied so did government revenues through export taxes. By 1882, 27 per cent of state income was accounted for by these duties; in 1889 it was over 45 per cent. This was the basis for the large public works programme planned by President Balmaceda's government and, by some reckoning, one of the fundamental causes of the revolution that would shortly follow. For the moment, the Chilean establishment was as keen for the new nitrate companies to succeed as were the stockholders of those companies in Britain.

It was a comfortable arrangement and lesser men than 'Colonel' North would have sat back. But the "Nitrate King" wanted to control the entire business, especially the railways. The principal lines linking the *oficinas* to the coastal ports were built by the Peruvian Monteros brothers between 1868 and 1875, financed by large loans contracted in London. The National Nitrate Railways Company of Peru was registered in London in January 1874. Even after the Pacific War and the financial strains it generated, the Monteros retained a large portion of the shares in a newly established London-based company, the Nitrate Railways Company Ltd. However, in 1888, North snapped up most of the Monteros shares cheaply, becoming Chairman of the Board, in 1889.

The Nitrate Railways Company's near monopoly on services in Tarapacá, and the high tariffs it was able to charge as a consequence, had long been a sore point for nitrate producers. In essence they had no option but to pay up since their product had only one means to get to the ports of Pisagua and Iquique and into ships for export. Only one producer stood out, the Agua Santa Company, whose *oficina* was sited at a point from where nitrate could reasonably be transported by cart to the small port of Caleta Buena, some twenty miles away. Agua Santa was registered in Chile but dominated by the British firm of Campbell, Outram and Company.

In 1881, in an effort to circumvent the railway monopoly, Agua Santa and a handful of other companies sought new railway construction concessions from the government in Santiago. As they expected, their initiative was soon bogged down in legal complexity and political obstruction. However, in 1886, a government decree annulled the original Monteros concessions on the basis of non-fulfilment of contract. The Nitrate Railway Company appealed and the case steadily climbed the juridical ladder and became a jurisdictional cause celèbre. The Supreme Court ruled eventually that annulment of the concessions could not be solely an administrative act (government decree) which deprived the company of the right to a juridical appeal. On the other hand, the Chilean Council of State asserted that an ordinary court of law had no jurisdiction over the company's petition. This jurisdictional conflict between the courts and the government provoked a political confrontation, in 1889, just as North was cementing control of the Nitrate Railway Company in London.

But the tangle of interests would become more complicated still. North's ambitions to exercise an effective nitrate transport monopoly in Tarapacá also required control of the Patillos railway and the Lagunas nitrate fields in the south of the region. The rights in the line were also owned by the Montero Brothers while the nitrate rights were in the hands of a Chilean group. By 1887, through a series of complicated financial manoeuvres North had effective control over both. But the control was far from secure. Both the Nitrate Railway Company and the Patillos deals were under consideration by the Council of State, as was the control of the Lagunas nitrate fields. From afar, Gibbs and Sons were watching with increasing concern.

The Nitrate Railways Company Limited is registered in the City of London in 1882.

The Guildhall Library, London

In any event, absolute domination of the industry required control over water, finance and supplies. In September 1888, the Tarapacá Waterworks Company Limited was registered in London with £400,000 of share capital. Inevitably, the board included both North and Robert Harvey. The company soon dominated water supply in the region following a lengthy campaign by North to buy out, overwhelm or ruin the various alternative enterprises that sought to challenge him.

As for finance, the Bank of Tarapacá and London Limited was launched in London, with the support of N.M. Rothschild and Sons, in late 1888, with a capital of £1 million. North became Deputy Chairman of the Board of Directors. This time, North's associate John Dawson, himself a banker, secured the presence of the new bank in Chile, particularly, in Iquique, but with no licence to operate.

Given the many forms of general supplies required to operate the Tarapacá *salitreras* it must have seemed logical (and potentially profitable) to North to add a supplies business to all the other quasi-monopolies. Thus, the Nitrates Provisions Supply Company was floated on the London Stock Exchange with Robert Harvey as chairman, in 1889.

All of this new enterprise sustained and reinforced North's growing public popularity in Britain. The self-made man, succeeding through hard-work, iron nerve, good judgment and street-savvy, was the image he tirelessly cultivated. But the financial and commercial press was far from convinced. *The Economist* and *The Financial News* campaigned with increasing intensity on two fronts: the legitimacy of some of North's financial manipulation and the unpredictable nature of the world nitrate market. They questioned the intrinsic value of many of the companies whose shares British investors were rushing to buy up at inflated prices.

Both at home and in Chile, North's activities began to look vulnerable and in need of an injection of positive public relations. He decided to return to Chile, this time taking a posse of journalists – including from *The Financial News, The Times* of London (William Howard Russell) and Melton Prior, war artist from *The Illustrated London News*, which serialized the visit. Before leaving, North held a vast fancy dress ball for over eight hundred guests at the Metropole Hotel in London. It was a glittering and distinguished occasion with the cream of London society – among them, Lord Randolph Churchill, Lord Dorchester and Baron Rothschild and his wife. North dressed appropriately as King Henry VIII, and the lavish event may have cost him as much as £10,000.

North's stately progression through Chile duly impressed Russell, and the 'Nitrate king's' public standing in Chile was certainly boosted. However, while he was away from London, shares in North's companies collapsed as realization increased that even his magical powers might not be sufficient to correct the growing imbalance between the expanding productive capacity of the nitrate *oficinas* and the inability of markets to absorb the production. Nitrate stocks in Europe were already vast and being added to almost daily. Meanwhile the legal and constitutional clash over the nitrate railways and the Lagunas *salitreras* meandered on in the Chilean courts and Congress, adding to market uncertainty. Only at the end of 1890 was a combination agreement finally secured in London to again restrain production, but it would not operate fully until March 1891.

The terrain for a confrontation between the government of President José

Manuel Balmaceda and much of the European-based nitrate industry – as epitomized by John Thomas North – was set. Balmaceda was determined to ensure a permanent benefit to Chile from the exploitation of the nation's natural resources. Revenues from export taxes would be ploughed into public works projects and education. As an example of this remarkable effort in social engineering, official figures show enrolment in Chilean schools moving from 79,000 pupils in 1886 to 150,000 in 1890. Telegraph, railway, road, port and other infrastructure mushroomed in the same period with public buildings – hospitals, prisons and government offices – also proliferating.

Yet the emphasis on public works did not command a consensus among the political classes. Partisan critics charged that there were other priorities; but that Balmaceda could and did press on regardless reflected a much deeper constitutional division. The 1833 Chilean constitution had given much personal power to the president and its autocratic strands had only been reinforced since. Worse, presidents were free to avoid potential interference from the Congress by interfering in congressional elections and clipping congressional debate.

After his election in 1886, Balmaceda sought initially to be conciliatory with the Congress. In 1888, however, he reformed the cabinet, appointing only members of his Liberal Party, thus angering other groups, especially the previously supportive National Party. To shore up support, while flaunting the massive public works programmes that his nitrate policies had made possible, Balmaceda set out on an official visit to the Northern provinces of Tarapacá and Antofagasta. Coincidentally, the President only narrowly missed crossing the path of the Nitrate King who was about to descend on the same territories.

Some 150,000 people lined the dockside at Iquique when the president and a large delegation arrived on the warship *Amazonas* on 8 March 1889. It was the first visit ever by the Chilean head of state to the provinces taken in the Pacific War. The following evening, the President made a major speech on the government's approach to the nitrate industry. While he attacked foreign monopolies and the charges imposed by the Nitrate Railway Company, he avoided any direct promise to nationalize or to take part or all of the industry out of foreign hands. Indeed, quite what he was proposing was, and has remained, the subject of differing interpretation. Certainly the press of the time saw in the speech very much what their individual political inclinations required them to see.

Balmaceda toured the Tarapacá nitrate fields, in part courtesy of the Nitrate Railway Company's facilities, and stayed at North's house in the port of Pisagua. The delegation was lavishly entertained at two of North's *oficinas*. On his return to Valparaíso, Balmaceda found a request from North himself, just arrived in Chile, for a summit meeting.

The two met in Viña del Mar on 25 March, 1889. The encounter seems to have been cordial and, according to Howard Russell of *The Times*, Balmaceda was supportive of foreign capital helping to develop the country's natural resources. He had no interest in "making war on vested interests", and even praised the Nitrate Railway. Still, the meeting was essentially a social call and the habitually charming Balmaceda may have declined to show his teeth. There were two more such meetings in the following weeks. Overall, there is little reason to believe that North's affairs benefitted directly from his encounters with Balmaceda (or indeed the tour as a whole) or that they were damaged. North left for Iquique in early May 1889, staying at Humberstone's house at the Primitiva *oficina* during his tour of the nitrate fields. He spent a month inspecting his kingdom, before leaving for home on 7 June 1889, via Panama and New York. Among the many gifts he left behind was a new fire engine for Iquique which he had brought with him from England.

None of this deterred other powerful British firms from acting to dampen North's drive for absolute dominance. In September 1889, a few months after his departure for an increasingly sceptical London, Campbell, Outram and Company sought a concession to construct a new railway from its Agua Santa *oficina* to the little port of Caleta Buena between Pisagua and Iquique. Sensing the direction in which the political wind was blowing, the company proposed attractive terms on tariffs, access to the new service for other local *oficinas* and an option for the Chilean government to buy out the line whenever it wished. In response, the government put out an invitation for open tenders to build the Agua Santa line – with terms heavily set in Campbell, Outram's favour.

North and the Nitrate Railways Company's reaction was swift and heavy. They approached the Chilean Senate noting the constitutional issues already engaged with respect to the earlier railway concessions. Stressing the benefits the Nitrate Railway Company had brought to Tarapacá – essentially equating the country's interests to those of the company – a legal memorandum called on the Senate to refuse to allow the executive (government) powers that curtailed the responsibilities of the judiciary. Clearly, the intention was to influence an already sensitive domestic political stand-off.

North's political meddling embarrasses London

In London, North's company lobbied the Foreign Office, securing, initially, an instruction to the British minister in Santiago to support the company's interests there. But, just a few months later, the firm of Anthony Gibbs and

Sons intervened. The North monopolies and the "Nitrate King's" meddling in Chilean politics were damaging Gibbs's plans to develop a new nitrate field, called Alianza, which would need a railway concession to take the product to the port of Chucumata, south of Iquique. A power in the land – and probably the most distinguished British trading house in Chile - Gibbs began to pressure the Foreign Office, pointing out that many nitrate producers supported the Chilean government's position in questioning the monopolies. Embarrassment followed when the British government was pressed to explain why it was intervening diplomatically on one side only. Ultimately, the Foreign Office had no choice but to step back; the British minister in Santiago began taking a more nuanced line with the Chilean government. In any event, on 19 March 1880, the Agua Santa railway concession was granted to Campbell, Outram. That tender was followed by two others for nitrate railway projects to further seal the end of the Nitrate Railway Company's monopoly. Although legal advice in London was that these moves should be challenged in Santiago, the entanglement of issues affecting British nitrate interests and the wider political crisis were becoming acute. As the British minister, J G Kennedy, reported to the Foreign Secretary in London, in May 1890:

"...the President might profit by a renewed intervention of Her Majesty's Government ... to seek an escape from his serious political embarrassments by arousing the patriotic feelings of Chileans against what would be represented as an attempt by a foreign power to exercise pressure on the Government of Chile in a national matter."

That view prevailed in London. North was effectively set adrift. And it was not merely over the nitrate railway concessions; Gibbs had become a weighty counterbalance to North's urgent objective of constituting a new producer combination to cope with market demand difficulties and the overhang of excessive nitrate stocks. He started talks in London to find a means of creating buffer stocks of nitrate that would be held off the market. At the same time, Gibbs was strenuously pressing its interest in the Alianza-Chucumata railway directly with the Chilean President. Balmaceda's price was a concession which entailed a commitment to export nitrate at a set level. Naturally this would have maintained export revenues and permitted the President to pursue his popular public projects. At the same time, it would upset any combination commitment by other producers. So Gibbs became a wild card in the game being played in London and a joker in the pack in Chile where talk of revolution was growing.

While the nitrate railways controversy was not the cause of the domestic political crisis developing in 1889, it was a football to be kicked around by all sides. Balmaceda was drifting into intense trouble with Congress. Following ill-considered and divisive manoeuvres to fix the appointment of the next President (due in 1891), Balmaceda's cabinet resigned in October 1889. Forming a new cabinet was difficult, and the result only temporary, as political pressure was hardening all round for the President to be made subordinate to the will of Congress, while staying out of political party affairs and elections.

In January 1890, having refused demands for a Liberal Convention to elect a presidential candidate and with the resignation of the cabinet, Balmaceda dissolved Congress to widespread outcry. The Agua Santa case and the cancellation of the Nitrate Railway Company monopoly by government decree – whatever the rights and wrongs of the actions in terms of national interests – both added to the view of the opposition that Balmaceda would trample normal practices and laws to secure his party's political future and that of his pharaonic public works programmes. In the words of the historian Harold Blakemore, the stage was set for "the most profound constitutional crisis in the country's history."

Despite pressure from the opposition and a plea by the *Comisión Conservadora* (the guardian of the constitution) Balmaceda refused to reconvene Congress before the opening of a regular session on 1 June, 1890. When the President finally addressed the members of Congress he proposed a new constitution, but with presidential powers every bit as overbearing as those in the 1833 version. It was a mistake, he had misread the strength of sentiment in Congress and in much of the country. Within days, votes of censure against the government had passed in both the Senate and the Chamber of Deputies. The cabinet offered to resign, Balmaceda refused to accept the offer and the Chamber then passed a resolution refusing to consider the law authorizing the government to collect taxes.

The consequent economic crisis brought protests, notably in Tarapacá

President José Manuel Balmaceda

where there were deaths, and then in Valparaíso. Public and press opinion moved swiftly against Balmaceda; by the end of July there were calls for him to be declared unfit for office. Coincidentally, two of the most outspoken figures opposing Balmaceda were also the legal advisers in Chile of North's Nitrate Railway Company and Gibbs. Mediation efforts to bring the Congress and the President closer, initially failed. However, the Archbishop of Santiago intervened, in early August 1890, and secured a compromise under which a new cabinet was formed and the tax bill passed. The political ceasefire did not last. By early October the new government had itself resigned as relations with the President crumbled once more. Again, Balmaceda closed the Congress, while concern grew that he would seek to usurp the elections of 1891.

By December, the situation was so threatening that the British minister in Santiago wrote to the commander of the Royal Navy's Pacific fleet seeking the protection of two naval vessels in the ports of Iquique and Valparaíso. Balmaceda banned unauthorized public meetings after a murderous action by thugs at a meeting of Conservatives in Santiago. A few days later the congressional opposition drew up letters declaring the President unfit for office and sent them to the Admiral of the Fleet, Jorge Montt, and General Manuel Baquedano, the hero of the Pacific War. Montt pledged support in the event that Balmaceda violated the constitution. Baquedano declined.

On 1 January, 1891, Balmaceda challenged what he called a failure by Congress to perform its constitutional duty, and declared he would act by decree on the budget estimates and funding the armed forces. Several days later, at the request of leaders of the two houses of Congress, Admiral Montt took almost the entire Chilean fleet out of Valparaíso Bay with marines and many prominent politicians on board. Balmaceda reacted by mobilizing the army, imposing a state of siege, suspending the constitution and, when the Supreme Court, on 10 January, declared these acts unconstitutional, repressing the judiciary. Many political arrests were made, together with imprisonment, flogging and exile at will. Balmaceda even sought British naval assistance to destroy the Chilean fleet – a request politely declined by the British minister in Santiago.

The Nitrate Railway Company and anything associated with it became objects of hatred and suspicion by Balmaceda and his supporters. One of the President's decrees in January 1891, was to suspend all nitrate exports from Tarapacá. During the summer of 1891, when a Balmacedist Congress was sitting, direct charges were made against North suggesting he was complicit with Chilean bankers in fomenting the revolution. That was an exaggeration, but the sympathies of the British community in Chile were largely on the side of the "Congressionalists" and their revolution. No doubt North's companies did, indeed, supply the forces of the Congressionalists in Tarapacá, but these were normal commercial transactions – there were few other suppliers, after all. Furthermore, North did make some representations in favour of the anti-Balmaceda revolutionists to the British Foreign Office, but they were mild and limited. British firms certainly provided material assistance while British naval officers sided naturally with Admiral Montt as a respected fellow commander.

Another observer of the revolution was Maurice Hervey of *The Times* of London, sent out specially to seek the truth given the gathering interest in London, not least in the commodity and financial markets. It was assumed he would back the Congressionalists as did most English interests in the country. But Hervey was a pugnacious, strong-minded reporter who needed convincing. He attempted to provide a reasoned and balanced record of these ultimately tragic events.

"I had not travelled 12,000 miles merely to play echo to Congressionalist statements ... It was easy to denounce Balmaceda as a tyrant, a ruffian, a murderer; but I required evidence of his tyranny, of his ruffianism, of his murders."

The reporter was immediately inundated with offerings from the revolutionary side. Of one such representation he noted:

"As a document denunciatory of Balmaceda, his aiders and abettors, the paper left little unsaid; well-nigh every English adjective indicative of moral crookedness was introduced, in the superlative degree. But, it was all assertion. Not one atom of proof was adduced."

Having failed to sway *The Times's* correspondent directly, Hervey claimed the "revolutionists" then started sending poisonous cablegrams and letters to London. He believed North was behind the campaign. He held his ground, commenting, with an unconcealed disdain for his former *Times* colleague William Russell:

"I had not lived long enough to accept a commission as Descriptive Writer for a Nitrate King. I held no brief. And whether or not my conclusions should prove favourable or the reverse to Chilean agitators and their foreign sympathizers, I was resolved that these conclusions should be based upon the evidence of my own senses."

Finally, he decided to talk directly with the President. He met with Balmaceda at the Moneda Palace and promptly sought to lecture the Chilean leader. The response was caustic:

"Your records [those of England] indicate a continuous struggle between a dominant aristocracy and a liberty-seeking people. And, in the course of time, you have contrived to reconcile the pretensions of both. But your ways are not the ways of the rest of the world; and most certainly they are not our ways. Your hereditary throne, your hereditary House of Lords, and your popular elective House of Commons appear to harmonize with the character of the English nation. But they do not meet the views of younger nationalities, which invariably adopt a republican form of government. Now, here comes the great difference. With you, but one out of three powers is elective. In a republic, all three are elective. Your two hereditary powers are, more or less, automata; that is, neither Crown nor Lords dare oppose a strong expression of national will. We have no such automata; least of all is a Chilean president such an automaton, being invested by the Chilean constitution with powers greater even than those of Congress." His oath of office had been to uphold the constitution "as it stands", not as it may be interpreted through custom and practice. "Congress, by the express terms of that constitution, has no more right to dictate to me what ministers I shall choose than it has to ordain what food I shall eat or what clothes I shall wear."

David Davies continued to serve as an officer on the mail steamer "Imperial" after it was commandeered by Balmaceda to harrass the Chilean navy which had sided with the Congressionalists. *The Graphic*

Hervey understood the foreign entrepreneurs and traders: they were unsettled by the positions taken by the President and especially his threats to end those concessions and special favours granted to European syndicates exploiting the wealth of Tarapacá. In concluding his investigation of Balmaceda's behaviour, Hervey finds the charges against the President "not proven" and that Balmaceda had "a long way the best of the argument". He also believed that the Chilean leader would, in the end, prevail. However, getting a dispatch to that effect back to London proved tricky. The *Times* man discovered that all such communications were vetted by the Ministry of the Interior in Santiago and his would be no exception, even if it did offer unusual support for the Government's position. No *Times* correspondent could be treated that way. Hervey flounced off indignantly "to the Moneda, to interview the Minister for the Interior. I think I rather staggered Senor Godoy with my vehemence."

Hervey would accept neither that the clearance of his story was a matter of routine, nor the personal signature of the Minister on "any required number of blank forms," to permit him to file articles subsequently without challenge. Taken directly by Minister Godoy to see the President, he argued his case for the right to unmolested communication with his office in London. He went as far as to threaten to take one of the English ships, then in Valparaíso harbour, north to Iquique and to send his dispatches from the revolutionary headquarters there. He won his case. The President conceded.

One British reporter supports President Balmaceda

But his dispatches caused anger at *The Times* which, like other British newspapers, had been inundated by pro-revolutionary sentiment, much of it relayed by *The Times* correspondent in Rio de Janeiro. While a telegram instructing Hersey to return to the UK was subsequently reversed, giving him reluctant clearance to travel north with a government naval squadron to witness the events which would follow, he was indignant that his judgment could have been put in question, and probably ridiculed. He subsequently observed key actions of the civil war during three cruises up the coast. He travelled in one of the merchant ships commandeered by the President to harass the Congressionalist fleet. He admitted that the mail steamer *Imperial,* owned by the Compañía SudAmericana de Vapores and, like other requisitioned merchant vessels, still crewed largely by Europeans, offered him great luxury and a ringside seat at various naval engagements.

Hervey maintained his support for Balmaceda. When he arrived in Valparaíso after his third cruise, an instruction to return to London awaited him. Reviewing the local and international press he understood that he had been in a minority of virtually one. He left Santiago, generously offering the President the benefits of his military judgment and an affectionate, if outspoken, farewell:

"That was my last interview with the 'Bogieman' of London journalism – the great leader who stood between the Chilean people and the triple curse of a bankrupt oligarchy, a depraved Papist clergy, and the insatiable greed of parvenus foreign nitrate adventurers."

Hervey departed the country before the civil war had reached its violent and tragic conclusion. With the army staying loyal to the President and the navy siding with the Congressionalists, it was the latter who would command the military advantage throughout. Admiral Montt blockaded Valparaíso and the nitrate ports in mid-January 1891, with the President's forces ceding both Pisagua and Iquique in early February. A decisive land battle at Pozo Almonte handed the entire nitrate region to the Congressionalist forces, opening the way for a Junta government under Montt and others to harness the revenues for arms purchases. In the months that followed, both sides sought to rearm, the forces loyal to the President needing ships and the Congressionalists seeking guns. Once again, it was those backing the revolution that had most success, not only securing arms from Europe for 10,000 soldiers, but unexpectedly finding a key military strategist, General Emil Körner, joining them in the north. Körner had been brought from Germany in 1886 to modernize the Chilean army. Disillusioned with Balmaceda, he would be a vital asset as the Congressionalists prepared for the final phase of the civil war.

Back in Santiago, the President was able to oversee the election of a new, and relatively pliant, national assembly. Political posturing over the influence of foreign interests as well as anti-establishment feeling grew while most opposition voices – notably in the press and universities – were repressed harshly. The limits of repression were reached in August 1891 when several dozen young Congressionalist militants, meeting at the Lo Canas hacienda near Santiago, were cut down savagely by the army.

Within days, the navy brought a Congressionalist army of some 9,000 men from the north to the port of Quintero, near Valparaíso. The revolutionary force engaged Balmaceda's army first at Concón, on 21 August, and then at Placilla, seven days later. These two short battles were fierce, merciless and costly in deaths on both sides. They were followed by looting and arson in Valparaíso, quickly brought to order by the marines, leaving a reported 300 corpses in the streets.

The Congressionalists had prevailed bloodily – with around 6000 dead in all. Balmaceda transferred his authority to General Baquedano and fled to the Argentine legation in Santiago. Only when the Congressionalist army entered the capital was mob violence finally calmed. Three weeks later, unable to countenance a life in exile, Balmaceda shot himself through the head.

Yet the assessment of José Manuel Balmaceda by *The Times* reporter Maurice Hervey was not far off the mark. Six months after his death his body was disinterred and reburied in the family vault with great pomp and ceremony. His reputation restored, the tragic but, to many, heroic, passionate and decent, leader was reinstated in the nation's pantheon where he remains today. Hearing of the suicide of Balmaceda after the victory of the Congressional side, Hervey reflected sadly at the conclusion of his book "Dark Days in Chile":

"My chief regret is that I cannot see a silver lining to the cloud which so

The city of Iquique was destroyed by a naval bombardment during the civil war.
The Illustrated London News

many others have seen reflected from the revolutionary bayonets. My chief sorrow is that so many persons endeared to me during my stay in Chile are dead or in exile."

The British community and its nitrate interests were clearly relieved at the outcome, at least initially. As the British minister reported to the Foreign Secretary on 21 September 1891: "[they] make no secret of their satisfaction over the downfall of Balmaceda whose triumph, it is believed, would have involved serious prejudice to British commercial interests."

The sense of optimism was duly marred by *The Economist*[3]:

"...it will not do to be too sanguine that all questions between the nitrate companies themselves and between the nitrate companies and the Chilean Government have been put at rest..."

---

3   5 September 1891

The journal was right: nothing much changed. The new government confirmed the view that the high tariffs charged by the Nitrate Railway Company and the danger of monopolies were very much as Balmaceda had seen them. In the years that followed, succeeding governments made clear they were no less sensitive to the nation's dependence on foreign interests in the exploitation of natural assets (and export tax revenues) than was Balmaceda. At the end of 1892, with the foreign export cartel attracting increasing public criticism, and despite existing over-production, the government sought authorization from Congress to sell new nitrate concessions. Chilean national pride and patriotism were increasingly roused by newspapers and politicians. Foreign businesses saw the writing on the wall. There was also strong commercial resentment among trading houses and shippers in Valparaíso which were being circumvented by direct export shipments from the nitrate ports in Tarapacá. In a letter to his London headquarters the manager of Antony Gibbs & Sons in Valparaíso noted, on 27 July 1893:

"… [It is] very clearly the intention on the part of the government to do all they can to hostilize and if possible break up the Nitrate Combination and damage the Bank of Tarapacá, and the feeling is we fear developing into another period of dislike to foreigners generally and perhaps the English particularly as being more closely connected with Nitrate manufacture and combination."

Fortuitously perhaps, the local sense of bitterness was attenuated in early 1894 when the price-fixing combination fell apart in London and the Chilean government successfully sold to Chilean interests a number of new nitrate fields.

But the throne of John Thomas North was now more than insecure. Uncertainty in the nitrate business became generalized. North tried various manoeuvres to regain the upper hand, including opening up the Lagunas nitrate fields with a new syndicate and a stock flotation in London. The price of the shares in the new company initially rose strongly as had been the case for all his ventures. But *The Economist* attacked him violently. Still, his businesses had a short renaissance despite the criticism. Indeed, his public popularity was sufficiently restored for him to seek a parliamentary seat in Leeds – though he lost at the election. He then struck out on a series of new business initiatives around the world: factories in France, gold mines in Australia, a tramway in Egypt, a cement works and a hotel project in Belgium and rubber in the Congo.

These projects were in part intended to counterbalance the failing nitrate interests and sustain his public image. The revival of the nitrate market, in 1894, was brief. Managers at the Valparaíso trading house, Balfour Williams, reckoned the Lagunas syndicate had 30,000 tons of unsold product: "The result must be disastrous..." In autumn 1895, North, as chairman, had himself to move the winding up of the Primitiva Company. Other North companies in Tarapacá were ailing, dividends were falling and share prices collapsing. Yet the now crownless "Nitrate King" himself hardly felt the losses; it was discovered that he had earlier bailed out of most of the companies at a good price.

North died of a heart attack on 5 May 1896, after a banquet at his mansion. *The New York Times* and others reported that the attack may have been brought on by oysters consumed at the meal. His funeral was grandiose, telegrams of sympathy flowed in from around the world. In Chile, North's passing was not much noticed by the Spanish language press and he was mourned only by some in the British community. Over the following years enquiries revealed the extent to which he had manipulated the values and affairs of his companies, especially the Nitrate Railway Company. His reputation only declined with time: colourful, yes; a dubious and manipulative capitalist, certainly.

Of course, the demise of "Colonel" North did not spell the end of the Chilean nitrate industry, or anything like it. However, the amount of British capital invested began to diminish from the mid-1890s onwards. Chilean and German capital was rising. Export figures for 1910 indicate that over 31 per cent was accounted for by Chilean interests, 25 per cent by English and 24 per cent by German. The remaining 20 per cent was in the hands of Spanish, Peruvian, Austrian, French and Italian interests. Clearly, the face of the industry was changing even if Europeans maintained the lion's share.

Three foreign names stand out from those who profited from the subsequent period of nitrate exploitation in Chile: Sloman, Baburizza and Guggenheim. Although Henry Brarens Sloman was named the richest man in Hamburg in 1912 and was responsible for the construction of one of the architectural masterpieces of that city – the *Chile-Haus* – he was born in England, in Kingston-upon-Hull. The family fortunes were based on trading and shipping services, but when his father lost heavily during the Crimean War, young Henry was sent to the German branch of the family for his studies and an apprenticeship. In 1869, at the age of 21, Sloman decided to set sail for Peru, following a close friend, Hermann Fölsch. He suffered one of the more troubled passages, via Cape Horn, with his ship finally lowering its anchor in Peru after 160 days.

The new nitrate magnates: Henry Sloman and Pascual Baburizza

Initially working with the American Henry Meiggs, who was then engaged on the construction of the Central Peru Railway across the Andes, Sloman later picked up again with Fölsch and spent the next 22 years successfully building the nitrate business of the family firm Fölsch and Martin. In 1874, Hermann Fölsch returned to Hamburg to marry Henry's sister, Harriet, and sail back with her to Iquique. Sloman, having bought concessions in the unpromising area of La Pampa del Toco, outside the port of Tocopilla, mid-way between Iquique and Antofagasta, embarked on his own independent enterprise, Compania Salitrera de H B Sloman, in 1891. He built special loading quays at Tocopilla, constructed a dam to channel water to his *oficinas* and arranged with a Hamburg shipping line, Laiez, to take the nitrates to Europe. His first *oficina* was aptly named "Buena Esperanza" ("Good Hope") and was followed by several others nearby, "Rica Aventura" ("Wonderful Adventure") and "Prosperidad" ("Prosperity") among them. Prosper he did: his 1912 wealth was estimated at 16 million deutschmarks (around four million US dollars of the time). Hamburg toppled Liverpool as the most important port for European arrivals of nitrate. Sloman, a practising Lutheran, also built the town of Tocopilla its first Catholic church.

Like most of the rest of the nitrate industry in Chile, Sloman's *oficinas* suffered during the First World War, with many of his shipments lost in the sea war. At one point, he is reported to have approached the grand German Admiral Tirpitz with a plan to break the British naval blockade: using his own money to finance submarines. The reply was a polite no. In 1924, Sloman finally returned to Germany with most of his nitrate assets transferred to other companies.

The nitrate shipping losses of the First World War were severe. Exports fluctuated wildly, although demand for explosives as well as that for fertilizers remaining as high as ever. Erratic deliveries reflected the hazards facing the nitrate ships both in the Pacific and in crossing the Atlantic. The starkest example was the French shipping company Antoine-Dominique Bordes et Fils which had run its grand and distinctive steel-hulled sailing vessels from the nitrate ports of Chile to Europe, via Cape Horn, for several decades. The firm was taken over and renamed by the French state, Compagnie d'Armement et d'Importation des Nitrates de Soude, charged with maintaining a wartime supply. As many as sixteen Bordes ships were lost from U-boat (submarine) torpedoes and German surface warship fire, solely on the nitrate run.

Just as the Chile-Haus in Hamburg remains a startling and timeless monument to Henry Sloman's nitrate adventure, so the art-deco, art-nouveau Palacio Baburizza, on the hill above the port of Valparaíso, is the city's magnificent architectural inheritance from another remarkable European nitrate entrepreneur, Pascual Baburizza. The man who might reasonably be described as the heir of the "Nitrate King", John Thomas North, was born on Kolecep Island off

Dubrovnik, in what is now Croatia, in 1875. His was a poor fishing family in a troubled period of Habsburg domination of the Balkans. On his father's death, and at the age of just seventeen years, two of the three brothers decided to emigrate rather than suffer military service. They chose Chile, having heard about the promise of "white gold" and arrived in Valparaíso, in 1892, moving quickly

Henry Sloman (centre) and some of his *oficina* managers at the company guest-house, around 1925.   *Guillermo Burgos collection*

northwards to Iquique and the nitrate fields of Tarapacá. They would have felt reasonably at home: by the 1890s there was already a Croatian community in Tarapacá, numbering around four hundred out of more than eleven hundred Croats recorded in Chile as a whole.

Following a succession of modest jobs around Iquique, Baburizza became a small-scale trader of supplies, especially meat. By 1910 he was the principal shareholder in a new company formed specifically to deliver fresh meat to the nitrate oficinas throughout Chile. In parallel, from around 1902, he also invested in nitrate companies, taking minority shares in several before, in 1909, starting to build a significant stake in the powerful Compania de Salitres de Antofagasta. Then, unexpectedly, in 1912 Baburizza suddenly sold out. It was time for him to become a king-pin in the still fast-growing industry.

Valparaiso Bound!

In 1913 Baburizza, Bruna y Cia was formed in Valparaíso, quickly buying a group of producing nitrate fields north-east of Antofagasta, known collectively as the Salitrera Progreso. That was just a start. The firm weathered the First World War better than most competitors, while adding general trading activities, including importing machinery for other *salitreras*, becoming the local agent for a British insurance company and establishing links with major shipping lines, especially in Yugoslavia. The firm acted as agent for an English coal supplier, a Norwegian explosives manufacturer and even had a concession to distribute Chilean wines. In 1923, with the industry now consolidating, Baburizza took a stake in the giant, London-based, Lautaro Nitrate Company, which two years later swallowed the Companía de Salitres de Antofagasta. By then the Lautaro Nitrate Company accounted for 24 oficinas and 27 per cent of Chilean nitrate sales. With its capacity to transport, trade and distribute its own production it was in a powerful position and was soon quoted on the London, Paris and Brussels stock exchanges – as well as those in Valparaíso and Santiago. Baburizza had truly inherited North's crown while remaining a quiet, reserved and somewhat solitary individual – rather the opposite of his flamboyant, high-profile predecessor.

He was also canny and farsighted. Baburizza & Company Limited, the London-based parent company, as well as the branches in Chile, appear to have been operating increasingly prudently well in advance of the Wall Street crash and the onset of the Great Depression. Certainly, nitrate export figures for 1928 and 1929 were among the highest ever, but Baburizza had a sense of what was coming and seemed to understand instinctively that the industry would never be the same again. Demand for fertilizer in Europe was increasingly being met through synthetic products while explosives were being manufactured without the need for saltpetre-based nitrates. In any event, economic activity worldwide was already under threat when, in 1928, Baburizza decided to anticipate the coming financial catastrophe and sell out. His massive holding in the Lautaro Nitrate Company was snapped up by the Guggenheim Brothers in what was one of their most disastrous business decisions. The new Guggenheim technology that the family thought would make their *oficinas* so productive that they would halt the drift away from saltpetre nitrates, did no such thing. Despite getting into bed with the newly-established Chilean state enterprise COSACH – the Compañía de Salitre de Chile – the industry suffered badly in the mid-1930s, as did the Guggenheims. There were modest, short-lived recoveries in nitrate exports over the following decades but, by the 1950s, the *oficinas* were closing up fast and only a handful were left in the 1970s.

Pascual Baburizza had diversified however. He had turned the Banco Yugoslav into a major financial player by the end of the 1920s; he had played a big role in the reconstruction of the port of Antofagasta, using cement shipped from Yugoslavia; he developed his shipping interests and construction projects as well as investing in copper and other mining activities. Most of all, he pursued his greatest love, farming, through a multitude of agricultural development enterprises. Baburizza himself died from tuberculosis, in 1941, in Los Andes to where he had moved from Valparaíso in an attempt to get the better of the disease. Although Baburizza & Co Ltd, was voluntarily wound up in London in 1937, he left behind a vast heritage in addition to the remains of a business empire. His altruism had helped establish the Colegio Yugoslavo de Antofagasta, a new fire brigade in that same city, and a medical school in Valparaíso. Above all, in the 1920s, he bought and completed the construction of what would be known as the Palacio Baburizza. As the Museo de Bellas Artes de Valparaíso, this remarkable building came recently to house his large collection of paintings and other artworks which he bequeathed to the city.

Of course, it would be a gross distortion of the history of this immense industry, which transformed the economy of Chile, to see the nitrate business as simply a century-long parade of European capitalists. 'Colonel' North did not dirty his hands much, after his initial efforts to make a living as a railway engineer in Caldera. Nor were Henry Sloman and Pascual Baburizza – still less, the Guggenheims - well known for the physical effort they exerted in generating their fortunes from the assets of the desert. Certainly there were many foreigners present in the *salitreras* –including Chinese and other groups working, at times, in particularly slave-like conditions - but it was mostly ordinary Peruvians, Bolivians and Chileans who daily strained their muscles to feed nitrates to the Pacific ports. At the peak, in 1910, there were probably around 45,000 male workers with more than half as many women and uncounted children in the *oficinas*.

The end of the nitrate era – regrets as well as tragedy

Were they badly treated? It can be argued that in the isolated locations in which the *oficinas* had to be sited, there was no other option open to the owners than to provide conditions sufficient for their employees to work efficiently. Given the prevailing social conditions in the haciendas and in the large towns, the shelter, housing and other welfare provided by the nitrate companies were probably superior. A glance at conditions in the South Wales coal mines, those of West Virginia in the United States and New South Wales in Australia, or the goldmines of South Africa, at the time, would certainly suggest that life in the Atacama Desert was, at least, no worse. But that is not to say that social tensions were absent.

Indeed, the first decade of the twentieth century was marked in Chile by social disorder, the rise of labour unions and undercurrents of anarchism. In 1903, stevedores of the Pacific Steam Navigation Company in Valparaíso went on strike. When the employers tried to draft in replacement labour, large-scale riots broke out in the town. These were supressed by the army and navy at the cost of several hundred lives. Two years later, a demonstration against high meat prices was put down violently in Santiago, with two hundred left dead, while a railwaymen's strike in Antofagasta in 1906, ended when marines opened fire in the main square killing several dozen protestors.

The nitrate industry saw its share of labour militancy in that same period. The grievances were various, especially for the least-favoured daily work-

Striking nitrate workers marching in Iquique prior to the massacre at the Santa Maria school in December 1907. *www.memoriachilena.cl*

ers. In particular, the 'company-store' system was grievously exploitative. Employees, captive in their distant *oficinas*, could only buy their daily personal needs, as well as their entertainment, from shops and other facilities run by the company, and often pay for them only in a special currency issued by the employer Already low wages were, in this manner, effectively claimed back by the nitrate owners. These and other practices provoked industrial actions from 1900 onwards.

The most tragic instance took place in Iquique in December 1907. A strike, initially involving men from two *salitreras*, developed quickly into a major confrontation with the civil and military authorities as well as the owners. With an estimated 10,000 to 12,000 strikers gathered in the centre of Iquique, around the Santa María school, the leaders called on the governor to mediate with the nitrate companies involved. In the meantime, the army was being reinforced and naval vessels were sailing towards Iquique. The tension rose. Several strikers were killed. Finally, the military commander gave orders for the troops to open fire on the crowd. The number of fatalities from the machine-gun onslaught has never been confirmed, but estimates range from the official figure of just under 200 to claims of several thousand dead. The Santa María School massacre became a symbol for working class resistance in Chile, and remains so.

There were many less horrific examples of violent assaults on strikers. But that is not to say the *salitrera* communities were without social cohesion. Given the isolation of the villages whose existence depended on the *oficinas*, there was an intensity in the communal spirit perhaps even greater than that once found in the coal mining towns of Britain. Certainly, the passing of the nitrate era was a social disaster; the good days were remembered with nostalgia.

It is put well by Hernán Rivera Letelier, the Chilean novelist who grew up in the nitrate villages and found early work in the *oficinas*. His 2008 work, *"Mi nombre es Malarossa"*, traces the local social impact of one of the closures.

"In its heyday, the outsiders permeating the streets and squares during weekends could exceed two thousand people. Most were workers who came to whoop it up, body and soul, to exchange all their wages for wine and beer in barrels, jukebox music and the laughter of loose women, women with too much lipstick and flimsy dresses. Not for nothing, in this modest centre, as well as three hotels, boarding houses, a general shop, clothing stores, wine-sellers, billiards, pubs and taverns, seventeen brothels managed to operate."

But the nitrate crisis decimated the villages in the 1930s as, one after the other, the businesses and the population slowly departed for the towns.

"The first to go was the smoke; the smoke of the *salitreras*, the smoke of the *caliche* trains, the smoke of the mud-brick stoves; after the gringos disappeared (already they were no longer seen in the brothels, with their safari jackets and their red faces like scavenging birds), then the police went and later the shop-keepers – first the established merchants and afterwards the peddlers – and in their turn the whores vanished, and then, ineluctably, the village was gone. And there, standing in the sand, under the white desert sun, we realized that all these years we had lived, we had loved, we had conceived our children and buried our dead in a mirage."

14.

The legacies: families, teachers and priests

Fare ye well, Chiliano ladies,
We now bid you fond adieu,
And we never will forget you,
Or the times we spent with you,
But we leave you our best wishes,
As we leave your fertile shore,
For we are bound across the ocean,
To return to you no more.

Rolling home, rolling home,
Rolling home, across the sea.
Rolling home to Merrie England
Rolling home, fair land, to thee.

Song sung by the crew of the *British Isles[1]*, 1901

Power and influence in Chile remains, to this day, dominated by a relatively small number of families whose roots date back to colonial times – when Spanish soldiers wedded local women – and the nineteenth century when new European immigrants married into those clans and established their own. The melange of Spanish family names with those that boast of origins in England, Wales, Scotland, Italy, France and Croatia, among others, constantly grace the business and political news pages of modern newspapers, not to speak of the social columns. One British traveller and naturalist, in 1907, put it bluntly:

"But Chile is only nominally a republic; it was then (around 1890) and is now, an oligarchy governed and directed by a few very rich Santiago families whose influence was of the same nature as that of the great British families – the Cecils and others in England – only more so."

Who are the Chileans? The conquistadors did not bring their women-folk along when they were conquering Latin America for their King and

---

1   See Chapter 1

Church. From their arrival, Spanish men and native women produced babies and, according to the historian and early president of independent Argentina, Bartholomé Mitre, those offspring were normally immediately regarded as of "pure Spanish descent". In most colonies the fighting, if any, was over quickly, and soldiers moved on. In Chile it was otherwise, at least from the region of Araucanía southwards. Three centuries were insufficient for conquest. So soldiers took their native women with them; according to some writers, not just one. Nicholás Palacios, a Chilean physician, wrote extensively on the subject. His conclusions have been summed up as follows:

"The Spanish trooper fared south to the frontier with from four to six native women to attend him. Four to one was the ratio of the sexes in the frontier garrisons, and soon there was a swarm of half-breed children. In a single week in 1580, sixty such children were born in a post with one hundred and sixty soldiers. In 1550, the married men in Valdivia had up to thirty concubines apiece. Aguirre, one of the conquistadors, left at his death fifty legitimate sons, to say nothing of daughters."

If true it would be a remarkable performance for men fighting against the odds in a debilitating, savage war, often going for months without adequate food and supplies. Indeed, the commentator Mark Jefferson, writing for the American Geographical Society in 1921, extols this amazing martial fecundity:

"It is doubtful if the exploits in parentage of the Chilean pioneers can be matched in history. The men of two of the most bellicose breeds the world has ever known wore each other down by endless warfare, so that innumerable native women became the booty of the surviving white men and bore them children."

Whatever the exaggeration, as Jefferson pointed out, the offspring of the couplings of soldiers and Indian women were not simply fodder for general population growth but the underpinning of the Chilean aristocracy:

"Even the singular group of families with English or Irish names – the Edwards, Walker, Williams, Tupper, Clark, Holly, Miller, Thompson, Lynch, O'Brien, Cochrane and Mackenna families – all so prominent in the Chilean [society], have Indian blood by their marriages with Creole families."

John Miers, the British engineer and long-time resident of Chile in the 1820s, took a predictably dim view of the tendency of European gentlemen to wed local women, no matter how well-heeled the families of their brides may have been:

"The laws respecting dowries are likewise very singular: the husband can under no circumstances dispose of the property of the wife without her express consent; and in the case of separation, divorce or bankruptcy, she can always claim her own dowry, together with one-half of all profits he may have accumulated since their marriage...

"In cases of adultery and divorce, it seems singular that a woman should claim her own dowry as well as her husband's profits; but in all instances the Spanish colonial laws display a remarkable tendency in favour of the woman, rendering her in fact quite independent of her husband. ... The privileges claimed by the woman seem quite incompatible with the customs of commercial persons, and yet it is surprising to see Englishmen marrying the native women: two or three instances I have known where our countrymen have been most fortunate in their selection, but it is a hazard of too great risk for a prudent man to venture upon: should the wife please, she can prevent the husband from

The English Tearoom in Calle Prat, Valparaiso, around 1922. The place for port gossip and deal-making.

being master of his own house, she can introduce and maintain as many of her relations as she chooses: it may indeed be said that, in marrying a Chilena, he marries her whole family.

"A singular instance of this occurred to an Englishman, who kept an inferior type of tavern in Valparaíso: soon after his marriage with a Chilena woman, she began to introduce her sisters into the house, till at length she brought together, one after another, no less than eighteen persons , whom she claimed as her relations: the poor Englishman, who bore a reasonable encroachment without grumbling, took fire at so monstrous an intrusion, and was about to turn all out by force, when he was taken before the governor, who declared his conduct unwarrantable, and that he would be liable to severe consequences were he to transgress in like manner in future: there was no alternative, and the wife and friends soon ate the poor fellow out of house and home."

The British journalist William Howard Russell, writing of his observations during the tour of Chile by John Thomas North in 1889-1890, had his own thought on the matter:

"At the exchange, the bourse, and the quay all these gentlemen, foreign and native, meet as business men, but out of business they have generally no relations. It is said that the Germans have a remarkable facility in learning Spanish, and I believe that saying is true. But I have reason to think that the number of Englishmen who marry Chilian women, though it is small, is far greater than the number of Germans who seek wives among the natives of the country. They have their musical reunions, their kneips[2], and their fire brigades, and as far as they can, they carry about the manners and customs of the Fatherland with them, but they are not quite so prone as the English to marry and settle in the country. English names are borne by men high in the service of the State, and by politicians and landowners the descendants of English, Irish and Scotch, who married Chilian ladies and settled in the country, and who for the most part, if not always, become intensely Chilian in feeling, and generally adopted the religion of the people."

Certainly, a visit to the "Dissidents' Cemetery" in Valparaíso today gives substance to Russell's suspicions. The German names rival those of British and other nationalities in this plot reserved for those outside the Roman Catholic Church. The Germans did, indeed, keep themselves to themselves. English, Welsh, Irish and Scottish surnames, on the other hand, are more easily observed, hyphenated with old Spanish family names, in the two cemeteries reserved for those of the Roman Catholic faith above and below the dissidents' patch.

What we can be sure of, however, is that whatever their distant origins and religions may have been, the offspring of the nineteenth-century arrivals who chose to stay, regarded themselves as wholly Chilean. According to Burton Holmes, the American travelwriter:

"The Irish, the English and the Scotch (sic) have played a noble part in Chilean history. Sons of those British adventurers bearing their Irish, English and Scotch names are the men who are today ruling the destinies and shaping

2   Probably kneipe, or bar.

the civilization of the nation. But they do this as Chileans, they are in no sense foreigners, they are patriotic sons of Spanish-speaking mothers – their Christian names all have a Spanish ring: Carlos, Juan, Eduardo and Enrique."

One of the most dominant families in Chile, for some two centuries, has been the Subercaseaux, hailing not from the British Isles, but from France. Francois Pierre Pascal Suber de Casaux arrived in Chile in 1754, a son of a noble line that dates from the fifteenth century in the Gironde region of Southwest France. A junior naval officer, he is said to have left France in the wake of a duel. Having met with some success in the development of silver mining around Copiapó, he was soon persuaded to lend his military skills against the British who had declared war on Spain. He organized the defence of the port of Coquimbo and subsequently rose up the ranks, in part because of his effectiveness as a commander and in part because he put his own money into equipping his army units. He was known for his sense of charity and was appointed mayor of Copiapó in 1791 having received his naturalization papers two years earlier. He died in the early years of the nineteenth century. Suber de Caseaux's marriage to Manuela Mercado y Corvalán, had produced a family that would soon link the name Subercaseaux with other powerful and influential Chilean lines like Vicuña, Mackenna, Browne, Perez, Larrain, Errázuriz and Concha. Many would hold high political office; there would be writers, historians, artists as well as engineers, wine-growers and businessmen.

We could go on reciting the hundreds, if not thousands, of Chilean family names that spring directly from the original Spanish colonists, from the post-independence influx of new immigrants from across Europe or from the entanglement of both. As mentioned earlier, a visit to almost any cemetery in the country would also do the job effectively. More interesting is to explore how those grand and not-so-grand families attracted others, those with a calling and the will to withstand the rigours of the voyage and the environment and who perhaps did most to inspire a sense of identity within a proud Chilean community which, nevertheless, clings to distant European roots. For this we need finally to consider the influence of the teachers and the priests.

Teachers unwelcome except to train priests

If it is possible to refer to a colonial system of education under Spanish rule, it was a very rudimentary and selective one. As the capital of the Vice-royalty, Lima in the sixteenth century was a prime centre for education, but of a tiny elite – mainly offspring of the ruling administration and the clergy. For that limited purpose, the Universidad Mayor de San Marcos was founded in the city, by royal decree, in 1551. Run by the Church, it was the very first university in the whole of the Americas and remains one of the top educational establishments in Peru to this day.

For ordinary children, no such instruction was possible, especially for the Indians repressed in the systems of servitude that marked the first centuries of colonialization. As we have seen earlier (Chapter 9), attempts to improve their conditions, including offering at least some basic religious training, as in the ordinances of Santillán, came to nothing. Indeed, real schooling was not favoured by the early Spanish monarchs in their dominions. They feared the undermining of power structures, insurrection and even the formation of independence movements by informed subjects. This went even for the colonists of Spanish birth. Thus, throughout most of the sixteenth century there were no colleges or printing presses in Chile. The attitude was not very different from that prevailing in Spain at the time, certainly as it applied outside the wealthy and powerful strata of society. The conquistadores had come to fight, not to bother with educating their many offspring.

Eventually, some basic education became available. First it was through personal instruction by priests – in reading, writing and the scriptures – for the sons of families having the necessary means. By the end of the sixteenth century the first primary schools began to spring up in Santiago, run by the Dominican fathers and later, the Jesuits. However, the absence of serious education meant that the only option for colonist families with some ambition for their children – meaning their sons – was to send them to the colleges in Lima. It was a hazardous option that few took.

James Thomson brought the Lancasterian school system to Argentina, Chile and Peru.

By the eighteenth century, the situation had improved. Jesuit schools and colleges were especially favoured since they offered not only religious and classical instruction but training for employment in the vast network of haciendas and other businesses that the priests had developed and administered. At least that was the case until 1767 when the Jesuits were expelled from the colonies by royal decree. By then, Chile had its first university. The Real Universidad de San Felipe – named after the Spanish king, Philip IV – opened its doors to students in 1758, finally ending the country's dependence on Lima for tertiary education. Not that there was much distancing from the predominance of the church in teaching. Instruction was largely provided by priests, and exclusively in Latin. While law studies were popular, theology dominated, and the professors of medicine and mathematics had very few students. Nevertheless, the Real Universidad, started the evolution of a solid intellectual base in the country which, in turn, encouraged the broader availability of primary education. It also attracted students from Argentina, Uruguay and Paraguay who were yet to have access to advanced education in their countries. In the nineteenth century, the institution was renamed and re-founded as the University of Chile.

Still, by the time of independence, the system of education remained highly selective, dominated by priests, hopelessly expensive for most parents (although a small number of poor pupils were admitted free of charge), and fixated on religious instruction. There were no schools for girls, even if some rich families paid for their daughters to receive limited instruction in convents. There were almost no secondary schools for boys or girls.

Bernardo O'Higgins, Supreme Director of Chile, and General José de San Martín, the Argentine commander of the Army of the Andes and, for a while, 'Protector' of Peru, were both prime movers in driving the cause of popular education. Both turned to James Thomson who, from 1821, would set up three 'Lancasterian' schools in Santiago, one in Valparaíso, one in Coquimbo and then three in Lima. Founded in England by Dr Andrew Bell and Joseph Lancaster, the 'monitorial' system relied on the best students passing on their knowledge to those down the line, thus cutting the expence of additional professional teaching staff. This was initially strictly religious education which, at least, led children to read and write.

Maria Graham, the English traveller and writer, staying in Valparaíso at the time of Thomson's departure northwards, commented:

"Yesterday a very interesting person sailed from hence to Lima, Mr Thomson, one of those men whom real Christian philanthropy has led across the ocean and across the Andes to diffuse the benefits of education among his fellow creatures. He had spent some time in Santiago, where, under the patronage of the supreme director, he has established a school of mutual instruction on the plan of Lancaster. He has been in Valparaíso some time superintending the formation of a similar school, to the maintenance of which part of the revenue of a suppressed monastery has been appropriated. … It is now, though so recent, well attended, and I have met many of the country people bringing in their children in the morning to go thither."

However, these schools were short-lived; those in Chile surviving only a decade or so. Claudio Gay, the French writer and naturalist, referred to the work of Thomson and the value of the Lancasterian schools as a means of moralizing the people. As to the schools, he declared that they were costly, in the extreme, and, besides, "gave no result whatever".

In the 1830s, a Chilean national commission on education reported unfavourably to the President, finding the Lancasterian system fundamentally flawed because of the incompetence of the monitors. Nevertheless, the approach was resurrected briefly in the 1840s in the form of Sunday schools which were established through the initiative of Don Andrés Bello, the great Venezuelan who gave to Spanish America the first complete treatises on Spanish grammar and, in Chile, was influential in the writing of the civil legal code. Bello had originally opposed the Lancasterian system in the public schools, yet when, at his suggestion, the Sunday schools were established for the instruction of the soldiers of the Chilean army and other adults, this was the approach chosen. However, the absence of suitable monitors or assistant teachers, condemned the initiative from the start and it was soon abandoned once more.

Reformers finally began to make progress with a true public education system in the 1840s – with the country's first teacher training college opening in 1843, the new University of Chile that same year and then a scattering of technical colleges and secondary schools. But there were huge gaps. The Chilean historian Luis Galdames notes that there were less than fifty primary schools across the country instructing little more than three thousand children in a population which ought to have had not less than two hundred thousand of school age. So the Europeans, who were by then arriving in relatively large numbers, took upon themselves the task of providing at least some portion of the schooling that the state failed to provide.

Schools would be set up in all forms, sizes and degrees of competence. One amused commentator, writing at the turn of the century, produced an impressive list of often back-room educational establishments in Valparaíso and Santiago from the 1820s onwards: John E Gray had a school in Valparaíso in 1828; Magdalena A Cobbett had a school for girls in 1830; John Burney, one for boys in 1831 and 1832; Edmund W Edwards taught boys in Santiago from 1837; around 1839 Catherine Swett ran a girls' school in Valparaíso; Charles

Black, part of the famous Edinburgh publishing family, went to Chile for his health and taught English in La Serena and then Santiago; Mrs Helsby set up a girls' school in Valparaíso; the brother of William Wheelwright, the railway constructor, had a girls' school in the same town, which, from 1845, was transformed into a boys' school, eventually under the name 'English and Classical Seminary'; in 1850 William Lackington ran the 'Colegio Comercial Inglés' while his wife kept the 'Colegio Inglés para Niñas"; and so on.

It was a boom period for European teachers and schools, with well-off Chilean families also taking advantage of the largely superior teaching standards for their own children. Not all thrived commercially however. A certain W Watkins took over 'The English Academy' of Valparaíso in 1839, later adopting the Spanish equivalent: 'El Seminario Inglés'. It was successful enough until 1852 when the school became the 'Liceo de Valparaíso'. Watkins would teach in the mornings and operated a small discount (trade finance) house in Calle Aduana in the afternoons. He did well, and with a fortune of $60-70,000 decided to take a passage back to England and comfortable retirement. Sadly he stopped on his way in Caldera and was seduced by the silver prospecting business. His mining investment failed, he lost everything and ended up teaching English in Copiapó. Watkins died poor, in the 1880s.

Thomas Somerscales, an unconventional teacher in Valparaiso, before becoming one of Chile's most celebrated painters.

Early on many successful merchants brought out their own personal tutors for their children. Gradually, more enduring and credible teaching establishments emerged. In 1858, the Valparaíso Artisans' School was launched by the British community through their own contributions. The firm Balfour, Williamson was a prime mover in the 'Artisans' School' and its director in Valparaíso, Alexander Balfour, was responsible for appointing Peter MacKay as headmaster. A few year later, with the school gaining popularity, Balfour recruited George Sutherland, another Scot, trained in Edinburgh, as the assistant headmaster. The company also funded scholarships for poorer students at the school whose roll rose from an initial 62 pupils to 307 by 1873. By then some 60 or 70 children were receiving free education, financed by subscriptions among the British community.

In 1870 the teaching staff was joined by yet another Scot, Thomas Somerscales, a sailor who had been stranded by illness in Valparaíso. He taught English and mathematics but also drawing, his artistic skills eventually revealing themselves in epic, often marine, paintings that would make him one of Chile's most gifted and cherished painters. Somerscales was also a man of character and profoundly-held principles. In particular, he did not believe in morning prayers and bible readings for the pupils. He confronted the board of governors which was led by the school's initial promoter, the Reverend David Trumbull, vicar of the Union Church. In the test of strength that followed, Mackay and Sutherland seem to have sided with Somerscales. The outcome was the closure of the Artisan's School in 1877 and the opening, shortly afterwards, of the Mackay and Sutherland School. Mackay died in 1905 and the school, under the management of Sutherland and yet another Scot, George Robertson, has continued to function – as simply 'The Mackay School' – apart from a ten-year break in the 1930s, until today.

If it seems that the development of foreign schools in the early days was heavily skewed towards British, not to say Scottish, initiatives, that largely reflected the predominance of Anglo-Saxon immigrants and travellers in the first decades after independence. Certainly, sons and daughters had to be furnished with an education on a par with their origins. At the same time, administrators, artisans, accountants, engineers and other professionals needed to be trained to support the British community's mushrooming commercial activities up and down the Pacific Coast.

Yet that did not mean other Europeans did not strive to provide schooling that reflected their own traditions and local needs. In the middle of the nineteenth century, when new German communities were arriving and often struggling for survival in the south of Chile, what schools there were had a precarious existence, for the lack of finance, the pressing need for youngsters to help parents on the farmsteads and local differences pitting secular against religious education. However, by the end of the century German schools were blossoming. Again, they often met a commercial need or filled gaps in the skills required within the farming communities. But, while seeking to produce fine young Chileans, these schools also aimed to promote and safeguard the German language and cultural traditions. The first Colegio Alemán opened in Valparaíso in 1858 and by 1910 had around 400 pupils enrolled each year. Another, in Valdivia, was active from the same year, while the German school in Santiago and a majority of the others opened their doors in the 1890s onwards. By 1909, some twenty-three German schools, from Valparaíso southwards, were instructing over 2,800 pupils, a large majority Protestants and with German as their mother tongue. Eventually German schools prospered in Peru and Bolivia also.

Among the other European communities that sought to offer a familiar, if basic, education to their own nationals, the Greeks of Valparaíso had their own primary school from 1864, the Italians from around 1886. The French had their schools as did the Croats. According to the 1875 national census, there were fifty-five teachers of British nationality throughout Chile in that year, and thirty-two French. By 1895, there were a little over four hundred foreign teachers in the country while the 1910 census figures record some 530 out of a national total of almost seven thousand.

S. PAUL'S SCHOOL
FOR BOYS
Principals: The Misses Merington
Casilla 464. — VIÑA DEL MAR
Boys are prepared for Public Schools at Home.

The Mackay School
VALPARAISO — FOUNDED 1857.
SCHOOL HOUSE: CALLE SANTA ISABEL
BOARDING HOUSE: "LOS OLIVOS", CALLE HOSPITAL,
CERRO ALEGRE
General and Commercial Education and Preparation for
Public Schools at Home.
Prospectus on application to Casilla 373, or to "Los Olivos",
Calle Hospital 28, Valparaiso.

S. PETER'S SCHOOL CHILE
Incorporated with "The Association of Preparatory Schools"
of Great Britain.
Application to Rev't. C. McDonald Hoble
G. P. S. Crofts
Address VILLA ALEMANA
English Phone 10, VILLA ALEMANA.

THE BELL VIEW SCHOOL FOR GIRLS
VILLA ALEMANA
For Prospectus apply to Mrs. Oswald Evans.
CASILLA 46. — VALPARAISO.

GIFFEN SCHOOL FOR GIRLS
CALLE CERRO No. 50, MIRAMAR.
Garden School—Private Tennis Court.
Pupils prepared for Cambridge Local Examinations and for
the Royal Academy of Music.
Special morning Kindergarten Classes for boys and Girls.
Sports:—Tennis, Hockey, Cricket, Gymnastics,
Girl Guides.
BOARDERS — HALF-BOARDERS — DAY PUPILS.
Principals: Mrs. Giffen; Miss Bertha M. B. Giffen, L. I. S. M.,
L. C. M, Miss Dall, M. A., L. L. A,
English Phone: 22 Viña. — Casilla 394, Viña del Mar.

No shortage of English schools for European residents in 1925. *South Pacific Mail*

Religious tolerance scarce, even in the ground

One legacy of the Spanish colonial epoch would never be erased: these were and would remain deeply Roman Catholic nations. Religious tolerance in countries so intensely Catholic could not be taken for granted. Those "dissidents" who built new lives on the Pacific West coast long practised their faiths surreptitiously and without even the opportunity to bury their own dead in consecrated ground. Some passively accepted the situation while others pushed against it. Some Chileans, including the editorialists of *El Mercurio*, accepted the case for religious tolerance. But it took decades for the Chilean Congress to pass laws permitting worship by non-Catholics in private buildings and the establishment of Protestant schools.

The history of the Anglican Church in Valparaíso begins earlier but is little different from that of other similar churches up and down the coast. It all started in private houses: Thomas Kendall began reading the Anglican service in his sitting room in 1825 and when he left Chile in 1828, John Sewell continued in his Calle Leighton dwelling until 1835. In the same period, local British Protestants would also have had the option to attend services aboard British naval vessels anchored in the bay. In the 1830s a simple building on Cerro Alegre was used as a makeshift and strictly unofficial church.

In 1835, an English pastor, John Rowlandson arrived in the town as tutor to the children of a Richard Price. Before long, Rowlandson was writing to the Bishop of Exeter, in whose diocese he had previously worked, on behalf of the five hundred Protestant souls reckoned to have been in Valparaíso at the time, to seek support for establishing an Anglican church. The community itself lobbied the Foreign Secretary, Lord Palmerston, and diplomatic efforts led to unusual permission from the Chilean government for a "school room" – nothing that *looked* like a church – to be made available for Protestant services. The local community agreed to raise at least £450 as a salary for Rowlandson as chaplain. However, he never received an official appointment, the Bishop of London instead sending out the Reverend William Armstrong in 1841 as the first consular chaplain. Armstrong distinguished himself by fighting for the establishment of a Protestant cemetery (see below). He also experienced a resurrection when, in the middle of one burial service, sounds were heard from inside the coffin and the 'deceased' was discovered to be ... not deceased!

Only in 1858 was a real Anglican church constructed. The initial proposal had divided the community. Official policy, as represented by Consul H W Rouse in Valparaíso, was cautious; in 1856, he had warned that British citizens not read too much into the treaty of friendship between the two countries and, in 1858, he advised members of the church to "worship in a quiet and unostentatious manner". Nevertheless, the church was built and belatedly dedicated in 1869. The 'honorary' architect was the British railway engineer, William Lloyd, who had surveyed and managed the construction of many Chilean lines, including that between Valparaiso and Santiago. For a railwayman he designed a remarkably beautiful church, in the Early English style. St. Pauls Church remains open to this day and is one of the finest restored buildings in Valparaíso, even if it no longer has a congregation.

Any visitor to the Iglesia San Pablo will be struck by the magnificent organ, which remains in excellent condition and can be heard at regular concerts. It was constructed in Hull, England, and shipped out to Chile in 1903 as a tribute to the then late Queen Victoria. The cost of £1600 was met by donations from the local community. The instrument's installation took months, during which time the regular worshippers were welcomed by the German Lutheran Church a few metres away. That elegant church had been constructed only in 1897-98 and would be severely damaged in the 1906 earthquake. Lutheran services for the local community had been launched earlier, in 1865. These were abandoned during the Pacific War, largely because of the accompanying economic recession. They were restarted in 1890.

The state of worship in Valparaíso also fascinated US Navy Lieutenant J M Gilliss, whose report of the US Astronomical Expedition, in the early 1850s, noted that there had previously been bigotry and intolerant oppression, "proportionate to that which still remains at Santiago":

"By sufferance, the Protestants have been allowed to put up an unpretending building back of the residences on Cerro Alegre, where service is performed every Sabbath morning according to the rubric of the Church of England. Indeed, it may be considered an exclusively English church, for Her Majesty Queen Victoria is the only sovereign prayed for, although American and German families are among its attendants and supporters. It is proper to add, however, that England and the English pay the lion's share, government by act of Parliament appropriating a sum for the support of churches abroad equal to that voluntarily subscribed by its citizens.

"A free Protestant chapel has also been permitted. To this end a room near the custom-house is used, and it is more especially intended for 'those who go down to the sea in ships'. Its expenses are borne by voluntary subscription from residents and one of the American missionary societies. The Rev. David Trumbull, in charge of it, devotes a portion of his time to editing *'The Neighbour'*..."

With so many mariners constantly roaming the streets of Valparaíso, Callao and other West coast ports, often separated from their ships, destitute and as likely as not drunk, their welfare was frequently assured only by charities, notably the seamen's missions. As with the launch of the Artisans' School, Trumbull was the pioneer of work in support of sailors, aided later by a fellow countryman, Frank Thompson. Trumbull founded the Valparaíso Seamen's Mission in 1846. The mission's work was largely conducted directly on board vessels in the bay although, from 1888, the mission had its own boats on which to conduct services and provide welfare. In 1906, the Valparaíso mission was absorbed into the Missions to Seamen Society based in London. A year later, the Seamen's Institute, on Avenida Errázuriz, was established to provide, as the *South Pacific Mail* would later put it, "a sorely needed counter attraction ... against the manifold temptations of sailor town." Also in 1907, the Reverend Thomas Hardy was sent from London to head the mission. Hardy was famed for his near-daily visits to seafarers under treatment in the local hospitals as well as for ensuring that the sailors' wages were banked on arrival in port and sent on to their families rather than dissipated in the more traditional nautical manner.

The Reverend Thomas Hardy set up the Seaman's Institute in Valparaiso to look after visiting mariners.   *The South Pacific Mail*

While it may be excusable to imagine the foreign business community of the nineteenth century as exclusively grasping, neo-colonial capitalists and exploiters of the region's natural resources, there is some reason to believe also that they played a benevolent role in Valparaíso society and in commercial ports up and down the coast. Perhaps there was a degree of paternalism and Protestant religiosity of the Victorian kind, but the idea of 'doing good' when endowed with the advantages of a successful business life, was not uncommon among the folk on Cerro Alegre. Take the Williamson family: Stephen and Annie. He headed the successful

Liverpool-based trading house of Balfour, Williamson in Valparaíso in the 1850s and 1860s. As the company's official history – which may naturally exaggerate – insists, the company was a benevolent influence in the city. Its senior staff, even if they lived in those comfortable houses on the hill were naturally austere, coming from Scottish Presbyterian stock.

Both Alexander Balfour and Annie Williamson were teetotallers while Stephen Williamson was described as 'abstemious' which presumably left space for the occasional dram of scotch whisky. For the Williamson family, Sundays consisted of church (twice), Sunday school tuition, bible reading in Spanish to the servants and visits to the sick in the English hospital. They waded in when life in the town was especially tough; helping with soup kitchens, for instance, after the 1866 bombardment by the Spanish fleet and donating for the care of the wounded from the War of the Pacific.

The firm also ensured that the Rev Trumbull of the Union Church – non-denominational but mostly attended by Scottish Presbyterians – was paid an adequate salary. And it backed the Valparaíso Bible Society, which opened a shop to provide appropriate religious books in Spanish, as well as the seamen's charities in the port. Alexander Balfour was one of the founders of the YMCA in Chile.

The right to a Christian burial was a struggle that continued well after independence. In 1821, the Captain of the English naval vessel *HMS Conway*, was confronted by the problem when he and his crew provided the funeral honours to an American officer who had died in Valparaíso:

"On achieving the grave, even the most unreflecting were shocked to find that the body was to be laid in un-consecrated ground; for the former masters of the country, it appeared, had systematically denied to all foreigners, except such as were Catholics, the privilege of a Christian burial. But it is very gratifying to learn that the new government, in a spirit worthy of the times, has since expressed the utmost readiness to grant a piece of ground to be consecrated and set apart for this purpose."

This was premature. Even Lt Gilliss was aware of the problem thirty years later:

"Even quiet sepulture was denied the unfortunate heretics who died thus far away from home and kindred; it being regarded commendable to disinter bodies, and leave them on the surface of the ground, after committing on them indecencies of every kind. Of course, they were not in the ground deemed consecrated by Catholics, nor has it been many years since a cemetery has been publicly permitted. But in spite of the wry faces of the priests, the influx of Protestant population has forced measurable toleration at last; and, in consequence, the larger number of the long-robed and broad-brimmed gentry have retreated to the capital, where hypocrisy and indolence meet neither opposition nor criticism."

The "heretic" foreigners had drawn up a petition to Supreme Director O'Higgins in 1819. They did not seek to be given special ground, merely to be free to acquire some and use it in perpetuity as a graveyard. They included some powerful figures, like Joshua Waddington and Henry Cood, and their submission explained graphically how they were forced to bury the remains of friends in the beach below the high-water mark. Thus a few days later, it was common to see the corpses floating in the bay; presenting a horrific sight as well as prey for scavenging birds. The community wanted a burial plot in Santiago and one in Valparaíso. The church establishment in the capital was not ready at that time, but the petition succeeded in the old port. A subscription was raised and what became the Dissidents' Cemetery, next to the town's prison, was founded in 1823, serving not only Valparaíso but non-Catholics from other cities, including Santiago. (One of the original signatories, George Perkins, did not live long enough to make use of the newly hallowed ground when it was finally granted. He was murdered five months after the petition; his three murderers being executed within 48 hours of their arrest, the entire judicial process having been duly completed!) A law prohibiting religious discrimination in municipal cemeteries was not passed until 1883.

Nevertheless, the new graveyard did not meet with universal admiration. Arriving in May 1867, the Scottish naturalist Robert Cunningham, as well as reporting copiously on the wildlife, plants and geology of the region had an opportunity to observe the religious customs of the foreign community:

"The 21st [May 1867] was our first Sunday on shore at Valparaíso, the weather having been too bad on the previous one to allow of our landing. After attending morning service in the English church on one of the hills, some of us whiled away our time at the inspection of the Protestant and Roman Catholic cemeteries, which lie side by side. It was amusing to observe how the taste for turgid and ridiculous inscriptions, so marked in cemeteries and churchyards in Great Britain, was maintained abroad, contrasting strangely with the touching simplicity and pathos displayed in most of the German epitaphs, which generally began with 'Hier ruht,' which will be admitted to be an improvement upon 'Here where this silent marble weeps,' and such like effusions."

Still, a decent burial place was not a small matter for the residents. So many of the foreign, especially European, communities were there to stay. Some became Chilean or Peruvian citizens, some did not. Some married into Spanish families, others stayed within their own national societies. But tens of thousands died in the countries to which they had sailed years before, often braving Cape Horn and the rigours of life in the most extreme conditions on earth. Dead or alive, they had no wish to go home: they had found their home. As the traveller George Scott Elliott wrote of Europeans in Chile in 1905:

"The author failed to find a single German who had the slightest wish for the government of William II. Nor did he discover a Briton who had any desire for the methods of the British House of Commons and of English political parties. These wanderers do sing of the Vaterland, of 'dear old England' and of 'bonnie Scotland', but in so doing, they simply indulge that necessity of romantic enthusiasm, of poetic yearning for something ideal, which is innate in everybody.

"They do not really want to return 'home' for a permanent residence. ... No one who has lived long in Southern Chile would seriously desire to return to live in Glasgow, London, Liverpool or Manchester.

"There is a liberty and a freedom to which, in aged nations, one is quite unaccustomed. The sunshine and the invigorating air no doubt account for much, but certainly the Chilean people themselves are largely responsible for the indefinite attraction which everyone experiences in the 'England of the Pacific.'"

Valparaiso Bound!

15.

Conclusion: a spirit of enterprise and adventure, with faults

That final sentence quoted from George Scott Elliott would likely be echoed by today's travellers, even if they would hesitate to refer to Chile as the "England of the Pacific." More the Switzerland, perhaps, or the United States. And the adjectives used so often in the stories of the new European arrivals in the nineteenth century – like brave, ingenious, tough, entrepreneurial, adventurous and steadfast – have been employed copiously in news reports about Chile and Chileans in modern times. The resilience of the nation in the face of natural disasters – the capacity to recover from horrifically destructive earthquakes and tsunamis, to bounce back after rapacious fires, to devise the most ingenious rescue operation from a deep mine accident – has been observed and admired by visitors and television viewers across the globe.

Of course, there is a wholly different set of adjectives also employed in any discussion of the colonial period and the era of nineteenth-century European engagement on the Pacific coast. This would include: exploitative, opportunistic, cruel, unscrupulous, paternalistic, intolerant and discriminative. The Spanish showed some of the very best and much of the very worst of what the culture of the Old Continent stood for during some three hundred years. To suggest that the conquistadors bought no more than savage disruption to idyllic indigenous tribes, empires and lifestyles – as modern movies sometimes depict – is false. At the same time, with their sometimes evangelical missionary zeal and sense of superiority, the new arrivals in the nineteenth century, after independence, though usually well-intentioned, brought social breakdown to ancient tribal societies and often virtual extinction.

Yet none of this detracts from the pioneering spirit and the remarkable resilience the Europeans brought to the region. They were farmers and traders, miners and businessmen, bankers and engineers, adventurers and explorers, pirates and naval officers, teachers and preachers, botanists and astronomers, prostitutes and entertainers. They came from the lowest ranks of European society and from its aristocracy. It hardly matters; they all contributed to building new nations. And they were almost all united by one experience: a sea passage, a voyage, a long, debilitating, exhausting submission to the whims of unspeakably vicious natural forces. Many were lost, but mostly they arrived at their destination, and so often it was Valparaíso.

And such a collection of personalities: "Colonel" John Thomas North, Inés Suárez and Pedro de Valdivia, Maria Graham, Ferdinand Magellan, Ambrose and Bernardo O'Higgins, Pedro Sarmiento, Charles Darwin, Lord Thomas Cochrane, George Beauchef, Pascual Barburizza, Francis Drake, Isaac Le Maire, Commodore George Anson, Diego de Almagro, Henry Sloman, General John Mackenna, Carlos Andwanter, James 'Santiago' Humberstone, Hernando

The ugly side of European intervention in Patagonia. Onas (Selk'man) people on display at the Great Exhibition in Paris, 1889, with businessman Maurice Maitre. Later they were exhibited in London at the Westminster Aquarium.

de Santillán, Luis de Valdivia, Joshua Waddington, Baron Henri Arnous de Rivière, Richard Trevithick, John Edwards, William Myers, Alexander Balfour, Rear Admiral Casto Méndez Núñez, William Wheelwright, Peter Mackay and so on. And alongside the celebrated characters in this drama lasting more than 400 years are all the other European bit players whose names festoon the cemeteries the length and breadth of Chile, Peru and Bolivia – and, indeed, whose surnames live on in many families today.

There were heroes and villains and a few fools. Among the fools can be found the French king of Araucanía (and Patagonia). And this story would not be complete without paying the respect due to one of the most outlandish and comic adventurers who ever stepped foot on any continent intent on establishing a realm if not an empire.

The first King of Araucanía was born Antoine de Tounens in the Dordogne town of Chourgnac, France, in 1825. Despite having a minor legal qualification he was essentially an adventurer, with plenty of nerve and more than his share of charisma. He left France for South America, travelling by steamer from Southampton to Coquimbo where he arrived in August 1858. He seems to have had no solid plans, not even to make a fortune. Instead he learned some Spanish, spent time in Valparaiso and Santiago and studied the country and its history before setting out for Araucania in 1860.

Once across the "border" he made contact with several *caciques* (tribal chiefs) before not only declaring himself King of Araucanía, Oréllie-Antoine I, by decree, but also issuing a constitution for the vast territory which he considered ungoverned by the Chilean state and in need of a unification among the many tribes. Establishing an autocratic constitutional monarchy with all the trappings – at least on paper – of a modern, but repressive European state of the period, he then notified the Chilean President, the foreign minister in Santiago and the press, of the new nation. Not only that, but he claimed the tribes of Patagonia had signalled their interest in being assimilated into his kingdom. Obligingly, he issued a new decree to submit that even larger territory to his rule. All this he wished to offer to France as a new colony. He travelled quickly back to Valparaiso where, surprised at the lack of attention he was receiving from the authorities in Santiago – and shocked not to have been arrested – he sent official letters to the government in Paris and to the French newspapers.

Silence followed. The French press had fun at de Tounens' expense, but from the French administration there was nothing. Deducing that he needed to consolidate his status in some way, the "King" headed back south – alone, none of his French associates would accompany him – to set up a series of meetings with "electors" in the various tribes forming his nation. On Christmas Day 1861, the Canglos were duly assembled and, according to the record, unanimously declared allegiance to the new ruler. Two days later the Quicheregua submitted willingly and the Traguén, shortly after, happily did the same.

At least, that was de Tounens' story. What was the deal? He denied it vociferously afterwards, but the attraction for the various *caciques* appears not to have been the rosy prospect of becoming French subjects but the new king's assertion that they had a collective right to the territories south of the BioBío

River. This had, indeed, been the de facto frontier for several centuries while the Spanish tried and ultimately failed to bring the Araucanian people under colonial rule. However, in 1861 Chile had been independent for over forty years. The government in Santiago was in no doubt that the nation extended, unbroken, southwards to the southern shore of Tierra del Fuego. Nevertheless, it was struggling to pacify Araucanía and territory to the south for the arrival of new, state-sponsored German and other European settlers.

King Oréllie-Antoine I may have been a joke to his fellow countrymen, but he was an irritant to the Chilean authorities and needed to be removed. During an excursion to enlist yet another tribe, in early January 1862, he was betrayed, arrested by the police and imprisoned. There followed months of

Patriotic silliness. Chilean and British flags held aloft in a tableau mounted at Valparaiso's Victoria Theatre in 1887 to mark the Jubilee festival of Queen Victoria's ascent to the British throne fifty years earlier. *The Graphic*

legal manoeuvring since neither the civil courts nor the military authorities would accept the responsibility of trying de Tounens for insurrection. Finally, in October, a local magistrate declared him insane and had him sent north to a lunatic asylum in Santiago. The French chargé d'affaires retrieved him and put the disgraced monarch on a ship back to his homeland. That did not entirely end the bizarre story; de Tounens tried three times more to take back what he regarded as his rightful throne in Araucania. He was, of course, unsuccessful and, although he established a farcical court in exile in a Parisian apartment, he died unrecognized back home in the Dordogne, in 1878.

Naturally, de Tounens was not the only unwelcome arrival on those distant shores. Indeed, by the turn of the nineteenth century the level of overt xenophobia directed explicitly at what were portrayed as useless and undesirable European residents had become acute. Newspapers railed at the 'abject dregs' of European cities placed on Chile's doorstep while politicians attacked the recruitment policies of the Agencia General de Inmigración in Paris.

And yet, the sentiment that only large-scale immigration could create a great nation to stand its ground with the likes of the United States, Australia and, above all, Argentina, remained prevalent. In reality, the days of significant government-sponsored immigration came to a close as the nineteenth century ended. Newcomers would continue to arrive: some accidentally, some spontaneously, lured by irresistible opportunity, others meeting contractual obligations, a few escaping oppression and war, and yet others for family reasons. Chile would largely remain open and inviting – receiving new flows of Palestinians, Syrians, Iraqis; Russians and Yugoslavs – while establishing its own character, its own solid democratic institutions, the rule of law and a sense of patriotism. So it has remained until the present day; albeit with a few aberrations along the way, though less so than any other South American nation.

For the most part Chile was constructed by waves of invaders, adventurers and immigrants mixing, not always comfortably, with its original indigenous peoples. Chile *became* that melange, just as the United States is a weave of immigrant and indigenous threads and the nations of Europe have their roots in the flows of peoples that have not ceased in several millennia, if not since the beginnings of human existence. The author's own Anglo-Saxon ancestors probably came many centuries ago from across the North Sea; his Jewish forbears arrived freely from Poland in the mid-nineteenth century to do business as tailors in the north of England. A nation is a construction of circumstance and opportunity. It is good to feel pride in what is constructed, as do Chileans so acutely and admirably; it is also often worthwhile to understand and take pleasure in roots and heritage.

Valparaiso Bound!

Bibliography

Many of the following books and articles are out of print. However, digital versions are often freely available on the Internet. Two sites are especially valuable in this respect:

http://www.memoriachilena.cl which is an excellent, highly professional, source managed by the Biblioteca Nacional de Chile.

https://archive.org which provides digital access to many very old, rare and valuable volumes.

Alvarado, Rodrigo. *Chilean Wine - The Heritage.* Santiago: Origo Ediciones, 2004.

Anson, George. *Voyage Round the World in the Years 1740-1744.* Edited by Richard Walter. London: John & Paul Knapton, 1748.

Arlettaz, Gérald. *"Emigration et colonisation suisses en Amérique 1815-1918. Chapitre 6: Le Chili."* In Etudes et Sources, 135-148. Berne: Archives fédérales suisses, 1979.

Astaburuaga, Ricardo. *"El agua en las zonas aridas de Chile."* ARQ 57 (July 2004): 68-73.

Beauchef, Georges. *Memoires pour servir à l'indépendance du Chili.* Translated by Patrick Puigmal. Paris: Librairie La Vouivre, 2001.

Bengoa, Jose. *Historia Social de la Agricultura Chilena: Tomo 1, El Poder y la Subordinacion.* Santiago: Edicions Sur, 1988.

Berguno-Hurtado, Fernando. *Les soldats de Napoléon dans l'indépendence de Chili (1870-1830).* Paris: L'Harmattan, 2010.

Berry-Bravo, Judy, and Pedro Bravo-Elizondo. *Tres Britanicos en la Era del Salitre.* Santiago: Libreria y Editorial Ricaaventura, 2013.

Betagh, William. *A Voyage Round the World.* London: T. Combes, 1728.

Blakemore, Harold. *British Nitrates and Chilean Politics 1886-1896: Balmaceda & North.* London: The Athlone Press, University of London, 1974.

Bravo Quezada, Carmen Gloria. *La Flor de Desierto.* Santiago: LOM Ediciones, 2000.

Bridges, Stephen Lucas. *Uttermost Part of the Earth.* London: Hodder and

Stoughton Ltd, 1951.

Browning, Webster E. *"Joseph Lancaster, James Thomson, and the Lancasterian System of Mutual Instruction, with Special Reference to Hispanic America."* The Hispanic American Historical Review (Duke University Press) IV, no. 1 (February 1921): 49-98.

Bucher, Gilberto Harris. *Emigrantes y Inmigrantes en Chile - 1810-1915, Neuvos Aportes y Notes Revisionistas.* Valparaiso: Universidad de Playa Ancha Editorial, 2001.

Burgos, Guillermo. *Photografia Del Salitre Siglo XX.* Santiago: Libreria Editorial Ricaaventura, 2013.

Burmeister, K. *"Los hospitales alemanes."* In *Los Alemanes en Chile,* 338-353. Santiago: Imprenta Universitaria, 1910.

Burney, James. *A Chronological History of the Voyages and Discoveries in the South Sea and Pacific Ocean. Vol. II.* London: Luke Hansard, 1806.

Byron, John. *The Narrative of the Honourable John Byron, the Loss of the Wager.* London: S. Baker & G. Leigh, 1766.

Caldcleugh, Alexander. *Travels in South America during the years 1819-20-21.* London: John Murray, 1825.

Casa Mackenzie. *El Esfuerzo Britanico en Valparaiso.* Valparaiso: R. V. y V. Editores, 1925.

Centner, Charles William. *"Great Britain and Chilean Mining 1830-1914."* The Economic History Review (Blackwell Publishing) 12, no. 1/2 (1942) (1942): 76-82.

Chichester, Francis. *Along the Clipper Way.* London: Hodder and Stoughton, 1966.

Collier, Simon, and William F. Sater. *A History of Chile, 1808-1994.* Cambridge: Cambridge University Press, 1996.

Collins, Esteban. *"British Influence on Education."* In *British Legacy in Valparaiso,* by Michelle Prain, 254-277. Santiago: RIL Editores, 2010.

Couyoumdjian, Juan Ricardo. *"Apuntes Sobre un Periodico Inglès de Valparaiso; "The South Pacific Mail" entre 1909 y 1925."* In *Valparaiso: 1536 - 1986.* Valparaiso: Universidad Catolica de Valparaiso, 1987.

Crommelin, May. *Over the Andes - from the Argentine to Chili and Peru.* New York: The Macmillan Company, 1896.

Crozier, Ronald D. *"El Salitre hasta la Guerra del Pacifico."* Historia (Instituto de Historia, Pontificia Universidad Católica de Chile) 30 (1997): 53-126.

Cunningham, Robert O. *Notes on the Natural History of the Strait of Magellan and West Coast of Patagonia.* Edinburgh: Edmonston and Douglas, 1871.

Dana, Richard Henry. *Two Years Before the Mast.* New York: D. Appleton & Co. 1899.

Darwin, Charles. *Journal of Researches into the Geology and Natural History of the Various Countries Visited by the H.M.S. Beagle, Under the Command of Captain Fitzroy from 1832 to 1836.* London: Henry Colburn, 1839.

Davis, Charles G. *Around Cape Horn.* Edited by Neal Parker. Camden, Maine: Down East Books, 2004.

De Robiano, Comte Eugène. *Chile - Le Chile, l'Araucanie, le Détroit de Magellan et retour par le Sénégal.* Paris: E. Plon et Cie., 1882.

Defoe, Daniel. *A General History of the Pyrates.* London, 1724.

Dictionnaire de biographie française. Paris, 1939.

Edmundson, William. *A History of the British Presence in Chile.* New York: Palgrave Macmillan, 2009.

Elliott, L. E. *Chile Today and Tomorrow.* New York: The MacMillan Company, 1922.

Encina, Francisco A. *Resumen de la Historia de Chile.* Santiago: Zig-Zag, 1964.

Enock, C. Reginald. *The Great Pacific Coast.* New York: Charles Scribner's Sons, 1910.

Espinosa, Felipe. *"Valparaiso y su larga historia de incendios."* Revista El Topo, 18 February 2013.

Estrada Turra, Baldomero. *"Importancia económica de los alemanes en Valparaíso, 1850-1915."* América Latina en la Historia Económica , 2013.

Foxley, Juan H. *"Everton: British Seed, Germinated in Valparaiso."* In *British Legacy in Valparaiso,* by Michelle Prain, 297-303. Santiago: RIL Editores, 2010.

Frey, Juan. *"Las Escuales Alemanes."* In *Los Alemanes en Chile,* 353 - 362. Santiago: Imprenta Universitaria, 1910.

Galdames, Luis. *A History of Chile.* Translated by Isaac Joslin Cox. New York: Russell & Russell, 1964.

Gautier, Ferdinand. *Chili et Bolivie.* Paris: E. Guilmoto, 1906.

Gilliss, Lieutenant J. M. *The U.S. Naval Astronomical Expedition to the Southern Hemisphere during the years 1849, '50, '51,'52.* Washington: House of

Representatives, 1855.

Glaser-Schmidt, Elizabeth. *"The Guggenheims and the coming of the Great Depression in Chile, 1923-1934."* Business and Economic History 24, no. 1 (1995): 176-185.

Golusda, Pedro. *La Introduccion del Salmon en Chile.* Government, Ministerio de Industria, Santiago de Chile: Anales Agronomicos, 1907.

Gonzalez Ochoa, José Maria. *"Dos Callagurritanos en la Conquista de America y su intervencion en Mexico y Peru-Chile."* Kalakorikos 8 (2003): 47-61.

Graham, Maria. *Journal of a Residence in Chile in the year 1822...* Charlottesville & London: University of Virginia Press, (Ed. Jennifer Hayward, 2003).

Hall, Captain Basil. *Extracts from a Journal written on the Coasts of Chili, Peru, and Mexico in the years 1820, 1821, 1822. Vol. II.* Edinburgh: Archibald Constable & Co., 1826.

Halsey, Frederic M. *Railway Expansion in Latin America.* New York: The Moody Magazine and Book Company, 1916.

Hamy, Ernest-Théodore. *"Les voyages de Richard Grandsire de Calais dans l'Amérique du Sud (1817-1827)."* Journal de la Société des, 1908: 1 - 20.

Hernandez, Roberto. *El Salitre.* Valparaiso: Associacion de Productores de Salitre de Chile, 1930.

Hervey, Maurice H. *Dark Days in Chile - An Account of the Revolution of 1891.* London: Edward Arnold, 1892.

Hillman, Charles Fletcher. *"Old Timers" - British and American in Chile.* Santiago: Imprenta Moderna, 1901.

Hollett, David. *More Precious than Gold - The Story of the Peruvian Guano Trade.* Teaneck, New Jersey: Fairleigh Dickinson University Press, 2008.

Holmes, Burton. *Burton Holmes Travelogues, Volume Thirteen.* Chicago, New York: The Travelogue Bureau, 1917.

Hough, Richard. *Captain James Cook - A Biography.* London: Hodder & Stoughton, 1994.

Humberstone, James. *Huida de Agua Santa en 1879.* Santiago: Editorial Andres Bello, 1929.

Hunt, Wallis. *Heirs of Great Adventure. The History of Balfour, Williamson and Company Limited.* Volume One. 1851-1901. 2 vols. London: Balfour Williamson and Company Limited, 1951.

Hunter, Daniel J. *A Sketch of Chili - expressly prepared for the use of emigrants from the United State and Europe.* New York: Hallet, 1866.

Jefferson, Mark. *"Recent Colonization in Chile."* American Geographical Society (Oxford University Press) Research Series No. 6 (1921): 1-52.

Jocelyn-Holt Letelier, Alfredo. *La Indepencia de Chile: Tradicion, Modernizacion y Mito.* 2e. Santiago: Planeta/Ariel, 1999.

Jones, William. *The Cape Horn Breed.* London: Andrew Melrose Limited, 1956.

Kelsey, Harry. *Sir Francis Drake.* New Haven and London: Yale University Press, 1998.

Kerr, Robert. *A General History and Collection of Voyages and Travels.* Vol. X. Edinburgh: William Blackwood, 1824.

Koerner, Victor. *"Influencia alemana en el desarrollo de la medicina en Chile."* In *Los Alemanes en Chile.* Santiago: Imprenta Universitaria, 1910.

Korth, Eugene H. *Spanish Policy in Colonial Chile: The Struggle for Social Justice, 1535-1700.* Stanford: Stanford University Press, 1968.

Kuethe, Allan J., and Kenneth J. Andrien. *The Spanish Atlantic World in the Eighteenth Century -War and the Bourbon Reforms. 1713-1796.* New York: Cambridge University Press, 2014.

Lambertie, Charles de. *Voyage Pittoresque en Californie et au Chili.* Paris: Ledoyen, 1854.

Lavin, Alfredo Larreta, and Julio Hurtado Ebel. *Valparaiso al Trasluz.* Santiago: RIL Editores, 2010.

Lloyd, William. *A Railway Pioneer.* London: Baines & Scarsbrook, 1900.

Mackenna, Benjamin Vicuna. *Ensayo Historico sobre el Clima de Chile.* Valparaiso: Imprenta del Mercurio, 1877.

Mackenna, Benjamin Vicuna. *Bases del Informe Presentado al Supremo Gobierno Sobre la Inmigracion Estranjera.* Comision Especial, Santiago de Chile: Imprenta Nacional, 1865.

Mackenna, Benjamin Vicuna. *El Libro de la Plata.* Santiago: Imprenta Cervantes, 1882.

Mansfield, Robert E. *Progressive Chile.* New Yrk: The Neal Publishing Company, 1913.

Markham, Sir Clements. *Early Spanish Voyages to the Strait of Magellan.* London: The Hakluyt Society, 1911.

Martinez, Sergio. *"British Doctors in Valparaiso."* In *British Legacy in Valparaiso,* by Michelle Prain, 304-332. Santiago: RIL Editores, 2010.

Martinez-Busch, Jorge. *La Armada de Chile - En Busca de la Excelencia, 1818-1952.* Valparaiso: Imprenta de la Armada, 2010.

Mathew, W. M. *The House of Gibbs and the Peruvian Guano Monopoly.* London: Royal Historical Society, 1981.

Mayo, John. *"The British Community in Chile before the Nitrate Age."* Historia (Instituto de Historia, Pontificia Universidad Catolica de Chile) 22 (1987).

McCall, Alejandra L. *"Ad Maiorem Dei Gloriam: The Expulsion of the Jesuits from Chile and their Journey into Exile."* Bachelor of Arts thesis. University of North Carolina at Asheville, 2008.

Merwin, Mrs George B. *Three Years in Chile.* New York: Follett, Foster and Company, 1863.

Miers, John. *Travels in Chile and La Plata.* Volumes I & II. London: Baldwin, Cradock, and Joy, 1826.

Monaghan, Jay. *Chile, Peru and the California Gold Rush of 1849.* Los Angeles: University of California Press, 1973.

Ortega, Luis M. *"Acerca de los Origenes de la Indistrializacion Chilena, 1860-1879."* Nueva Historia, 1981: 3-56.

Ortleib, Luc. *"Las mayores precipitaciones históricas en Chile central y la cronología de eventos ENOS en los siglos XVI-XIX."* Revista Chilena de Historia Natural 67 (1994): 463 - 485.

Ovalle, Francisco Javier. *La Cuidad de Iquique.* Iquique: Imp. Mercantil, 1908.

Pastene, Luis A, and Daniel Quiroz. *"An Outline of the History of Whaling in Chile."* Human Culture from the Perspective of Traditional Maritime Communities, International Symposium Report No. 1. Kanagawa: Kanagawa Shimbun Press, 2010. 73-98.

Pattillo Bergen, Alejandro. *"El conjunto portuario : Valparaíso, Quintero y San Antonio."* Colección Terra Nostra, Instituto de Investigaciones del Patrimonio Territorial de Chile, Universidad de Santiago de Chile., no. No.16 (1989): 76.

Perez-Rosales, Vincente. *Essai sur le Chile. Report to the President,* (French Translation of Spanish), Hambourg: Nestler & Melle, 1857.

Pocock, H.R.S. *The Conquest of Chile.* New York: Stein and Day, 1967.

Pytches, David. *Foreigners and Religious Liberies in 19th Century Chile.* Nottingham: University of Nottingham, Thesis, 1984.

Quadra, W. A., and P. M. Dunkerley. *"A history of gold in Chile."* Economic Geology 86 (1991): 1155-1173.

Rivera Letelier, Hernán. *Mi Nombre es Malarossa.* Santiago: Alfaguara, 2008.

Rodriguez, Antonio. *"Chilean Coal Consuls in Britain and Australia at the Beginning of the 20th Century."* In *British Legacy in Valparaiso,* by Michelle Prain (Ed), 65-75. Santiago: RIL Editores, 2011.

Rogers, Woodes. *A Cruising Voyage Around the World.* London: A. Bell, 1712.

Russell, William Howard. *A Visit to Chile - Nitrate Fields of Tarapaca.* London: J. S. Virtue & Co. Ltd, 1890.

Scott Elliott, G.F. *Chile - Its History and Development.* London: T. Fisher Unwin, 1907.

Serrano, Gonzalo. *"Football in Chile: Santiago Wanderers, an outstanding case."* In *British Legacy in Valparaiso,* by Michelle Prain, 278-293. Santiago: RIL Editores, 2010.

Torres-Dujisin, Isabel. *La vida de un croata: Pascual Baburizza Soletić.* Valparaiso: Ediciones Universidad de Playa Ancha, 2003.

Urrutia de Hazbrun, Rosa, and Carlos Lanza Lascano. *Catastrofes en Chile 1541 - 1992.* Santiago: Editorial La Noria, 1993.

Vallejo, José Joaquín, and Frederick H. Fornoff (Translator). *Sketches of Life in Chile 1841-1851.* New York: Oxford University Press, 2002.

Vega, E M. *Album de la Colonie Francaise au Chili.* Santiago: Imprimerie et Lithographie Franco-Chilienne, 1904.

Vega, Nicholas. *La Inmigracion Europea en Chile 1882-1895.* Memorandum, Paris: Agencia General de Colonizacion del Gobierno de Chile, 1896.

Vial, Sara. *"Cae el viejo Teatro Victoria de Valparaiso."* In *Memorial de Valparaiso,* by Alfinso Calderon, 455-457. Valparaiso: Universidad Catolica de Valparaiso, 1986.

Villalba, Ricardo. *"Fluctuaciones climáticas en latitudes medias de América."* Revista Chilena de Historia Natural 67 (1994): 453-461.

Villiers, A. J. *By Way of Cape Horn.* New York: Garden City Publishing Co., 1930.

Villiers, Alan, and Henri Picard. *The Bounty Ships of France.* New York: Charles Scribner's Sons, 1972.

Wiborg, Frank. *A Commercial Traveller in South America.* New York: McClure Phillips & Co., 1905.

Valparaiso Bound!

Wiener, Charles. *Chili & Chiliens.* Paris: Librairie Leopold Cerf, 1888.

Wilcox, L. A. *Anson's Voyage.* London: G. Bell & Sons, 1969.

Maps

The following maps of Chile are taken from the 1907 book *"Chile"* by G.F. Scott Elliot. While they are helpful in placing locations mentioned in this book, it should be kept in mind that borders, territories and administrative areas have changed since that time. Tacna in the North, for instance, is again part of Peru, while the territory of Tierra del Fuego is now divided between Chile and Argentina.

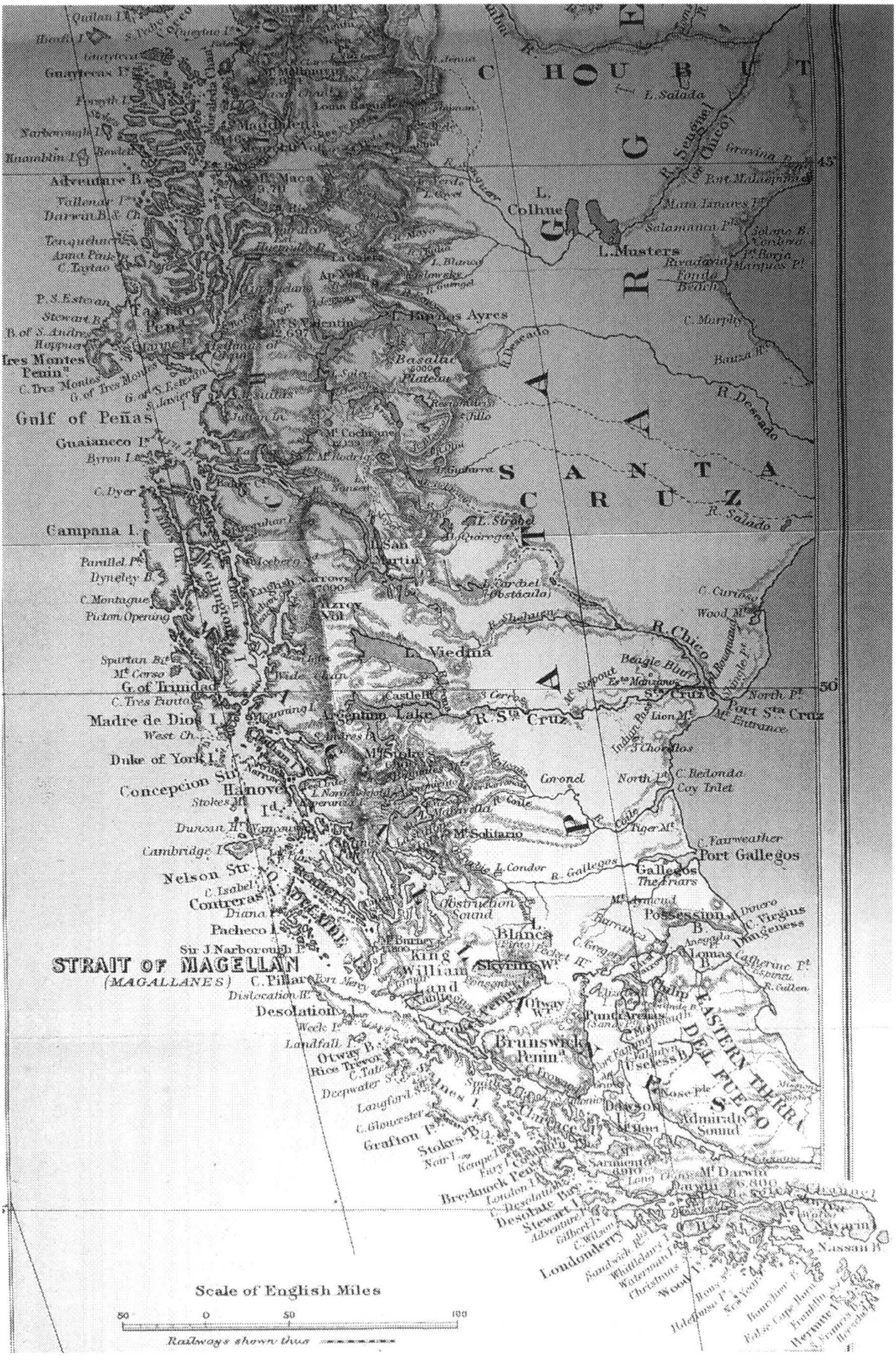
C H O U B U T
L. Salada
Gravina
45°
L. Colhue
L. Musters
Adventure B.
Gulf of Peñas
Guaianeco I.s
Byron I.
C. Dyer
Campana I.
S A N T A
C R U Z
R. Salado
R. Deseado
L. Buenos Ayres
L. San Martin
English Narrows
L. Viedma
Fitzroy Vol.
Dyneley B.
C. Montague
Picton Opening
R. Chico
Beagle Bluff
North P.t
Port S.ta Cruz
G. of Trinidad
C. Tres Punta
Madre de Dios I.
West Ch.
Duke of York I.
Concepcion Str.
Hanover I.d
Argentino Lake
R. S.ta Cruz
Castle H.
Lion M.t
C. Redonda
Coy Inlet
M.t Solitario
Tiger M.t
Cambridge I.
Nelson Str.
C. Isabel
Contreras I.s
Pacheco I.
Sir J. Narborough I.s
C. Fairweather
Port Gallegos
L. Condor
R. Gallegos
Gallegos
The Friars
Possession B.
C. Virgins
Dungeness
Obstruction Sound
Blanca
STRAIT OF MAGELLAN
(MAGALLANES)
C. Pillar
Dislocation H.r
Desolation I.
Landfall I.
King William Land
Skyring W.r
Otway W.r
Punta Arenas
Brunswick Penin.a
EASTERN TIERRA DEL FUEGO
Dawson I.
Admiralty Sound
Otway B.
Rice Trevor
Deepwater Sd.
Langford Sd.
C. Gloucester
Grafton I.s
Stokes B.
Breaknock Pen.a
Desolate Bay
Stewart I.
Londonderry I.
Sarmiento
M.t Darwin
Navarin
Nassau B.
Scale of English Miles
50 0 50 100
Railways shown thus

298

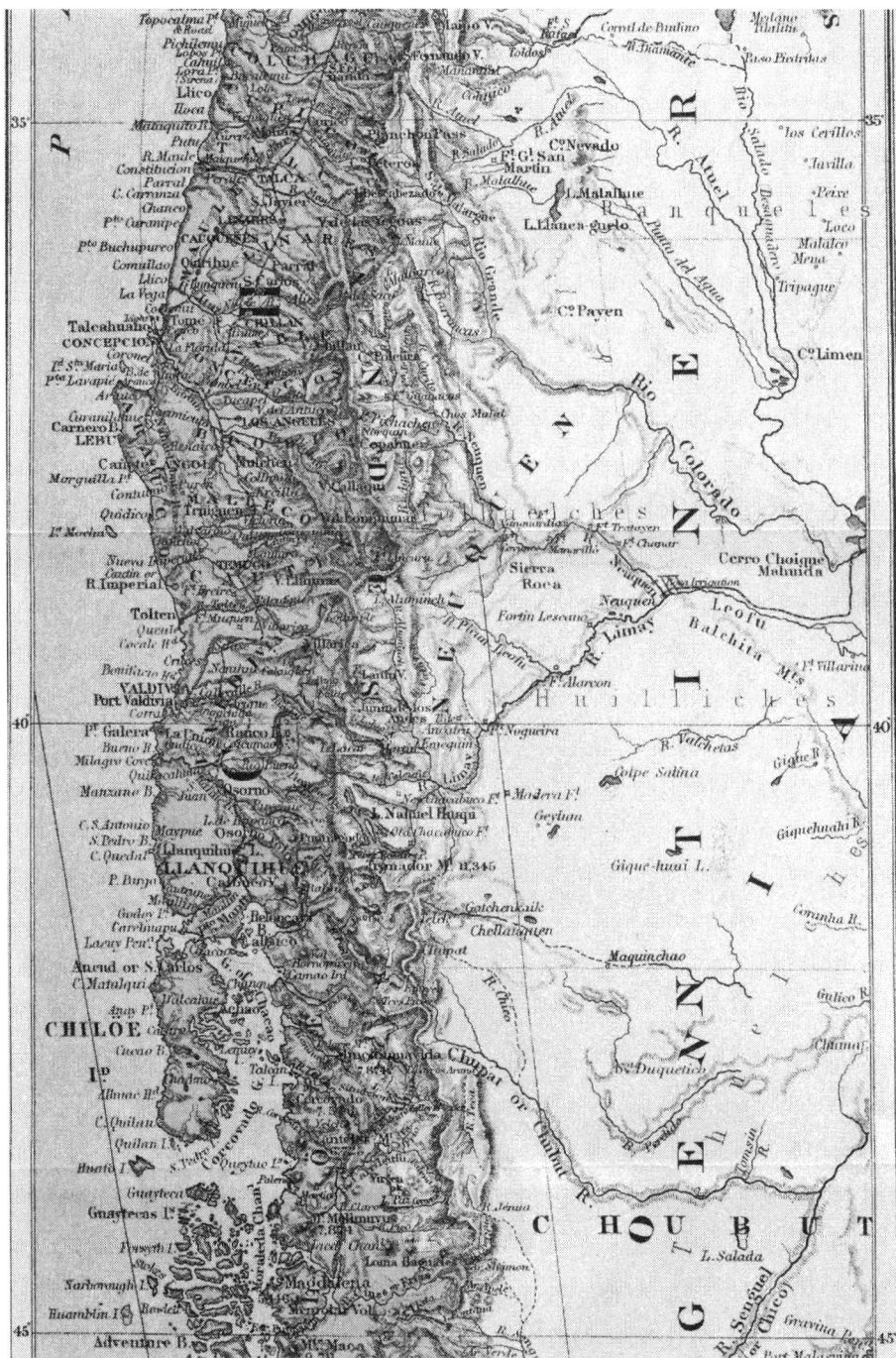

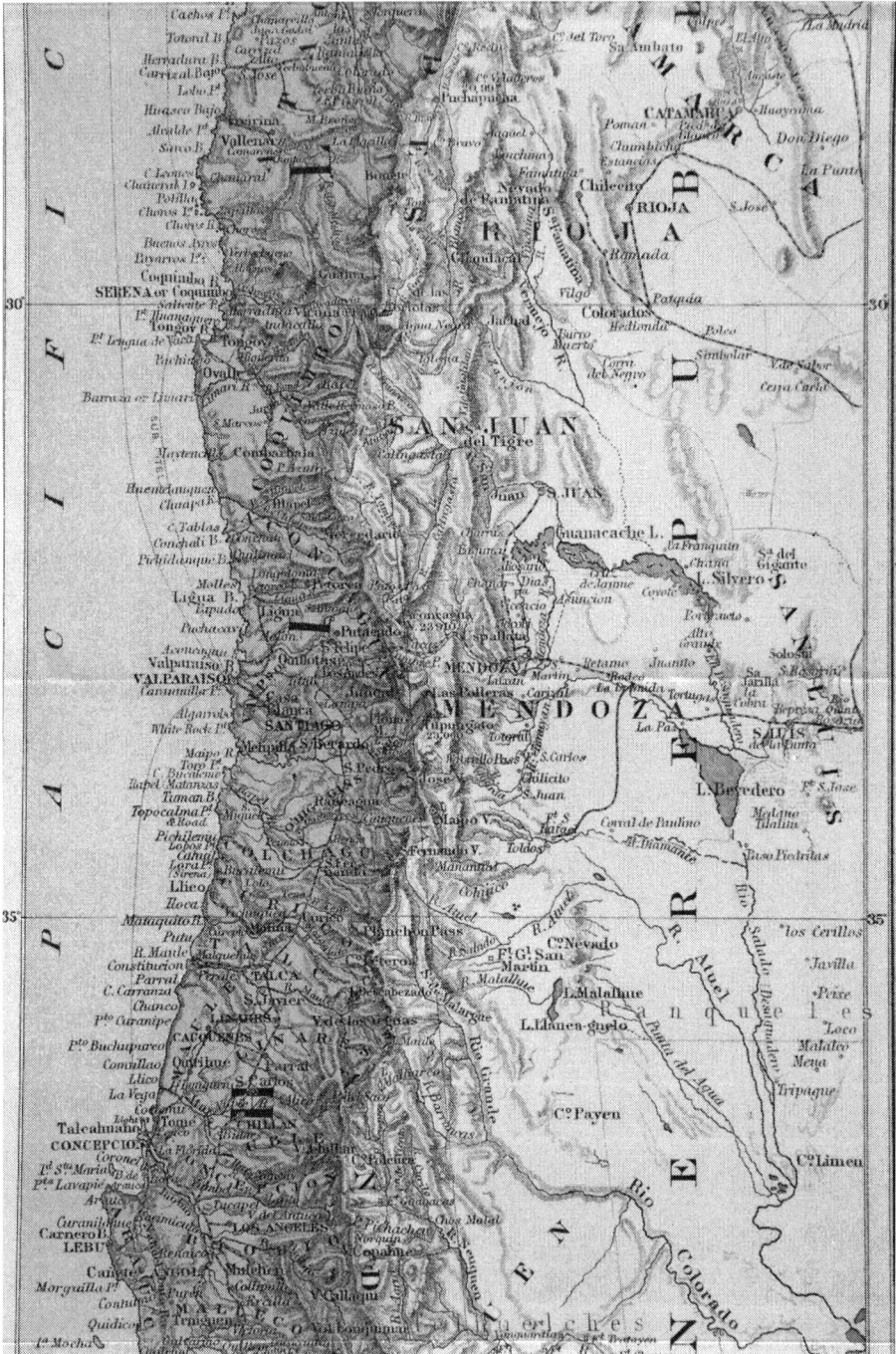

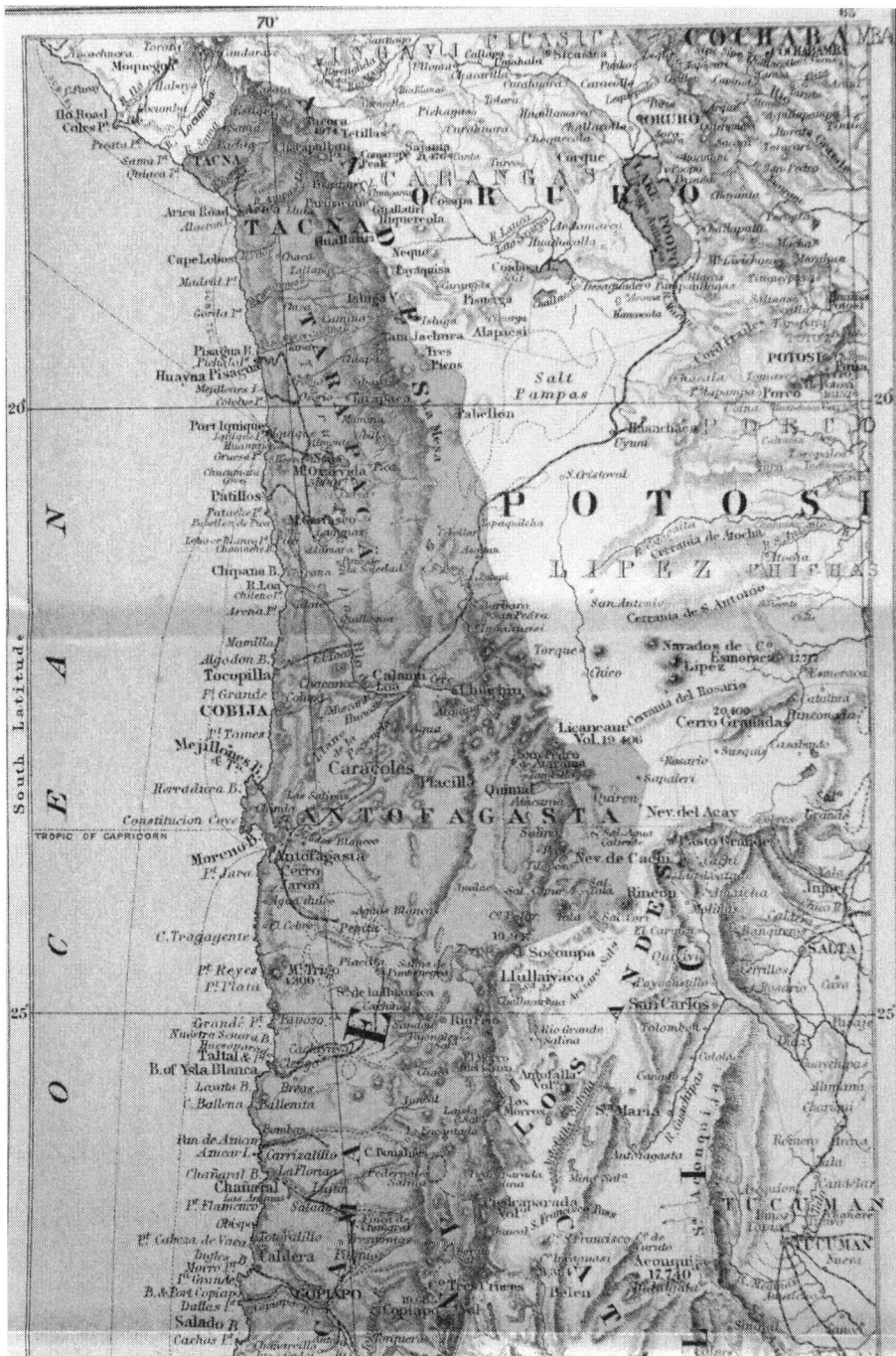

Valparaiso Bound!

Index

311

Typhus 151

Valparaiso Bound!

Valparaiso Bound!

Printed by Amazon Italia Logistica S.r.l.
Torrazza Piemonte (TO), Italy

45444217R00189